Contents

How to use this book

Introduction – interviews with real industry practitioners give invaluable insights into a wide variety of career paths

Case studies – in-depth focus on industry-specific scenarios show you how the theory works in real-life situations

Evidence activities – short activities are spread throughout the unit giving you the opportunity to practise your achievement of the grading criteria in small steps

edexcel

advancing learning, changing lives

BTEC National
Travel and Tourism

Book 2

Specialist units

Andy Kerr
Victoria Lindsay
Diane Sutherland
Jon Sutherland

A PEARSON COMPANY

Contents

Grading criteria – learning outcomes and grading criteria are located at the beginning of every unit, so you know right from the start what you need to do to achieve a pass, merit or distinction

To achieve a pass grade the evidence must show that the learner is able to...	To achieve a merit grade the evidence must show that, in addition to the pass criteria, the learner is able to...	To achieve a distinction grade the evidence must show that, in addition to the pass and merit criteria, the learner is able to...
P1 Explain different methods that can be used to research a current issue	**M1** Explain how the proposed research plan enables exploration of the current issue	**D1** Evaluate the research undertaken and recommend improvements to your own research skills in the future
P2 Propose a research plan to investigate a current issue that is affecting the travel and tourism industry	**M2** Conduct independent research into a current issue, using at least four different types of sources of information, showing awareness of limitations of sources	**D2** Use findings from research into the current issue to recommend actions for the travel and tourism industry
P3 Use appropriate sources of information to research a current issue, using a standard referencing system	**M3** Communicate information about a current issue clearly, concisely and coherently, using specialist vocabulary and making connections and synthesising arguments	
P4 Communicate a current issue that is affecting the travel and tourism industry, using appropriate conventions to convey findings	**M4** Provide a comprehensive analysis of the current issue researched, combining and recognising different points of view	
P5 Explain how a current issue affects the travel and tourism industry		

Think – questions help you reflect on your learning and to think about how it could be applied to real-life working practice

Research Tips – direct you to useful websites and key organisations to help you take your study further

Laissez-faire management

This is management through delegation. Employees have set objectives and targets and are left alone to achieve these goals. Laissez-faire management is sometimes mistaken for bad management and a lack of caring, but this is not the case. Laissez-faire management involves developing the employees' skills and **empowering** them to be able to achieve targets and giving them the space to do the tasks, although managerial support must be always available if required.

Teamwork

Teams are important in any workplace. Two people doing the same job separately are not as productive as two people working together. For a team to work effectively, it requires a number of different skills and abilities.

Dr R. Meredith Belbin developed a team inventory while studying at Henley Business College in the 1970s. In the team inventory, Belbin identified each role.

Research tip

To find out your individual team roles try the test on *www.belbin.com*.

Key words

Empowerment – giving individuals the power to be able to do their jobs independently

Belbin's team role	Strengths	Weaknesses
Plant	Comes up with original and sometimes unconventional solutions to problems	Finds explaining ideas difficult
Resource Investigator	Good at finding opportunities and contacts Not afraid to ask for directions	Loses momentum towards the end of projects
Coordinator	Good at seeing the 'big picture' Helps to stabilise the group	Spends too long managing and not enough time working
Shaper	Drives the team forward Tackles problems head-on	Can be insensitive to the needs of others and their feelings Can act without thinking
Monitor Evaluator	Brings fairness and a detached overview Sees all available solutions and judges on merit	Can seem robotic in their behaviour and finds motivating others and themselves difficult
Team worker	Maintains the team concerns with others and how the group is working together Talent for smoothing over conflict in the team	Unwilling to take sides Can be paralysed in decision-making process, due to their need not to offend
Implementer	Makes things happen Efficient and effective and can be relied on	Closed minded and inflexible when the plan is set
Completer Finisher	A perfectionist and will make sure everything is just right Very meticulous and strong sense of duty	Worries about the smallest detail Cannot delegate tasks they feel they can do and have tendencies not to trust other people's standards
Specialist	Brings a high level of skill in their specific area Good concentration and ability in their specialisation	Can only contribute in specific area Often loses others in the detail of their specialisation

Table 6.5 Belbin's nine team roles

58

Application forms

Application forms are used by many organisations. They benefit the organisation as each candidate's information is in a standard format making it easier for the organisation to short-list candidates. There are two main formats for application forms:

1) Written – the traditional paper-based method of an application form. They are used by many companies in travel and tourism and tend to be **generic**

2) Online – job vacancies and applications for jobs are increasingly online. Online application forms are similar in structure to the paper-based version, except that you complete them online and then e-mail them to the company.

Key words

Generic – a general purpose rather than a specific use

Research tip

Most large travel and tourism organisations will have a career section on their website with information on jobs that are available

Letter of application

A CV and an application form only tell the recruiter about the experience, attributes, skills and qualifications that you have. They do not tell the recruiter what your motivation is for applying for a new job or what you specifically have to offer the company to which you are applying. You should always include a letter of application when you return your CV or application form. If it is an online application form, most companies also give you the opportunity to include an e-mail of application with your application form.

Personal statements

Personal statements can be included in an application form or in the covering letter. However, people are now providing a personal statement within their CVs. This is a statement of what you are good at and what you have managed to achieve in your career and personal life. You should include many positive examples.

Example

Rather than saying "I am good at customer service," a statement about the numbers of letters of praise that you have received would give the argument more strength. Never say that you feel or think something as this introduces doubt into the mind of the person who is short-listing applications.

INTERVIEW SKILLS

If you have been successfully short-listed, then you are likely to be called for an interview. There are many skills that you need to prepare before the interview takes place.

Advance preparation

You must prepare in advance for an interview. You need to know where it will be held, how to get there and how long it will take to get there. You also need to prepare yourself for the types of questions you could expect to be asked. Although all interviews are different depending on the company, level of job and what the company wants to get out of the interview, there are some general questions that you can prepare. You could even organise a mock interview with a friend or member of the family to give yourself some practice.

Think How would you answer the following:
• What are your main strengths?
• What are your main weaknesses?
• Where do you see yourself in five years time?
• Why should I employ you rather than any of the other candidates?
• Tell me about the company.

Key words – easy to understand definitions of key industry terms

Examples – industry-specific examples show you what the theory looks like in practice

Track your progress

This master grid can be used as a study aid. You can track your progress by ticking the level you achieve. The relevant grading criteria can also be found at the start of each unit.

To achieve a pass grade the evidence must show that the learner is able to...	To achieve a merit grade the evidence must show that, in addition to the pass criteria, the learner is able to...	To achieve a distinction grade the evidence must show that, in addition to the pass and merit criteria, the learner is able to...
Unit 5		
P1 explain the factors affecting marketing using examples from different travel and tourism organisations	**M1** analyse the constraints of marketing in relation to a selected travel and tourism organisation	**D1** recommend how the selected travel and tourism organisation could adapt to the constraints of marketing
P2 describe the marketing mix of a selected travel and tourism organisation	**M2** explain how the 4 Ps work together as a marketing mix in a specific travel and tourism organisation	**D2** recommend how the organisation can use the results of their market research activity
P3 prepare a plan and documentation for a market research activity in a travel and tourism organisation	**M3** explain how their plan and documentation will meet their market research objectives	
P4 conduct a market research activity for a travel and tourism organisation	**M4** explain how the planned campaign would enable the objectives to be met	
P5 plan a promotional campaign for a selected travel and tourism organisation to achieve stated marketing objectives		
P6 prepare an item of promotional material as part of a planned promotional campaign for a target market		
Unit 6		
P1 describe career opportunities in the travel and tourism industry and produce a description of two chosen jobs	**M1** compare two jobs in the travel and tourism industry taking into account the entry levels and opportunities for promotion and progression	**D1** evaluate own suitability for a chosen job and prepare an action plan to meet all training and development needs
P2 produce a personal skills audit in preparation for employment	**M2** produce guidelines for success in the different stages of the recruitment and selection process and use these to evaluate personal performance	**D2** analyse the factors that contribute to an effective workplace, highlighting good practice from different travel and tourism organisations
P3 describe the stages of the recruitment and selection process	**M3** explain how different travel and tourism organisations motivate staff in the workplace	
P4 demonstrate suitability for employment during different stages of the job selection process		
P5 describe the factors that contribute to an effective workplace in travel and tourism organisations		

To achieve a pass grade the evidence must show that the learner is able to...	To achieve a merit grade the evidence must show that, in addition to the pass criteria, the learner is able to...	To achieve a distinction grade the evidence must show that, in addition to the pass and merit criteria, the learner is able to...
Unit 9		
P1 describe the retail and business travel environment including the relationship between retail and business travel agents and other sectors of the travel and tourism industry, giving examples where appropriate	**M1** explain how relationships operate in the retail and business travel environment and its impact on the travel industry as a whole	**D1** evaluate the effectiveness of retail and business travel organisations and how they operate in the travel industry environment
P2 describe how technological advances have affected retail and business operations	**M2** compare the effectiveness of two retail travel organisations seeking to gain a competitive advantage	**D2** recommend how two retail travel agents can gain a competitive advantage
P3 explain how retail travel organisations seek to gain a competitive advantage		
P4 use appropriate resources to produce two complex travel itineraries for retail travel customers to given client briefs		
P5 use appropriate resources to produce two complex travel itineraries for business travel customers to given client briefs		
Unit 11		
P1 describe the impacts of tourism development in one specific short-haul and one specific long-haul destination	**M1** explain how the positive impacts have been maximised and the negative impacts minimised in a selected destination	**D1** assess the effectiveness of measures taken in a destination to put the objectives of sustainable tourism development into practice
P2 describe the roles of agents involved in sustainable tourism development at a selected destination	**M2** explain how the agents involved in sustainable tourism development could have conflicting objectives in a selected destination	**D2** recommend how the travel and tourism industry could adapt to support sustainable tourism development in a selected destination, justifying recommendations by drawing on examples of good practice
P3 explain how the objectives for sustainable tourism development are put into practice at a selected destination	**M3** analyse how effectively the industry is supporting sustainable tourism development in two destinations	
P4 describe how the travel and tourism industry supports the development of sustainable tourism at one specific short-haul and one specific long-haul destination		
Unit 12		
P1 describe the tour operations environment	**M1** explain the challenges facing the tour operating sector	**D1** evaluate the effectiveness of tour operators in responding to challenges facing the sector
P2 describe the products and services provided by different categories of tour operator	**M2** analyse how a selected tour operator's portfolio of products and services meet the needs of its target market(s)	**D2** recommend, with justification, how a selected tour operator could expand its range of products and services for its current target market or adapt its range of products and services to appeal to a new market
P3 describe how tour operators plan, sell and administer a package holiday programme	**M3** identify and explain ways of maximising the profitability of the planned package holiday	
P4 describe how tour operators operate a package holiday programme		
P5 plan and cost a package for inclusion in a tour operator's programme		

To achieve a pass grade the evidence must show that the learner is able to...	To achieve a merit grade the evidence must show that, in addition to the pass criteria, the learner is able to...	To achieve a distinction grade the evidence must show that, in addition to the pass and merit criteria, the learner is able to...
Unit 21		
P1 use different contacts and resources to identify and describe potential work experience placements in the travel and tourism industry, taking into account constraints	**M1** explain how two potential work experience placements could provide opportunities to meet personal, career and curriculum objectives	**D1** analyse the career progression potential of roles within the chosen work experience organisation and from that organisation into other areas of the travel and tourism industry
P2 prepare for work experience by completing relevant documentation and setting objectives for the placement	**M2** demonstrate effective skills, qualities and behaviours in a work placement, explaining how work undertaken has contributed to the key activities of the placement organisation	**D2** evaluate own performance on work experience and produce an action plan with justified recommendations for future personal development
P3 undertake work experience, monitoring progress of activities including skills used and adherence to code of conduct	**M3** explain the factors that contributed to the success of the work experience placement and provide supporting evidence to demonstrate personal effectiveness throughout the placement	
P4 describe the nature of the work experience organisation, including own roles and responsibilities		
P5 describe factors that contribute to an effective work experience placement, including supporting evidence used to track this		
Unit 26		
P1 explain different methods that can be used to research a current issue	**M1** explain how the proposed research plan enables exploration of current issue	**D1** evaluate the research undertaken and recommend improvements to own research skills in the future
P2 propose a research plan to investigate a current issue affecting the travel and tourism industry	**M2** conduct independent research into a current issue, using at least four different types of sources of information, showing awareness of limitations of sources	**D2** use findings from research into the current issue to recommend actions for the travel and tourism industry
P3 use appropriate sources of information to research a current issue using a standard referencing system	**M3** communicate information about a current issue clearly, concisely and coherently using specialist vocabulary, making connections and synthesising arguments	
P4 communicate a current issue affecting the travel and tourism industry, using appropriate conventions to convey findings	**M4** provide a comprehensive analysis of the researched current issue, combining and recognising different points of view	
P5 explain how a current issue affects the travel and tourism industry		

Research Skills

Before you start your research project you need to know where to find information and the guidelines you must follow.

Types of information

Primary Sources

This is information you have gathered yourself, through surveys, interviews, photos or observation. Ensure that you ask the appropriate questions and people. You must get permission before including someone's photo or interview in your work.

Secondary Sources

This is information produced by somebody else, including information from the Internet, books, magazines, databases and television. You need to be sure that your secondary source is reliable if you are going to use the information.

Information sources

The Internet

The Internet is a useful research tool, but, not all the information you find will be. When using the Internet ask yourself if you can trust the information you find.

> Acknowledge your source! When quoting from the internet always include author name (if known)/document title/URL web address/date site was accessed.

Books, Magazines and Newspapers

Information in newspapers and magazines is up to date and usually researched thoroughly. Books have a longer shelf life than newspapers so make sure you use the most recent edition.

> Acknowledge your source! When quoting from books, magazines, journal or papers, always include author name/title of publication/publisher/year of publication.

Broadcast Media

Television and radio broadcast current news stories and the information should be accurate. Be aware that some programmes offer personal opinions as well as facts.

Plagiarism

Plagiarism is including in your own work extracts or ideas from another source without acknowledging its origins. If you use any material from other sources you must acknowledge it. This includes the work of fellow students.

Storing Information

Keep a record of all the information you gather. Record details of book titles, author names, page references, web addresses (URLs) and contact details of interviewees. Accurate, accessible records will help you acknowledge sources and find information quickly.

Internet Dos and Don'ts

Do

- check information against other sources

- keep a record of where you found information and acknowledge the source

- be aware that not all sites are genuine or trustworthy.

Don't

- assume all the information on the Internet is accurate and up to date

- copy material from websites without checking whether permission from the copyright holder is required

- give personal information to people you meet on the Internet.

Marketing travel and tourism products and services

unit 5

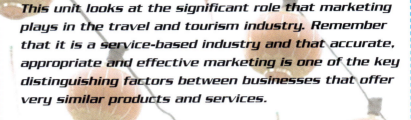

This unit looks at the significant role that marketing plays in the travel and tourism industry. Remember that it is a service-based industry and that accurate, appropriate and effective marketing is one of the key distinguishing factors between businesses that offer very similar products and services.

You will have the opportunity to look at marketing in the industry and how marketing activities can be limited under certain circumstances. You will also have the opportunity to conduct your own market research and design and use your own research documents. You will also find out about the marketing mix, which is an important marketing principle. Finally, you will have the chance to plan your own promotional campaign and design your own promotional material.

By the end of this unit, you will:

5.1	Understand the factors affecting marketing in travel and tourism	page 13
5.2	Know the marketing mix of a travel and tourism organisation	page 18
5.3	Be able to conduct a market research activity for a travel and tourism organisation	page 28
5.4	Be able to organise a promotional campaign for a travel and tourism organisation.	page 31

So you want to be a...

PR Manager

My name Dan Kaye
Age 24
Income £23,000

If you are a confident communicator with the ability to project manage and self motivate then PR has the financial rewards you're looking for...

What do you do?

My job is to work with the media to build, maintain and manage the reputation of my employer. The better the reputation, the more understanding, support and influence the company has in the industry.

What responsibilities do you have?

Research and analysis, surveys, market research, planning PR campaigns, analysing and dealing with problems, writing and editing press releases, using corporate advertising, answering queries from individuals, groups and the media. Quite a few really!

How did you get the job?

Experience in the media or the communications industry is a must. Ideally, a degree is needed, too. I wrote for my university newspaper and helped to organise events, which proved to be really handy. After applying I had three interviews in a month, which was challenging, but fortunately I did enough to be offered the job.

What training did you get?

I'm studying for my Chartered Institute of Public Relations Advanced Certificate. It's designed to give me a knowledge and understanding of theory and practice in PR. After that, the company has said I can go straight on to do the diploma.

What are the hours like?

Nine to five in theory, but in practice they're a lot more elastic. Most of the media do things at the last minute and work weird hours, but I don't really mind the hectic lifestyle - it suits me at my age.

What skills do you need?

Good communication skills, interpersonal skills, drive and a willingness to learn. Multi-tasking is usual, so that's also important. The ability to cope with pressure, creativity, initiative and having an enquiring mind are important as well. Having knowledge of the industry and being confident are also important.

> **I could end up earning £2000 a day!**

How good is the pay?

I'm on £23,000 and that's after 2 years here. The top pay for my scale is £26,000, so I hope to get to that in 18 months. I'm pushing for a proper management position, which will put the potential pay scale up to around £30,000.

What about the future?

More work, better pay I hope. I have a 10 year goal to move to a bigger company where the pay can be anything from £40K to £100K. Eventually I want to go freelance; if everything goes according to plan I could end up earning £2000 a day!

Grading criteria

The table below shows what you need to do to gain a pass, merit or distinction in this part of the qualification. Make sure you refer back to it when you are completing work so you can judge whether you are meeting the criteria and what you need to do to fill in gaps in your knowledge or experience.

In this unit there are 4 evidence activities that give you an opportunity to demonstrate your achievement of the grading criteria:

page 17   P1, M1, D1

page 28   P2, M2

page 30   P3, P4, M3, D2

page 33   P5, P6, M4

To achieve a pass grade the evidence must show that the learner is able to...	To achieve a merit grade the evidence must show that, in addition to the pass criteria, the learner is able to...	To achieve a distinction grade the evidence must show that, in addition to the pass and merit criteria, the learner is able to...
P1 Explain the factors affecting marketing, using examples from different travel and tourism organisations	**M1** Analyse the constraints of marketing in relation to a selected travel and tourism organisation	**D1** Recommend how the selected travel and tourism organisation could adapt to the factors affecting marketing
P2 Describe the marketing mix of a selected travel and tourism organisation	**M2** Explain how the 4 Ps work together as a marketing mix in a specific travel and tourism organisation	**D2** Recommend how the organisation can use the results of their market research activity
P3 Prepare a plan and documentation for a market research activity in a travel and tourism organisation	**M3** Explain how their plan and documentation will meet the market research objectives	
P4 Conduct a market research activity for a travel and tourism organisation	**M4** Explain how the planned campaign would enable the objectives to be met	
P5 Plan a promotional campaign for a selected travel and tourism organisation to achieve stated marketing objectives		
P6 Prepare an item of promotional material as part of a planned promotional campaign for a target market		

5.1 Understand the factors affecting marketing in travel and tourism

FACTORS

More than other industries, travel and tourism businesses rely on maintaining a strong and positive image as far as the public and the media are concerned. This means that businesses always need to project a strong and responsive image that is reliant on mutual trust as this is a service-based industry.

Marketing plays a vital role in establishing and maintaining the company's image and helping to frame its responses to various factors, which could have an impact on the business's reputation, the products and services it sells and the public and media's views on its behaviour and approach.

Company ethos

Company ethos is having a marketing-orientated approach within the organisation. This means recognising that marketing claims through advertising, public relations and promotions need to be supported and proven by real actions in the market place. Increasingly, this means taking on social responsibility in terms of fair trading, waste reduction, openness, environmentally considerate activities and having an effective, cooperative and collaborative relationship with employees.

Company ethos also means being customer-focused. The customer focus needs to be part of every decision made by the business. It needs to be applied by every single manager and employee. It has to be proven everyday by the company's attitudes, responses and behaviour.

In a service-based industry such as travel and tourism, customer focus and being market-driven is often the difference between two or more very similar businesses. The travel and tourism industry is highly competitive and customers often view one business more favourably if they feel that the company projects and actually behaves in a customer-focused manner and displays social responsibility.

Research tip

Find out more about social responsibility by looking at some of the websites of the major travel and tourism organisations.

Think Why do you think customers prefer companies that are customer-focused and show social responsibility?

Consumer protection

As you have seen in other units, there are basic requirements regarding consumer protection. These extend to all dealings that a business has with its customers. It must be remembered that legislation represents the basic minimum requirements as laid down by law.

Another key marketing tool is a company's assurance that they not only adhere to these laws, but also exceed them by protecting consumer rights and offering assurances above and beyond the basic requirements laid down by law.

Businesses will often offer money-back guarantees with the statement that 'this does not affect your statutory rights'. This suggests that the business is prepared to behave in a socially responsible manner beyond the requirements of law.

- All contracts concluded between Co-op Travel and you the customer are subject to our standard terms and conditions. A contract is only concluded when we accept your offer by sending you confirmation of our acceptance. Our acceptance is effective when sent by us. The contractual document is contained in the acceptance from us of your offer, and our terms and conditions which are incorporated into the acceptance and excludes any other representations. This does not affect your statutory rights as a consumer.

Figure 5.1 Extract from a brchure, clarifying the customer's statutory rights
Source Co-op Travel

The relationship between travel and tourism businesses and customers is a close one. It is closer than many other transactions that customers routinely enter into on a day-by-day basis. Many transactions undertaken by customers are rather anonymous.

Example

A customer enters a store and makes a purchase. If they pay in cash, the store has no knowledge of the identity of the customer. If they use credit and debit cards, they only reveal their name.

Many travel and tourism businesses require additional information about their customers. A tour operator needs to know the full names, dates of birth and nationality of customers. This is in addition to other basic data, such as contact details or their travel insurance company.

Other information may also be revealed, such as whether a customer has a full driving licence, which is necessary if the customer intends to hire a vehicle abroad. This means that a travel and tourism organisation has the potential to hold a considerable amount of personal data about each customer. This includes bank details, methods of payment, the regularity of purchases, consumer likes and dislikes, and the size and make-up of families. Much of this information falls under data protection legislation, which requires the business to reveal, if requested, what information is held about a particular customer, why it is kept and for what purpose it is held.

Think Why do you think businesses keep data about their customers?

Customer data provides great marketing potential for a travel and tourism business. Analysis of this information reveals the most likely times of the year when customers are considering making a travel or tourism-related purchase. They can also be targeted at particular times of the year if a booking has not been made in order to offer them additional incentives to purchase from the business, rather than buying from one of the competitors.

Standards of practice

Businesses usually have their own standards of practice, which require employees to adhere to certain levels of service and interaction with customers. These standards of practice have been built up over time. They are the results of numerous interactions with customers. They create precisely the correct approach in dealings with customers in order to foster a long-term relationship.

In addition to internal standards of practice, travel and tourism businesses that are members of organisations, such as ABTA, also adhere to their codes of practice. These lay down the basic minimum standards of behaviour when dealing with customers. They aim to make sure that the interaction is transparent and that no unreasonable or untrue statements are made by the organisation in encouraging the customer to make a purchase.

Imposing effective standards of practice and adhering to industry standard codes of practice are also seen as key determining factors when customers decide which organisation to contact for travel and tourism products and services. Businesses with poor reputations and with impractical or ineffective standards and codes will tend to be avoided by many potential customers.

Political factors

In considering the political factors that could potentially affect marketing in travel and tourism, the main reference is with regard to relationships with other countries. The vast majority of countries, such as Spain, Greece and France, all have long-term and solid relationships with the UK. Other countries that are less popular or those that are less developed as tourism destinations often have rather more strained or imprecise relationships with the UK.

Sometimes this means obtaining specific permission for holiday-makers to visit or pass through that country. This is usually achieved through the visa system. Many countries have **reciprocal arrangements**. Other countries retain the visa requirement, but this is almost always automatic, such as the USA. Some countries have a less developed relationship with the UK. These may have undergone serious political change or have only just become a tourist destination by the establishment of direct flights to and from the UK. While it is not the role of the travel and tourism industry to establish international relations, the industry does play a key role in illustrating the benefits of freely accepting tourists from the UK to these countries and showing them the economic benefits of tourism.

> **Think** Which countries have you visited that required a visa for you to go there on holiday?

Research tip

Find out more about UK visas and reciprocal arrangements on the UK Foreign and Commonwealth Office website www.fco.gov.uk.

Key words

Reciprocal arrangement – an agreement that allows each country's nationals to enter and leave the countries involved freely without a visa requirement

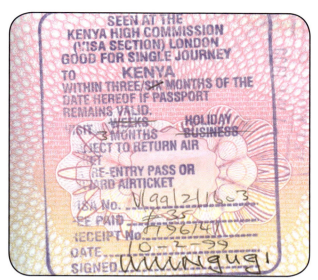
Figure 5.2 A visa must be acquired before travelling to Kenya

Economic factors

At various times, the travel and tourism industry, just like all companies that do business abroad, may need to borrow money in order to finance operations, which are affected by economic change.

Exchange rates

Exchange rates are a key economic factor. When sterling is strong and it is able to buy more foreign currency, the travel and tourism industry can use marketing in the resort to highlight the strength of the pound against the local currency. Tourists' money goes further when buying local products and services. On the other hand, when a foreign currency is strong, the costs of products and services in the resort may be high, which requires the travel and tourism organisation to adapt their marketing strategy. They may choose to focus on the fact that fewer British tourists are visiting the area.

Figure 5.3 Exchange rates effect the customer's value for money

Interest rates

When interest rates increase, it is more expensive to borrow money. This means that travel and tourism organisations can be affected in two ways. Firstly, if the organisation needs to borrow from banks, it is more expensive to do so and the profits will be reduced. Secondly, higher interest rates may mean that customers are less willing to borrow money in order to fund their holidays or leisure activities. They are reluctant to use credit cards or to take out bank loans. This means that demand for travel and tourism products will be reduced. Marketing comes into play by attempting to persuade customers that they are missing out on opportunities despite the cost. This is sometimes achieved by price reduction in order to appear to offset some of the additional costs.

Unemployment

This is another serious economic issue. Although the UK has a very low rate of unemployment, it is still a factor as travel and tourism is considered a luxury rather than a necessity. When customers' funds are short, necessities are purchased first and any remaining money can be spent on luxuries. Travel and tourism businesses use marketing to highlight the fact that holidays can still be affordable, even if disposable income is limited. This is particularly true of the domestic travel and tourism market, as well as cut-price package holidays.

Social factors

Social factors have a major impact on the travel and tourism industry. The two key issues are trends and fashions, as well as demographic change.

Over the years, the travel and tourism industry has seen constant changes in fashions and tastes with regard to the type of travel and tourism products and services required by customers. Before the 1970s, it was relatively rare for families to holiday abroad. However, during the 1970s and 1980s, the cheap package holiday, particularly to Spain, became the most common type of travel and tourism product purchased. Their popularity has begun to wane and newer, more exciting destinations are becoming more popular with customers.

Fashions and trends are not only driven by the desires of customers. They are also driven by the marketing efforts of travel and tourism organisations.

Example

A family of four has a budget of £2,000 for a 14-night overseas holiday. In theory, many thousands of different businesses are competing for that money. This means that tens of thousands of hotels, resorts, flights, transfer companies, car hire firms and insurance companies are all trying to earn a slice of that £2,000.

By using marketing, a travel and tourism organisation can position itself towards the top of the list of potential suppliers for that family. They need to match the specific requirements of the family. Therefore, an exclusive tour operator with holiday packages beginning at £4,000 cannot compete, but all of those within the price range can do so. There may also be other requirements that are specific to the family and it is the role of the tour operator or travel agent to identify those requirements and match a suitable holiday package to the customer.

Think Consider your own family and friends. What special requirements might they have on holiday?

Demographic change has also been a key factor that has affected the travel and tourism industry. We are often told that the UK is an ageing society. This means that people are often retiring earlier and living longer with a greater disposable income during their retirement. Family sizes have also tended to shrink. There are far more single parent families or families with just one child. There is a greater trend for unattached groups of individuals to holiday together. There is also an increasing multicultural mix in this country, which has an impact on the preferred locations of resorts.

Technological factors

Just as marketing can be a key factor in creating demand for particular travel and tourism products, it can also work hand-in-hand with technological developments. Until recently, air travel was expensive. The aircraft were much smaller and could carry fewer passengers. The development of wide-bodied jets has meant that more passengers can be packed on to a single flight. This makes better economic sense for the airline.

Other transport developments have also taken place. The Channel Tunnel was finally completed after many years of debate. Although it does not match the original purpose of people being able to simply drive from the UK to the European continent, it does provide an all-year-round route that is not reliant on the weather.

Transport integration has also been a key area of development, with transport hubs being developed where passengers can transfer from one mode of transport to another, such as the train station at Victoria in London, which is in close proximity to the coach station; or the express trains that run out of central London and connect with Heathrow or Stansted.

Technological developments are not only restricted to transport. Computer booking facilities have streamlined the travel and tourism industry and they have reduced the need to generate paperwork. Many transactions are now carried out electronically, including flight searches, reservations, bookings and confirmations. These systems can also generate tickets. In fact, some parts of the travel and tourism industry work without tickets, such as easyJet's ticketless online booking and confirmation service for flights, hotels and car hire.

EVIDENCE ACTIVITY

P1 – M1 – D1

Until recently the travel and tourism organisation for which you work has been relatively small and has used a marketing and advertising agency to deal with their marketing needs. Continued expansion means the establishment of a new marketing department, which the business wants you to lead. The board has asked you to prepare a report, which will systematically look at marketing in the travel and tourism industry.

1. Using examples from different travel and tourism organisations, explain the factors that affect marketing. You should include at least six different factors, drawing examples from the past ten years and consider both positive and negative factors. (P1)

2. Provide a detailed analysis of the factors which affect marketing for a selected travel and tourism organisation. Whether analysing adverse effects on marketing, or effects that may open up new opportunities for it, make sure that all chosen factors are relevant to your chosen organisation. (M1)

3. Make realistic recommendations as to how your selected organisation could adapt to the factors affecting marketing. (D1)

Figure 5.4 The Stansted Express provides a direct transport link from the airport to central London

5.2 *Know the marketing mix (the 4 Ps) of a travel and tourism organisation*

The marketing mix is at the centre of all marketing activities, not just in the travel and tourism industry, but in any type of organisation that has dealings with customers. The marketing mix has four basic elements. Together they seek to describe all of the various components and options available to a business when it frames the way in which it does marketing.

These four basic elements are known as the 4 Ps: Product, Price, Place and Promotion. In some industries, however, marketing specialists will refer to 5, 6 or 7 Ps and they include other factors beyond the basic four components. It is important to remember that no matter how many Ps are considered, they are all elements of marketing and represent choices and techniques that have to be made or used by the business.

PRODUCT

It is important to remember that whenever the term 'product' is used, it is interchangeable with the term 'service'. A product can therefore be any type of physical or intangible product or service provided by a travel and tourism organisation. As far as the definition is concerned, it is irrelevant whether the product is a theme park, baseball cap or an insurance policy.

The product is either the physical product or the service that is sold to a customer by the travel and tourism organisation. The component product is always considered first as it is probably the most important of the 4 Ps. It is the product itself that the customer requires.

The other 3 Ps are designed to make it as easy as possible for the customer to acquire the product. Not all products are the same and even products that have the same description can be remarkably different. A description such as 'holiday package' brings a certain mixture of characteristics to mind, but there can be considerable variety with regard to the characteristics or package. The first job of a business is to be able to clearly explain and highlight the key characteristics of the product or service that they are selling. It is also vital to convince the customer that there is something unique and special about the product or service that sets it above all of the competitors' similar products or services.

Key words

Intangible – something that cannot be physically touched

Nature of product

Travel and tourism products have three common features: intangible, perishable and service related.

Intangible

These products and services cannot be touched. They are not a physical product.

Example

An airline seat is only hired by the customer for the duration of the flight, although the seat itself is physical. The customer does not keep the seat when they leave the aircraft.

All services are intangible and, since the travel and tourism industry is mainly a service-based industry, most of its products or services are intangible.

Perishable

Most travel and tourism products and services are 'perishable' – meaning they have a sell-by date. A flight will leave at a particular time on a particular day and the product cannot be sold once it has departed. Equally, once the date has passed, hotel availability for that period has gone forever. This means that most travel and tourism products and services have a limited life. They are sold in advance of the time that they become available and no longer exist once that date has passed.

Service related

The vast majority of products and services offered in the industry are service related, including information services, booking, payments, confirmations, ticketing, services provided in the resort, at attractions, entrance tickets and ancillary services, such as car hire and insurance.

Example

A restaurant in the tourism industry provides a mix of tangible and intangible products to its customers. The tangible parts of the product range are the actual food and drink provided to the customers. All of the other aspects, products and services offered by the business are intangible. This includes the work of the waiters and waitresses, bar staff, chef and kitchen staff, cleaners and those responsible for the layout and decor of the restaurant.

Figure 5.5 A restaurant provides both tangible and intangible products

Think Make a list of the various products and services that you have learned about in the travel and tourism industry. Divide them between the categories: intangible, perishable and service related.

Characteristics

A key element of marketing in the product component of the marketing mix is to make the products or services offered by the organisation instantly distinguishable from other similar products and services offered by competitors. This is known as branding.

Branding requires the business to create, promote, protect and preserve a recognisable name or set of features that can be instantly recognised by existing and potential customers. This is not simply naming the business. It goes beyond that and it is the foundation of product brands and product ranges.

Example

Thomas Cook has the Club 18–30 brand, which is designed to attract customers who enjoy clubbing, beach holidays and travelling with others of a similar age. They also have Thomas Cook Signature, which has high-end, more expensive resorts and packages. There is also Thomas Cook Sport, which focuses on sport centred or themed holiday breaks.

Figure 5.6a Thomas Cook Signature brand

Figure 5.6b Club 18-30 brand logo

A vital part of branding is to identify the key features of a product or service and to emphasise them whenever the product is marketed.

Example

The Disney Corporation is ranked 7th in the world's top 10 brands and has a value of over £30 billion. It is the only organisation in the travel and tourism industry that is found in the top 10.

Brand building incorporates several key factors:

- quality – identifying the key benefits that customers expect

- positioning – how the customer views the product and compares it to similar products

- re-positioning – what steps the business may have to take if its original market goes into decline and how it can reinvent itself for a new market

- communications – these need to be clear and build customer awareness of the product

- credibility – that any claims made about the product or service can be backed up and proven by the business

- internal marketing – this is an important consideration as anyone selling or being involved in the product must fully support it and reflect the brand image at all times

- long-term perspective – this means that the business may need to be patient as they gradually build the brand's identity and the customers become aware of it.

Research tip

Look at another major tour operator's brochures and research the different brands that they offer.

An essential part of building a brand is to identify and emphasise something that is truly unique about that product or service. Customers need to be made aware of at least one feature or characteristic that differentiates the product or service from anything else that they could buy. This is known as a unique selling point (USP) and can be emphasised in all of the marketing. If the unique selling point is copied or no longer relevant, then the business will need to look for, or develop, a new USP in order to maintain the brand and its differentiation from the competitors.

Features

An independent travel agent sells a wide range of different brands or packages, which are supplied to them as agents by a number of different businesses. If a customer purchases a ready-made package from a tour operator, it will already include a number of features or characteristics that the customer probably already knows about and prefers.

Tailor-made packages generally contain products or services from a variety of different suppliers. The customer may not necessarily know some of the features or the names of some of the suppliers. All of the product features and characteristics are created to satisfy customer needs.

Businesses need to carefully manage their products, so that they continue to meet customer needs. For many larger travel and tourism organisations, if not for all businesses involved in the industry, gradual change is absolutely essential. The bigger the business, the more difficult the challenge will be as they have to manage groups of brands and different product lines. They must be aware of changing customer needs and wants and then adapt the features and characteristics of their products to match these changes. If a product always remains the same, regardless of changing needs and wants, customers will eventually stop purchasing it. The features and characteristics will no longer match customers' needs and wants. Businesses need to be acutely aware of this factor.

Example

Theme parks constantly monitor the number of customers using particular rides. They use this as a key factor in their decision-making process to replace a ride with a newer one. They are also aware of the fact that by not adding new rides each season, customers may become bored with the variety of products or services available in the theme park and visit another park instead.

Figure 5.7 New and exciting rides are essential to the continued popularity of a theme park

Product lifecycle

Every product has a lifecycle. It is created, it grows, it reaches a stage of maturity, begins to fade and then eventually dies.

Businesses need to manage this lifecycle, control the various stages and extend the product's life for as long as possible. They must also make the key decision to kill off the product if nothing can be done to save it. However, they need to have a replacement product at hand, otherwise their sales could be drastically affected.

The product lifecycle was originally designed to look at the profitability of a product over a period of time. It therefore looks at sales over a period of time. The key stages can be seen in figure 5.8.

Introduction

This is when the product is brought on to the market. At this stage, it requires the maximum amount of help to establish itself on the market and for customers to become aware of it. A great deal of spending on marketing is necessary, otherwise it will fail, regardless of how good the product may be.

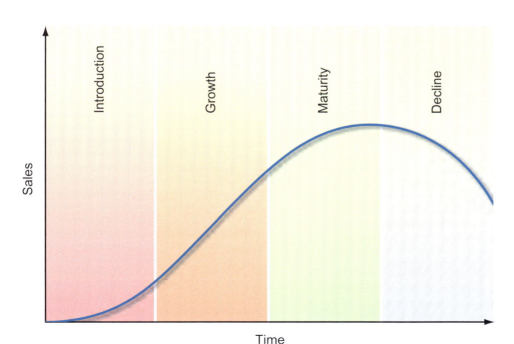

Figure 5.8 Product lifecycle curve

Growth

By this stage, a large number of customers should have learned about the product and more people are buying it. In order to continue the growth, the business may make small alterations to make it match customer needs and wants more closely.

Maturity

This is often shown as a flat level of sales, but the product is now well established and is enjoying steady sales. There are a large number of loyal customers who continue to buy the product, but the business needs to be aware of the fact that its success will have alerted its competitors and they will be trying to copy it and take sales away. This means that modifications may still be needed and new marketing ideas created to keep the sales high.

Decline

This stage shows that the product is reaching the end of its useful life. Demand is falling and sales are dropping. It is becoming less profitable. The business has three choices. It can either let the product die off naturally, try to modify the product in a radical way or spend a great deal of money on marketing to try to bring sales up to a better level again.

There are other stages that could be considered in the product lifecycle. The business spends money on developing the product and the brand before the introduction or launch of a product. At this stage they are spending, but not earning, so the income is negative. At the end of the maturity stage, there is often another stage before decline, which is called saturation. It shows a slight dip in sales before the product goes into steady decline. At this point, the business has a real chance to make adjustments before decline sets in. This could be in terms of price, features or marketing in order to stop the product from going into decline.

If the business can successfully stop the product from going into decline, it is said to have extended the lifecycle of the product. It can be re-launched, but it will have the benefit of having loyal customers already purchasing it, so in a

short period of time sales should be even higher. Extension strategies can involve re-branding, targeting different types of customers or looking to re-price the product or service and change its features.

PRICE

In a highly competitive market such as the travel and tourism industry, price can be a key part of effective marketing. It is important to remember that it is the only component of the marketing mix that actually generates any money for the business. The product itself, any promotional methods used and the ways in which the products are distributed all cost the business money.

In a service-based industry, price considerations are all about the perceived value of the product and this means value in terms of marketing. It is often shown in the following formula, which is used not as a mathematical calculation, but rather as a starting point.

$$\text{Perceived value of the product} = \text{the customers' perceived benefits} - \text{the costs to the customer}$$

As far as customers are concerned, the perceived value of a product offered by the industry can be increased in one of two ways:

1) by reducing the cost to the customer

2) by increasing the benefits that the product will give the customer.

By carefully manipulating these two features, a business will hope to create an effective pricing strategy, but not everything that can affect the demand for a business's products is controlled by the business.

Table 5.1 Factors affecting demand that can and cannot be controlled by the business

Factors affecting demand that can be controlled by the business	Factors affecting demand that cannot be controlled by the business
Advertising and sales promotion	Customers' tastes and fashions
The training of the business's sales force	The amount of disposable income customers may have
Distribution through as many outlets and points of contact with customers as possible	The price charged for very similar products by the competitors
Excellent after-sales service	The price of additional extras provided by partner businesses, such as car hire companies
Forward-thinking product research and development	
The actual price of the product	

Pricing strategies

Most consumers of travel and tourism products and services theoretically have a price ceiling beyond which they are reluctant to go. This means that businesses have to be very careful with their pricing strategies, so that they do not alienate potential customers by advertising relatively high headline prices. Prices are almost always quoted as being 'from' a certain price. In many cases, this is simply used as bait to attract customers. While a particular product may be priced at this low figure at a particular time of year, the cost is generally far higher for the majority of the time.

As there is considerable competition for customers in the industry, one of the major ways in which pricing strategies are created is to analyse the cost structure of the competitors. Broadly speaking, a business needs to be either slightly cheaper or in line with their nearest competitor, which offers very similar products and services to very similar customers.

It is not always possible to be able to do this with any great accuracy. Tour operator brochures are traditionally printed well in advance of the main summer seasons. At this time, information about competitors will be sketchy and price comparisons can only be made with pricing strategies that were adopted in the previous season.

A solution to this problem is to introduce discounting. For many businesses, discounting is a key part of their pricing structure. They give headline prices that are actually in excess of what they reasonably expect to receive for the product. This gives them room for manoeuvre to drop the price down to a level that will still provide them with a profit.

Discounting is not only used to dispose of products and services that are high in supply and low in demand. This was what discounting was used for in the past, but as the travel and tourism industry has perishable goods, any income from what would have been an empty seat or an empty bed provides valuable income that the business would otherwise have lost.

Like many other consumer products, those provided by the travel and tourism industry have a seasonal nature. By looking at the same holiday to the same resort and accommodation over the entire season, it is clear to see that there are peaks in terms of demand and price. Broadly speaking, the greater the demand, the greater the price. In order to stimulate additional demand when there is still supply that has not been taken up, the business will offer the products at a lower price.

Figure 5.9 Skiing holidays are priced according to the season

Example

Particular travel packages attract higher prices, according to the nature of the destination and the time of year. Traditionally, the most expensive periods when high demand is expected for beach-based packages are times when there are school holidays, such as Easter and July and August. Outside these periods, the same products are available at considerably lower costs. Equally, winter breaks for sports such as skiing tend to be more expensive when the resort has fresh falls of snow, rather than hotter periods where the skiing might not be so easy.

Think Can you think of any other times of year when prices may be higher or lower? Explain your reasoning.

PLACE

As the vast majority of travel and tourism products are intangible, the industry has many more options in terms of how it distributes its products to its customers than many other businesses.

Example

A washing machine manufacturer has to physically transport the products to warehouses and retail outlets. Once a sale has been made, the retailer must organise transport to deliver the washing machine to the customer's home.

For the majority of travel and tourism products, an envelope full of documents is the only distribution factor. This includes confirmation letters, flight tickets and hotel vouchers. This means that the options open to the industry are numerous.

Traditionally, many of the products were sold in the high street through travel agents. They fulfilled the same kind of role as any other type of shop, with an interested customer being shown a range of products and a financial transaction taking place. The travel and tourism industry has now increasingly moved over to either telephone sales or online sales. This means that the physical location of the business is no longer of any great importance. A tour operator does not have to be located in an expensive high street shop. It can be on a relatively cheap industrial estate anywhere in the country.

Place is a measure of how a business tries to maximise the ways in which its customers can access the business and its products. It wants to make this access as straightforward as possible. There should be no barriers and no difficulties. By promoting their services, the business hopes to attract customers by providing the easiest possible means to make a booking.

However, some travel and tourism businesses do have location concerns. Equally, some travel and tourism companies sell physical products, although these are usually in addition to the main product that is being sold.

Physical location and accessibility

All businesses want to have a highly visible market presence. For some companies, this means remaining in the high street as many customers prefer dealing face-to-face with company representatives. Others prefer to make their purchases by telephone, having looked through brochures and sales literature at their leisure. Increasingly, however, people are buying products on websites. This is the business's new shop window and many larger businesses have spent millions of pounds on ensuring that customers can easily navigate their websites, view video clips of resorts and make secure payments without any fear of using their bank details.

Actual physical location is therefore not a major concern for many tour operators or for providers of ancillary products such as insurance. Obviously there are many businesses in the industry that have no choice about their location, including:

- airlines – although head offices and booking systems can be located anywhere, points of contact have to be established at all major airports as their services run from these locations and sales can be made there

- attractions – for many attractions, such as historic sites, there is no choice with regard to location. Other newer attractions tend to locate where there is either a large population centre or excellent transport links, such as Alton Towers and Chessington World of Adventure

- businesses relying on suppliers – location may not simply be a question of being close to a large number of potential customers. It may also mean being accessible to businesses that supply the company. This would include restaurants and takeaway establishments.

Think Can you think of any other types of businesses that have no choice with regard to their location?

Channels of distribution

As you have seen in Unit 1, Book 1, the industry uses chains or channels of distribution to make sure that their products are available in as many locations as possible and are accessible to customers at all times.

For many years, airlines and tour operators simply sold their products through travel agents. It was the travel agent that usually had the only point of contact with the customer. Over the years, however, the channels of distribution have become more complex and flexible. It is now possible for customers to purchase directly from airlines and tour operators.

It is in the interests of all businesses to maintain both direct and indirect contact with customers for the following reasons.

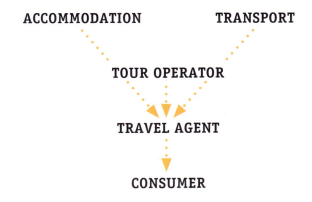

Figure 5.10 A simple channel of distribution

Direct contact

This allows direct dialogue between the actual supplier of the product and the customer. It also means that the supplier of the product retains more of the purchase price of the product as commission does not have to be paid to any intermediary.

Indirect contact

In order to maximise sales, other businesses in the travel and tourism industry can perform the selling task for the supplier. Airlines cannot hope to replicate the high street presence of a chain of travel agents. In some respects, this has changed with tour operators purchasing airlines and travel agent chains. This allows them to have direct contact with the customer, while still controlling the main components of the products that they sell.

PROMOTION

Promotion is the final component of the marketing mix. It involves creating and transmitting messages and information about the products and services sold by a business, either to its customers or to its suppliers. Promotion means far more than simply advertising products and services. The whole area of promotion has become increasingly more sophisticated, with larger numbers of television channels, radio stations, newspapers, magazines and, of course, the Internet. It is now

much harder to attract attention. It has also meant that it has become increasingly more expensive to run an effective promotional campaign. Only the largest organisations in the industry can afford to have a significant television presence.

Example

There are a number of advertising slots used for programmes on channels such as Sky Three. These advertising programmes tend to be used either by Sky Travel or by Thomas Cook TV. It gives both companies the opportunity to showcase particular packages and sell directly to customers through telephone contact.

Methods

The most common form of promotion is advertising. The purpose of advertising is to be as persuasive as possible in getting a message across to potential customers in order to encourage them to respond by making contact or making a purchase. Advertising has three key objectives:

1) to inform potential customers about a new product

2) to encourage customers to switch from one brand to another brand

3) to remind customers about the brand and where they can buy it.

Table 5.2 Advertising objectives and the measurement of their success in the travel and tourism industry

Advertising objective	How success is measured
Increase in sales	By the number of customer enquiries generated and the number of enquiries that actually become sales
Change in customer attitudes	Comparing the types of products ordered by customers to purchases that were made before the advertising campaign
Building customer loyalty	Number of repeat purchases and reducing the number of customers lost to competitors
Informing customers	To carry out tests of customer awareness, the number of enquiries from customers and the number of new sales
Reminding customers about the product	Testing customer awareness before and after the campaign and the number of enquiries from existing and new customers
Building a brand image	Testing whether customers recognise the brand name and asking them what they believe to be the perceived values of that brand

Advertising needs to be meaningful as far as the customer is concerned. They need to feel that the advertisement is relevant to them. This also means that the advertisement needs to be distinctive and recognisable in order to keep the attention of the customer. Another important consideration is that the advert should be factually acurate and believable.

Like many other techniques in promotion, advertising is judged in two different ways in terms of its effectiveness.

1) are more people aware of the product during or after the advertising campaign?

2) has the advertising stimulated sales?

For the most part, organisations in the travel and tourism industry have a key advertising objective in mind. They also have a fairly clear idea as to how they can measure whether that objective has been reached.

Public relations is another key part of promotion. The purpose of public relations is to establish and maintain goodwill and mutual understanding between the business and any groups or organisations it has dealings with. For businesses in the travel and tourism industry, this means that their 'public' includes:

- their own employees and shareholders

- their customers, past and present, as well as the general public

- pressure groups, environmental groups and professional organisations

- the government

- the media.

The idea behind public relations is to try to influence public opinion by communicating positive images and stories about the business. This is usually achieved by press releases, obtaining media coverage, getting celebrities to endorse their products, as well as running competitions that offer prizes and attending exhibitions.

Sales promotions can include:

- offering discounts

- issuing coupons and promotional codes

- gifts with purchases

- competitions and prizes

- loyalty incentives (such as frequent flyer programmes).

Sales promotions aim to encourage customers to buy a product. They are usually short-term and their goal is to attract additional interest in the products at the beginning of the sales period or if a particular period sees a slump in sales.

Direct marketing aims to establish a direct relationship between the business and its final customers. It includes:

- direct response advertisements on television and radio

- tour operator brochures

- websites

- magazine inserts and advertisements

- direct mail

- telemarketing.

The travel and tourism industry makes more and more use of databases containing customer names and contact details. Companies regularly contact their customers in order to encourage them to purchase directly. They can also buy mailing lists from other businesses or from brokers who compile lists of potential customers with similar characteristics to the business's own customers.

Think Can you think of any other types of direct marketing?

Materials

There are many common types of promotional material as far as the travel and tourism industry is concerned. These include:

- brochures
- leaflets
- advertisements
- press releases (used for public relations)
- direct selling techniques
- in-store or point-of-sale material.

Businesses use a variety of different types of marketing communications, which is often referred to as their promotional mix. It is a blend of advertising, public relations, sales promotion and direct sales. These are the four most common components of any promotional mix.

EVIDENCE ACTIVITY

P2 – M2

The next part of your report requires you to describe the marketing mix. In order to assist your business in understanding the implications of the marketing mix you will need to focus on one travel and tourism organisation. Your employer is happy for you to either produce a written report or to make an oral presentation.

1. Describe the marketing mix of a selected travel and tourism organisation. (P2)

2. Explain how the 4Ps work together as a marketing mix in your selected travel and tourism organisation. (M2)

5.3 Be able to conduct a market research activity for a travel and tourism organisation

MARKET RESEARCH ACTIVITY

Unit 26 focuses on how to carry out research in general. Many of the techniques used for general research are applicable to market research.

Market research aims to assist businesses in their decision-making. Businesses need to be aware of the environment in which they operate. This could include the activities of their competitors, what their customers want and the potential size of markets. All market research begins with a basic requirement for information. The information needs to be able to assist decision-making or make the situation clearer, so a more informed decision can be made.

Planning

The first stage is to plan the market research. Planning has three major components.

Identifying objectives

This is an important first step as it seeks to identify the precise purpose of the market research and what the researchers hope to achieve or discover. This may mean answering specific questions, proving or disproving something or finding out about topics, attitudes or opinions that have not been researched before.

Research methods

Having established the objectives of the research, it is now important to identify how any necessary information will be collected. As we will see when the research design gets underway, certain documents have to be created in order to collect and collate the data.

Target group

This is essentially the source of the information that will be collected. What types of people need to be investigated or asked for their opinions? What are their characteristics? What assumptions are being made about their knowledge?

Design research documentation

Having identified the best means by which information can be gathered from the target group, professionally produced research documentation has to be created. Research documentation has to serve two major purposes:

1) it needs to look professional as it will be used and/or seen by the target group

2) it needs to be as easy as possible for the researcher to analyse the data from the documents.

There are various types of research documentation that could be used, as seen in table 5.3.

Since all of these different types of research only involve a limited number of people, they are classed as qualitative or in-depth research. If the researcher uses pure statistics and facts from a large number of sources, this would be known as quantitative research.

Table 5.3 Different types of research documentation and their descriptions

Type of research documentation	Description
Questionnaires	These need to have clear questions with a number of options that are relevant to the target group. Ideally, a number of multiple-choice questions are used, as well as some more open questions, allowing space for the respondent to make comments.
Observation checklists	These assume that the researcher is looking for particular types of behaviour in the target group that can be recognised and noted. Observation checklists generally include a list of key words or behaviours that can then be ticked as having been observed and any necessary comments added.
Focus group reports	These are small groups of carefully selected individuals that represent the target group. They are prompted to give their opinions through discussions, which are stimulated by the researcher. The researcher and, perhaps, an observer can then note the key aspects of the discussion. Ideally, the whole focus group session could be recorded and played back later for deeper analysis.
Feedback cards	These are usually given out to the target group after they have experienced something. The target group is asked to comment on their feelings towards a particular experience, product or customer service situation. These can provide very useful on the spot and instant information.

Secondary research sources

As mentioned, information such as statistics is classed as being quantitative. However, it can also be put into another category, along with company records and information published on travel and tourism organisations' websites.

When information is being collected for the very first time, regardless of whether it is qualitative or quantitative research, it is often referred to as primary research. This means that the data is being collected for the first time or, at the very least, it is being assembled and used for an entirely new purpose.

Existing data that has already been published by a business and perhaps used for another purpose is referred to as secondary research. It has not been collected or used for the purpose that the researcher now wishes to put it to. However, it can still provide valuable insights into the industry and can often form the basis of a market research activity and give clues and directions to whether primary research needs to be carried out.

EVIDENCE ACTIVITY

P3 – P4 – M3 – D2

In order to illustrate how market research could work, you have been asked to plan, document and then conduct a market research activity.

1. Prepare a sample market research plan that illustrates the various market research options. (P3)

2. Produce a questionnaire that has at least 10 questions. Make sure that it is neat and of industry standard. (P3)

3. Select a suitable sample of respondents to ensure that an appropriate number of the questionnaires are completed. (P4)

4. Describe and identify useful sources of secondary market research to support your own primary research. (P4)

5. Explain how your plan and documentation meet the objectives of the market research activity. (M3)

6. Analyse the findings of your market research and make realistic recommendations. (D2)

5.4 Be able to arrange a promotional campaign for a travel and tourism organisation

PROMOTIONAL PLAN

In organising a promotional campaign, the materials that are used should support the promotional technique and the objectives of the campaign. The travel and tourism industry uses a wide variety of leaflets, brochures, advertising, direct mail and special offers. There are literally thousands in use at any given time.

It is important to recognise that promotional materials have specific layouts and designs and that they are always written in a style easy for the customer to understand and to respond with the minimum of effort. There are many factors that determine precisely what goes into a promotional campaign. However, three key factors are the most dominant.

Availability of resources

This generally relates to the budget that is available for the campaign. It is important to remember that certain types of media are very expensive, particularly national newspapers and television. In many cases, the availability of funds for the campaign is a key factor as it limits the business's choices.

Size of the market

The larger the market, the more likely it is that the promotional campaign will be broad and use mass market media types. Small markets, where the number of potential buyers is even smaller, may mean that the business may use direct selling techniques in order to be cost-effective.

Amount of information needed by the customer

For complex products, customers need a great deal of information in order to help them decide whether to make a purchase. This means that small advertisements may not be appropriate and that leaflets or brochures containing in-depth information may be necessary. Some products do not require a great deal of information to prompt a sale.

Objectives

Ultimately, the primary objectives are two-fold for many travel and tourism organisations. Firstly, they want to increase potential customers' awareness of the products or services that they offer. Secondly, at the very least, they want to prompt enquiries, but preferably sales. The promotional plan needs to clearly identify the key objectives and how success or failure could be measured.

Promotional methods

There are five main promotional methods. Each method is more or less appropriate in different sets of circumstances. It is important to remember that businesses often use more than one promotional method at the same time.

1) Advertising – includes any paid-for non-personal communication, such as advertisements in newspapers and magazines. The intention is to persuade and inform.

2) Direct marketing – to create a direct relationship between the business and the customer by making contact with them either face-to-face, by telephone or e-mail.

3) Sales promotion – to stimulate demand for a product by offering incentives to customers.

4) Public relations – obtaining space in the media, but without actually paying directly for the space as the business would have to in the case of an advertisement.

5) Personal selling – usually contact is initiated by a sales promotion, public relations or an advertisement. The customer contacts the business and it is the role of the business to transform an enquiry into a definite sale.

Target group

The characteristics, such as the age, interests, gender, available income and a host of other demographic features of customers, determine the type of messages contained in a promotional campaign. Any messages included in the campaign need to be directly addressed and relevant to the target group.

Timing

Promotional campaigns need a considerable amount of organisation and forward thinking. Space needs to be booked in the relevant media and sales literature needs to be designed, approved and printed. The sales literature must be distributed and employees may need to be ready to begin receiving enquiries, which are stimulated by the promotional campaign.

The travel and tourism industry operates in cycles throughout the year. Depending on the type of organisation and the nature of their products and services, certain key seasonal periods will be relevant. Promotional plans need to be timed carefully, so that they give both the customer and the business sufficient time before the products or services are either consumed or lost, if they have not been sold.

Budget

The budget plays a key role in determining the limitations of a promotional campaign. Businesses expect a promotional campaign's costs to at least be covered by any subsequent sales that it has stimulated. Ideally, the promotional campaign's costs should only be a fraction of the increased sales. Businesses need to think very carefully about the budgets as these costs have to be met before any income is likely to be received as a benefit of the campaign.

Bad timing and poor budgeting can seriously affect the cash flow of the business, making it difficult for them to afford other operations and activities to which they are already committed on a financial basis.

Monitoring and evaluating

A business looks for a return on its investment. A promotional campaign represents a major investment in the business and the business has a particular target return in mind for the amount it has invested.

They judge the success or failure of the promotional campaign by how much extra revenue is generated. Some may take a long-term view and measure brand awareness or changes in attitudes towards the business and its products. Ultimately, however, it boils down to increased income and increased profit as the primary tools of measuring success.

PROMOTIONAL MATERIAL

Different types of promotion use different formats for their promotional materials. In addition to common promotional material, such as brochures, there are also other key types of promotional material, which are commonly used throughout the whole of the travel and tourism industry.

Leaflets

Leaflets are highly flexible promotional materials that can be inserted into magazines and newspapers, handed out to customers, left in leaflet dispensers or posted through household letterboxes. They can be designed to encourage direct contact and enquiries.

Advertisements

Generally, they can only hope to inform and to encourage the customer to make contact with the business, due to space constraints. They outline the key benefits of the business or its products and provide contact details or give an indication as to where the products can be purchased by the customer.

Direct marketing letters

These are personalised letters that are created using computer software and the business's customer database. They can be specifically addressed and mailed out, giving the impression of a personalised letter. They can also be personalised in the sense of offering particularly relevant types of products and services or offers in line with the types of purchases that the customer has made in the past.

Figure 5.11 A direct marketing letter sent out by Mark Warner
Source MarkWarner.co.uk

Press releases

These are created by the public relations department and are sent out to representatives of the media. The purpose of a press release is to provide the media with a ready-made story, usually with quotes, a human angle and relevant photographs or illustrative material. The idea is to make it as easy as possible for the reporter or editor to transform the press release into a news story.

EVIDENCE ACTIVITY

P5 – P6 – M4

As your final task for your employer you need to convince them that it is perfectly feasible for the organisation to begin planning and implementing their own promotional campaigns.

1. Plan a promotional campaign for a selected travel and tourism organisation, which meets the requirement of at least one key marketing objective. (P5)

2. Produce a suitable piece of promotional material, such as a leaflet or a pamphlet. (P6)

3. Ensure that the material is fit for purpose, well presented and attractive. (P6)

4. Explain how your planned campaign should meet its objectives. Make sure you give valid reasons. Ideally objectives should be measurable. (M4)

Preparing for employment in the travel and tourism industry

unit 6

The travel and tourism industry offers a wide range of interesting and challenging careers.

You will investigate a selection of careers in different sectors across the industry, looking at entry requirements, routes of progression and promotion, responsibilities, skills and qualifications required for specific career pathways.

You will also review your own skills, qualifications and experience, comparing this with your desired career path by identifying your own development and training needs.

Competition for some careers can be intense. You will learn how to prepare yourself by analysing the stages of the recruitment and selection process from the perspective of an employer and a candidate. This analysis will help you to develop an understanding of where you can gain information to promote yourself positively when applying for a post.

Working practices will also be examined, so that you will appreciate the factors that motivate employees and how this helps to develop an effective and positive working environment.

By the end of this unit, you will:

So you want to be a...

People Development Manager

My name   Lucy Ellis
Age   28
Income   £24,000 + benefits

If you are a driven individual who is comfortable leading large groups of people, here is an opportunity to have the responsibilities you crave...

What do you do?

I work for a hotel and my main duties are to help in the recruitment and selection of staff within my company and act as an intermediary between line managers and the General Manager.

What responsibilities do you have?

I am responsible for ensuring that the hotel has the right teams in place to deliver on the objectives we have set ourselves to deliver to the customer. It is my job to make sure line managers are recruiting the appropriate staff and to provide those staff with training and guidance. I also provide support to HR and on legal matters.

How did you get into the job?

I left college after completing a GNVQ Intermediate and then Advance in Travel and Tourism. An employment agency found me a vacancy in their office as a temp. I enjoyed the work and stayed there for a couple of year, until I started my current job which I have now been in for almost five years.

How did you find your current job?

The job was advertised on the website www.jobsearch.co.uk. The site is brilliant and allows you to refine your search, so you only get results for the jobs you're really interested in. I applied online and was offered an interview as a result.

> **❝ I applied online and was offered an interview as a result ❞**

What are the hours like?

I work a traditional nine to five day, any five of the seven days in a week; although I regularly have to work longer as I am juggling the training of new recruits with my other administrational responsibilities.

What skills do you need?

Exceptional people skills are vital in my job; I have to work at a fast pace to build a raport with all staff and sometimes have to deal with members of staff with problems that need to be handled delicately and thoughtfully. It takes a special kind of person to be able to help those who are feeling vulnerable or upset.

I also have to be exceptionally organised and am constantly having to make quick judgement calls on how best to divide my time. A commercial mind-set is essential.

How good is the pay?

The pay is good. Like most people I would love to get paid more but I feel that the pay I get is reasonable for the job I do.

Grading criteria

The table below shows what you need to do to gain a pass, merit or distinction in this part of the qualification. Make sure you refer back to it when you are completing work so you can judge whether you are meeting the criteria and what you need to do to fill in gaps in your knowledge or experience.

In this unit there are 3 evidence activities that give you an opportunity to demonstrate your achievement of the grading criteria:

page 44	**P1, P2, M1, D1**
page 54	**P3, P4, M2**
page 63	**P5, M3, D2**

To achieve a pass grade the evidence must show that the learner is able to...	To achieve a merit grade the evidence must show that, in addition to the pass criteria, the learner is able to...	To achieve a distinction grade the evidence must show that, in addition to the pass and merit criteria, the learner is able to...
P1 Describe career opportunities for four sectors of the travel and tourism industry and produce a description of two jobs	**M1** Compare two jobs in the travel and tourism industry, taking into account the entry levels and opportunities for promotion and progression	**D1** Evaluate your own suitability for a chosen job and prepare an action plan to meet all training and development needs
P2 Produce a personal skills audit in preparation for employment	**M2** Produce guidelines for success in the different stages of the recruitment and selection process and use these to evaluate personal performance	**D2** Analyse the factors that contribute to an effective workplace, highlighting good practice from different travel and tourism organisations
P3 Describe the stages of the recruitment and selection process	**M3** Explain how different travel and tourism organisations motivate staff in the workplace	
P4 Demonstrate suitability for employment during different stages of the job selection process		
P5 Describe the factors that contribute to an effective workplace in travel and tourism organisations		

6.1 Career opportunities in the travel and tourism industry

TRAVEL AND TOURISM INDUSTRY SECTORS

The travel and tourism industry is the world's largest industry with 2.1 million people employed in the UK alone. The travel and tourism industry in the UK is expected to increase by 100% within the next ten years.

Table 6.1 Employment in tourism-related industries. June 2003
Source: The Office for National Statistics

Type of employment	Thousands
Hotels and other tourist accommodation	393
Restaurants, cafés, etc.	590
Bar, public houses and nightclubs	568
Travel agencies and tour operators	117
Libraries, museums and other cultural activities	87
Sport and other recreational activities	413
Total	2,168

Example

Extract from 'Tourism to double' by 2016'
by Chris Gray

Travel Trade Gazette, 17 March 2006

Global tourism is set to double in size to become a $12 trillion industry within ten years, while the divide between mass-market 'mega resorts' and exclusive tailor-made holidays will become even greater, two reports claim.

A World Travel and Tourism Council study predicts the UK's spending on personal travel will grow from $169 billion this year to $228 billion in 2016, and the UK industry will grow at 3.1% per year for the next decade.

Think Do you think this growth will be sustained after 2016?

The travel and tourism industry is made up of a number of different components, including accommodation, transport, attractions, tour operators, travel agencies, tourism development and promotion, and trade associations and regulatory bodies. You will look at each of these sectors and the career opportunities within them.

Figure 6.1 Flow chart showing the structure of travel and tourism in the UK

Figure 6.2a Serviced accommodation can range from large hotels…

Figure 6.2b … to intimate bed and breakfasts

Accommodation

We tend to divide the accommodation sector into serviced and room-only accommodation. Serviced accommodation offers additional services rather than just a place to sleep and can include food and beverage provision, leisure and recreation facilities and business facilities. This leads to a range of career opportunities including reception work, housekeeping, chefs, waiters, porters, concierge services, conference and banqueting, and the management of each of these individual areas as well as general management. This sector is looked at in greater depth in Unit 19, Book 3.

Transport provision

Transport provision can be divided into three sectors: land, sea and air. There are a range of different career opportunities in each of these areas.

Table 6.2 UK residents' visits abroad 2001 to 2005
Source: The Office for National Statistics

Mode of transport	Number of visits
Air	53,626
Sea	8,102
Tunnel	4,713
Total	66,441

Road and rail

Road and rail transport includes trains, taxis, coaches, trams and even rickshaws and canal boats. This range of transport options leads to a large range of career opportunities from drivers, ticketing offices, security and guards to office-based roles in the management and orchestration of services.

Sea

Although a majority of long-haul passengers will travel by air, a substantial number of European tourists will travel by sea. There are a number of different ways of travelling to the UK by sea, including ferries, cruise ships, and catamarans.

These services offer different job roles, from sailors, navigators and engineers to operation on the ships themselves as duty–free shop staff, catering staff, entertainers and customer service agents who take care of the customers on board. The staff require supervision and management, thereby creating a range of job roles, such as purser and captains on board a ferry or cruise ship.

Air

The staff working for an airline can be divided into ground crew and air crew. The air crew includes the pilot, co-pilot, flight engineer and navigator, all of whom are responsible for the flying of the aircraft and have overall responsibility for the safety of everyone on board. Cabin crew are also employed to look after and maintain the safety of passengers during the flight.

The ground crew includes customer service agents, baggage handlers, dispatchers and airport management. There are also people involved on the land and in the air, such as air traffic controllers.

Visitor attractions

The range of attractions is as vast as the job roles. There are some general career paths, such as guides, security staff, customer service staff and management. There is also a huge range of specific career roles that depend on the type of attraction. Museums, galleries and stately homes may have curators who are responsible for the collections as well as restorers and conservation workers who keep the exhibits and maintain them. In theme parks, there are maintenance and engineering teams. A lot of attractions will also have shops and places to eat, ranging from fast food to high-class restaurants.

Figure 6.3 *The Tate Modern in London offers a restaurant with excellent views of the city*

Cruising

You will need to be over 21 to work onboard a cruise ship and most positions require either qualifications or experience of working in that particular area. There are many different job opportunities available including qualified deck officers, engineers, medical staff, entertainment staff, retail staff, cleaners, waiters, chefs and bar staff to name but a few. It is vital to have customer service experience and also be able to work well under pressure.

There are also some shore based job opportunities working as the ships agent, organising or accompanying the transfer of passengers from the airport to the ship or taking bookings and organising shore excursions. Cruise operators also employ staff in their offices to take and process reservations and organise the shore side activities.

Tour operators

Many tour operators' products are sold by travel agents, but they also sell directly to the public by telephone or over the Internet. A large number of different people are employed to create a package holiday. There are buyers who source the appropriate components of the holiday. This involves travelling to check that the accommodation offers what is required, booking charter flights and organising transport between the airport and the accommodation. People are also required to create the promotional materials to sell the holiday. These job roles include webmasters, text editors, copy editors, writers and photographers. Some tour operators may print brochures in-house, although most **outsource** them to specialist printers.

There are customer service agents who answer enquiries, solve problems and send out tickets and itineraries.

At the resort, there is a team of resort representatives, children's representatives and resort managers who are responsible for looking after the holiday-makers and for dealing with any problems and issues that may occur during their stay. Holiday representatives also sell excursions and provide entertainment. Children's representatives run Kid's Clubs to entertain the children. A growing area for tour operators is the disaster recovery team, which is sometimes also known as the crisis management team.

Key words

Outsource – to contract work to an outside organisation

Travel agents

Most high street travel agencies will employ travel consultants, who are also known as agents. They also employ a management team, including store managers and area managers. There are a number of head office jobs in administrative roles such as accounts, marketing and human resources. They may also have trainee consultants.

More and more travel agents are offering their products on the Internet. This has led to a number of different roles in web design and call centre staff to answer enquiries and provide bookings.

Tourism development and promotion

VisitBritain promotes the UK abroad in order to encourage incoming tourism. The countries in the UK also have their own tourist boards, which are known as VisitWales, VisitScotland, Enjoy England and the Northern Ireland Tourist Board. There are ten regional tourist boards for each part of England.

The tourist boards employ staff to work in tourist information centres, as well as centre managers and head office staff. People are also employed to link the industry's needs with education providers in order to improve the quality of training and skills in the industry. VisitBritain promotes tourism to Britain through trade shows and promotional events around the world.

Trade associations and regulatory bodies

There are many trade associations and regulatory bodies in the travel and tourism industry, including the AA, RAC and VisitBritain, all of which inspect hotels and give grading by stars. They employ hotel inspectors and there are jobs in the production of information booklets, which are similar to the job role for tour operators.

Example

The Association of British Travel Agents (ABTA) regulates the travel agency industry. There are a number of roles working for ABTA, including press officers, public relations, legal and other administrative job roles.

Ancillary services

Ancillary services are those which add value to the travel experience. These services include car parking facilities and hotels at airports, currency exchange and travellers' cheques, money transfers and car, bicycle and motorbike hire, as well as visa and passport services and holiday insurance.

Job roles will depend on the organisation. In car hire companies, there are customer service agents and store managers, as well as contract managers who organise large bookings such as car hire for fly-drive holidays. Airport car parks employ security guards, car park attendants and a management team to manage the overall operation. Bureaux de change employ customer service staff, as well as managers and accounting staff. Other ancillary services include production of maps and guide books.

> **Think** Why do you think that travel agents offer this service?

JOBS

Every organisation has a number of different tasks that must be done in order for it to function. In a small one-person company, all the tasks have to be completed by the same individual or the tasks have to be contracted out to other organisations.

Job title

All employees are given job titles reflecting what the employee does, but also the responsibilities and duties that they have within the organisation.

Job role

As well as a job title, employees also have clearly defined job roles, so that an organisation can be structured to include all the tasks and responsibilities that must be covered. Job roles also help with recruitment and aid in defining responsibilities and duties that are attached to the job title. These tend to be surprisingly uniform across different sectors of the industry, although there are variations in responsibilities in different organisations, which are mainly due to their size and areas of interest.

Main duties and responsibilities

The duties and responsibilities are defined in the job description and contract of employment, but they may develop or alter during the employment period as organisations change and develop new systems, structures, procedures and products.

Research tip

Good examples of employment websites are www.monster.com, www.workthing.com and www.fish4jobs.co.uk.

Think What do the websites have in common and how do they differ?

ENTRY REQUIREMENTS

Most jobs will have a number of entry requirements: the minimum standards that are required to do the job. Entry requirements tend to be grouped into three different categories: qualifications, personal skills and attributes, and experience.

Qualifications

Qualifications are certificates that demonstrate ability in a particular subject area or skill set. Qualifications can be divided into two types: academic and vocational.

Academic qualifications are taught in schools, colleges and universities. They are about a subject rather than being specifically applied to an industry, for example, a GCSE in Geography.

Vocational qualifications are either taught in the workplace or at college and university or a combination of both. They prepare you to do a specific skill or a training programme that is aimed at

a specific job. For example, apprentices working in a travel agency study a National Vocational Qualification (SVQ in Scotland) at the same time as training to be a travel consultant.

Qualifications are a legal requirement for some jobs, meaning you cannot carry out the job without the specific qualification. For example, a pilot is not allowed to fly a passenger plane without a Commercial Pilot's Licence.

Personal skills and attributes

Although qualifications show which courses you have attended and passed to an employer, they do not necessarily give them the whole picture. Everyone has personal skills that cannot be covered by a qualification. These skills could be learnt from everyday life.

Example

Many people in the UK speak a foreign language (without having any formal training) because of their ethnic and cultural background or because they have lived abroad.

The same applies for computer and communication skills and customer service skills. These skills are no less valuable than a qualification, but they may be harder to identify.

Attributes are similar to skills, but they tend to be reflected in your personality rather than being learnt, although some attributes can also be learnt. For example, it is possible to learn how to be patient with others. Some attributes are learnt with experience and time. This is particularly the case with attributes such as empathy and understanding.

Think What skills do you you have? Consider the skills that you have developed from the work that you have done, as well as from your everyday life. Make a list.

Experience

People learn from experience, regardless of whether the experiences are positive or negative. An experienced staff member may be much more effective in a job role than one without experience, but this is only the case if the experience is relevant. Some experience is transferable.

Other factors

There are many other factors that are taken into consideration when it comes to setting job roles and entry requirements. We are going to look at two main ones: age and Criminal Record Bureau disclosures.

Age

Although it is now illegal to discriminate on grounds of age, there are jobs where age will affect the entry requirement. For example, you have to be over 17 to learn to drive and therefore any job that involves driving is not available to people under the age of 17.

The other age issue is with people over the age of 65, which is the statutory retirement age. The anti-age discrimination law, Employment Equality (Age) Regulations 2006, has led to many organisations being obliged to reconsider their employment and recruitment practices.

Criminal Record Bureau disclosures (to work with children)

Children need to be protected both in terms of their personal protection and as regards the reputation of the organisations that work on their behalf. This is both a moral and a legal responsibility, which is covered by the Rehabilitation of Offenders Act 1974. Everyone who works with children is required to have a Criminal Record Bureau check to make sure that they have nothing in their past that could put children at risk.

PROGRESSION

As people develop their skills and gain greater experience and more qualifications, they expect to be rewarded with more responsibility and challenging work. This move up the corporate ladder is known as career progression. Not every employee wants to have more responsibility and, as there are fewer jobs in each higher level of a hierarchical structure, it is not possible for everyone to progress.

Opportunities for progression and promotion

Opportunities for progression and promotion are created in a number of different ways: promotion, retirement, staff leaving, staff being dismissed, an expansion of the organisation's services and the development of new services.

In order to always be ready to make the most of any promotion or progression opportunities, you need to make sure that you are developing your skills, experience and qualifications.

Training

We have looked at how training and developing staff can lead to a competitive advantage over competitors (see Unit 2, Book 1). In your own career, you may need to use training to develop your skills and gain qualifications to demonstrate them. For example, an agent in a travel agency requires a qualification to sell travel insurance.

Many travel and tourism organisations also offer in-house training courses. These may be organised in order to develop skills required for a current position or to help staff to hone their skills in order to help their career progression and to support promotion.

Further and higher education

You may be studying the National Diploma in Travel and Tourism at a Further and Higher Education College. It is likely that your college or another local college will offer a range of courses that often take place in the evening or one day a week. These courses are aimed at adults who are looking to develop their skills and gain qualifications. Many of these students are taking qualifications to assist their career progression or perhaps for a career change.

Distance learning

Distance learning is learning by yourself in your own time. It has the advantage of being able to fit studying around other responsibilities. The increased use of computers, e-mail, the Internet and video conferencing means that it is now much easier to receive support than it was in the past. The Open University is one of UK's largest providers of distance learning courses.

> **Think** Find out which travel and tourism qualifications are available for you to study in your local area. In which careers would these qualifications help you?

> ### Research tip
>
> If your school or college has a careers library or service, it can be a really useful source of information. Prospectuses from local further education colleges are also helpful.

FACTORS TO CONSIDER

There are many issues to be considered when choosing a job position and a career pathway. These issues not only affect your working pattern, but also your lifestyle choices and career options.

Seasonality

Some companies in the UK travel and tourism industry are seasonal. This is especially the case if the attraction or destination depends on the weather. Seasonality leads to issues of job security and short-term contracts.

> ### Example
>
> Thorpe Park is a large theme park in Surrey, which is owned by the Tussaud Group. Every year, it closes during the winter months when new rides are installed.

Temporary or fixed-term contract

Temporary contracts, also known as fixed-term contracts, are employment contracts that are only set for a specific timeframe, for example, a six-month contract. These fixed-term contracts are often used in the travel and tourism industry to employ staff for seasonal jobs, during busy periods or to provide cover when someone is on long-term sickness or maternity leave.

Working hours

The hours that you work affect your lifestyle. Many jobs in travel and tourism are involved with providing services to customers during their leisure time. As a result, this leads to working anti-social hours. This can affect personal relationships and family and personal commitments.

Level of pay

The level of pay in some areas of the travel and tourism industry can be quite low. Travel companies have been competing on price for years. This has led to the margins being cut and costs being forced down to provide increasingly cheaper products. As staffing is one of the largest operational costs for travel and tourism, this trend has led to a low salary culture.

Pay is not the main motivator for most people and there are a number of perks that you may feel compensate for the level of pay in some job roles.

Job perks

Job perks come in many forms. They may involve the location of the job – for example holiday representatives and cabin crew travel the world.

Travel agents are often sent on familiarisation (fam) trips in order to better understand the products that they are selling. Hotel staff often have the option of discounted accommodation from other hotels within the company for their holidays. Some employees receive issued uniforms.

Other perks can be financial. Tipping is quite common in some sectors of the travel and tourism industry, particularly in the accommodation and catering sector. Commissions are also common in the industry for travel agents and holiday representatives who earn commission on the sales they make.

Figure 6.5 Travel agents enjoying a 'fam' trip

EVIDENCE ACTIVITY

P1 – P2 – M1 – D1

In preparation for leaving college and looking for a job you have been asked to research the career opportunities that are available for you.

1. Describe career opportunities in the travel and tourism industry. You should cover a minimum of four sectors offering opportunities in the industry and consider presenting your findings as a careers leaflet, display or oral presentation. (P1)

2. Looking at two jobs in more detail, produce a job description for each, remembering to include job title, role, main duties, entry requirements and progression opportunities. This could be in the form of a fact file or information sheet.(P1)

3. Produce a personal skill audit in preparation for employment. Ensure that you have evidence to support any skills mentioned and think about the best way to present the audit, possibly as a written review or in a detailed table. (P2)

4. Compare the two jobs that you have produced a job description for in task 2. You need to take into account entry level requirements and opportunities for progression and promotion. (M1)

5. Evaluate your own suitability for employment for a chosen job. You may want to look at one of the two jobs you investigated in task 2 and compare it with your personal skill audit from task 4. (D1)

6. Produce an action plan to show how you will meet the training and development needs for the job role you evaluated in task 5. Include in the plan the ways in which further training, experience, higher education or new skills may aid your development and explain how you will achieve these. (D1)

6.2 The stages of recruitment and selection in travel and tourism

There are two parts to the recruitment and selection process. There is an organisational process of finding the right person and the application process where the candidate applies and finds out if a job is appropriate for them.

ORGANISATION

The organisation wants to find the best person to do the job from all the people who apply. By studying this section, you will start to understand that the recruitment and selection process is not an exact science, but that the risks of employing the wrong person can be reduced with a systematic and well-structured approach.

Identifying company needs

The reasons for a job vacancy can be varied, for example due to changes in business practice or the development of a particular area of interest. Expansion of the business and the replacement of staff who have left, retired, were dismissed or are on long-term maternity or sickness leave are also common reasons for job vacancies arising.

In order to employ a member of staff, the company must identify what tasks need to be done. This is to determine what level of skills an individual needs in order to carry out a particular job. The company also needs to know the time frame that the tasks will take to complete, so that it only employs someone for the time required.

The company's managers can identify these needs in a number of different ways.

If replacing an employee:

- ask the employee who is leaving the company in an exit interview
- interview the supervisor of the role
- interview other employees with the same job role
- job analysis
- time and motion studies.

If a new job role:

- interview the supervisor to identify the needs
- interview other employees to identify the needs
- management consultants could be employed to provide advice
- job analysis.

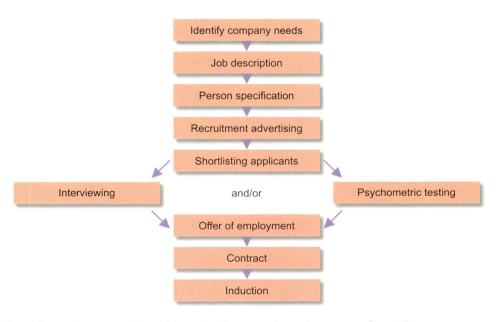

Figure 6.6 Flow chart demonstrating stages in the recruitment process from the viewpoint of the organisation

Job descriptions

A job description details the main roles and responsibilities of a particular job. It normally contains the following information:

- job title

- job location

- potential earnings

- brief overview of the business/industry

- main duties and responsibilities

- hours required (possibility of job-share and flexi-time)

This is often sent out to candidates to give them a better idea of what is involved with the job.

UK – Sales Consultant – Essex

Full time position

Various Locations including Central London, North London and Cambridge

First Year OTE £22K + bonuses

We are a market leading tour operator in the travel and tourism industry who have been voted into the Sunday Times '100 Best Companies to Work For' by our employees for the last two years. We have branches and offices throughout the UK and strongly believe that a happy workforce is the key to a prosperous business. We offer a focussed and flexible working environment and are sure it will prove the perfect environment for any dynamic and motivated individual who wants a chance to impress and progress.

As a Sales Consultant you will be given for own client base, for which you will have full responsibility. Your day to day tasks will include advising and selling a range of travel products and services, ensuring that a high level of customer care is provided at all times and hitting sales targets for your area.

Our fast-paced environment will offer you constant opportunity to shine and there are no restrictions on how quickly you can progress through the ranks. There is no cap on your potential earnings and it is worth noting that some of our top Sales Managers last year took home £45,000! We also offer extremely competitive benefits package on offer to all employees, including:

- profit share
- pension scheme
- health and dental insurance
- subsidising of travel

The ideal candidate will have vocational qualifications, 'A' Levels, or a degree, or be a sales executive with at least two years experience in the industry. You will be a strong written and verbal communicator, possess the ability to multi-task and problem-solve quickly and effectively, and enjoy the rewards that come with hitting sales targets. Do your career a favour and apply today.

Figure 6.7 A sample job description

Person specification

A person specification is a plan of the ideal candidate for the job. The personal attributes, skills, experience, knowledge and intelligence that are essential to carry out the job are all identified. The person specification can be sent out to applicants to help them to decide whether or not to apply. It is also used to help short-list applicants later on in the process.

Advertising

In order for candidates to apply for a job, they must know that there is a job available. Job advertisements can be placed in many different media.

Road shows

Road shows are used when a company is aiming to recruit a large number of employees. This is mainly due to the cost factor involved in this form of promotion. One of the most famous road shows is called the University Milk Round. This is when large companies go to each university with the aim of recruiting the brightest graduates to work for their company.

Recruitment agencies

These are agencies that specialise in the recruitment of staff for other companies. Agencies are increasingly online, giving employers and candidates the opportunity to access information regarding jobs more quickly and easily.

Recruitment agencies generate their income through charging a flat fee for each full-time member of staff employed. An hourly charge will be issued for temporary staff who are employed.

Trade newspapers and magazines

Many organisations will place advertisements in trade newspapers to recruit specialist or skilled staff. There are newspapers that are produced specifically for the travel and tourism industry, for example, *Travel Trade Gazette*, *Travel Weekly*, *Business Traveller* or *The Caterer*.

On the factory gates

It is common practice to put advertisements for junior positions up in shop windows. This is called 'on the factory gates' as this was the way in which factories advertised their job vacancies in the past.

Local and national newspapers

Local papers, especially free papers, are a good place to advertise operative level jobs. However, this isn't the best place to recruit specialist staff, unless there are many people with the skills required in the local area.

National newspapers are the best way to advertise for candidates if there are several vacancies available across the country. National newspaper advertisements can be expensive.

Job Centre Plus

Job Centres are run by the government as a place where people can find out about job vacancies, locally and nationally. It can be a good source of temporary or operative staff. However, experienced and skilled staff tend to use some of the other methods discussed to find out about job vacancies.

Short-listing applicants

Some job roles in travel and tourism are extremely popular and many applications will be sent when a vacancy is advertised. It isn't viable to interview everyone in terms of time and costs. Therefore the list of applicants has to be reduced. This process is called short-listing. The desired and essential criteria from the personal specifications are used as benchmarks to create a short-list of candidates.

Figure 6.8 Job Centre Plus focuses more towards temporary employment

Interviews

Interviews are used to assess the merits of the candidates that have been short-listed. An interview gives the organisation an opportunity to ask questions about the candidate's experience, skills and knowledge. It is also used as a chance to get to know the candidate better and assess whether they would fit into the organisation's culture. There are three main methods of interviewing.

Telephone

Telephone interviews are generally used as an initial screening when short-listing. There is fierce competition for some jobs and telephone interviews are a quick and relatively cheap way to interview candidates.

Example

Thomas Cook use telephone interviews to screen candidates when they have a large number of applicants for a post.

Group

Group interviews are used to see how candidates work with other people and how they react in a group situation. This method is used to select candidates who are likely to work in teams if they are employed.

Example

BMI Airlines use group interviews as part of their selection process when recruiting cabin crew staff.

Individual

Individual interviews are the most commonly used interviewing method. They can be done on a one-to-one basis where one person interviews the candidate, or panel interviews where a panel of people interviews each candidate. This gives the organisation an opportunity to ask questions when it feels that more information is needed in order to decide who to employ for a job.

The interviewing method really depends on what the organisation wants out of the interview. If they want the candidate to relax, a one-to-one interview over a coffee would be a better method than a panel interview. The organisation should have a standard list of questions that will be asked to all candidates. This will give all candidates the same opportunity, but also prevent any accusations of discrimination.

Psychometric testing

Psychometric testing can also be used to help decide which candidate to employ. Psychometric tests are made up of a number of multiple choice questions. There are no specific correct answers,

---

Think Produce a table listing the strengths and weaknesses of each of the three interviewing methods discussed. When would you use each method of interviewing?

---

but a range of different answers. By analysing the answers, the company will have a level of insight into the candidate's personality.

Offers of employment

When the organisation has identified which candidate they wish to employ, a formal offer letter needs to be sent to the successful individual. Unsuccessful candidates should not be informed until a written letter of acceptance has been received from the successful candidate. A contract of employment is often sent out with the employment offer.

Contracts

A contract is a formal agreement between two parties. In this situation, the contract would be between the employer and employee. The contract of employment sets out the main terms and conditions of employment, duties and responsibilities, who the employee reports to and who reports to them. It also states other terms of employment, such as holiday entitlement, sick leave and maternity and paternity conditions.

Induction

When a new member of staff starts in a job, they need to be inducted into the organisation's systems and procedures. These may be operational, meaning the company's way of doing things. Others are legal responsibilities, such as fire safety, COSHH (Control of Substances Hazardous to Health) regulations, lifting and handling, and health and safety.

Induction can last for a day or more, or it can stretch over a longer period, especially when there is specific training required in order to be qualified to do the job.

APPLICANT

The process will be different from the organisation's process for the applicant.

Figure 6.9 Steps to take in preparation for an interview

Researching opportunities

The first stage of the process is to research the possible options available for the candidate. Given the large range of opportunities in the travel and tourism industry, candidates need to identify what level of job and what type of job they are capable of doing.

Producing a Curriculum Vitae (CV)

To apply for a job, individuals need to provide information of what they have achieved so far in their lives. A candidate's Curriculum Vitae (CV) needs to tell a prospective employer about their skills, experience and education. There is no true standard for a CV, but there is certain information that needs to be included. This is looked at in more depth on page 51.

Speculative enquiries

Not all job vacancies will be advertised. If a candidate wants to work for a specific organisation, particularly a large organisation, they should write a letter to the human resources manager, including a copy of their CV. Speculative enquiries have two advantages. Firstly, if there is a vacancy and it has yet to be advertised, the candidate may be considered for the position. If the organisation does not have a vacancy, the fact that the candidate has approached the company shows willingness and enthusiasm and they may be considered when a vacancy becomes available.

Responding to advertising

When a candidate sees an advertisement for a job that they wish to apply for, they have to respond to the advertisement. It is not uncommon to telephone the organisation for an application form or to find out how to apply. When the applicant sends in the application form or a copy of their CV, they may also need to send a covering letter. The covering letter should explain why the applicant is applying for the job and what benefits employing them would have for the company.

Preparing for interview

If a candidate has been successfully short-listed, then he/she will probably be asked to attend an interview. There are several things that applicants need to do before the interview to give them every possible chance of being successful in the job application.

Attending interviews

The interview is the only opportunity the candidate has to sell themselves to the company. It is also an opportunity for them to find out more about the organisation.

It is very important to turn up on time; being five minutes early makes a good first impression. Candidates should always be polite and courteous.

Table 6.3 Tips on preparing for an interview

1. Check how you are going to attend the interview. If attending by public transport, check train and bus times and connections. If driving to the interview check the route and where you can park.

2. Consider what to wear as you can only make a first impression once. If you are not sure what to wear, you should dress conservatively. A smart business suit should be suitable for most jobs.

3. Research the job role and find out what the job is and what is expected from the job. From this research, the candidate can develop a list of questions to be answered at the interview.

4. Research the company to find out what it does and the range of products and services offered.

5. Prepare the list of questions and any other information, so you are ready the night before the interview.

6. Try thinking of the type of questions that might be asked in order to be prepared.

Responding to job offers

If a candidate is successful, they will be offered the job. This offer will be in the form of a telephone call or a letter. If the job is offered by telephone, it is usually followed up with a formal letter.

The successful candidate will also be sent a contract of employment. This is a legal document that confirms the acceptance of the job offer and legally binds the employee to the terms and conditions of the contract. Most job offers will have a clause concerning references. This is due to the timeframe of recruiting as it may take time to collect references after a job offer has been made.

References

Most employers ask for two references. It is usual for referees to be either previous employers or teaching staff at the employee's last school or college. These references concern the applicant's character and include issues such as attendance, punctuality, honesty and diligence. Permission needs to be sought from the referee before they can be used for a reference.

6.3 Applying for employment in the travel and tourism industry

Competition for employment in the travel and tourism industry can be very competitive and there are some job roles that are particularly popular. This leads to fierce competition for each position. Section 6.2 looked at the stages of the recruitment process. This section focuses on how to use this process to your best benefit.

PERSONAL SKILLS AUDIT

Before you apply for any job, it is important that you analyse your personal skills. This is called a skills audit. This audit identifies what skills you have and what skills you might need to acquire.

Attributes

These are personal characteristics including your appearance and manners. Attributes also refer to your personal traits. For example, you may be a naturally strong leader or an effective negotiator.

Skills

Skills means abilities that you possess. These skills may not be covered by qualifications that you have gained. For example, a student who has a part-time job in a supermarket has cash handling skills, customer service skills and skills in merchandising and stock control and rotation.

Experience

Experience is the amount of time that you have been practising the skills that you have already identified. The skills and experiences that you have developed through part-time jobs while at college or school are probably not directly related to the travel and tourism industry. Experience and skills can be transferable from one job to another. There is very little difference between helping a customer who is upset about a holiday or annoyed about the food they have bought.

Qualifications

Qualifications are certificates that show a level of competency in a particular task or field of study. Qualifications tend to be split between academic and vocational qualifications.

Academic qualifications are related to a subject and are quite abstract, such as a GCSE in History or Mathematics.

Vocational qualifications relate directly to an industry or a job task. They tend to be practice-based like a food hygiene certificate or an IATA fares and ticketing qualification.

Achievements

The earlier part of the audit looks at what qualifications, skills, attitude and experience you have. This part of the audit is about how you have used these tools.

> **Think** What successes have you had? This might help you to identify what skills you possess.

APPLYING FOR WORK

In order to get work, you need to apply for positions. This informs companies that you are available and that you have the appropriate skills, qualifications, experience and attitude to do the job successfully.

This is a competitive situation, and in most situations only the best candidate will be given the job. This means that you are competing with other candidates when applying for a job. There are several elements that you can use and develop to improve your chances of getting the job.

Research

There are two areas that you need to research to prepare for selection, which should be done before you write your CV or application form. The first issue to research is the organisation that you are applying to work with. This will show that you are interested in the organisation and it also helps to show your level of commitment to getting the job.

The second issue to research is the job that you are applying for. From this research you will be able to develop your CV or application form to demonstrate that you have the skills and experience that are required for the job. It is common practice to be asked about the job that you are applying for during the selection process.

Curriculum Vitae

This is the document that sells you to a potential employer. The information has to be easy-to-read and well laid out. Your CV should include:

- title of document: Curriculum Vitae
- name
- address
- telephone number – home, work and mobile if you have them
- e–mail address – this shows that you are computer literate
- if you have a driving licence – this is only important if driving is a part of the job
- work experience, including dates employed, job title, employer's name, main duties
- education – academic, including schools, colleges and university attended, dates attended, courses completed and grades
- education – vocational, including training course attended, dates attended, grades if appropriate
- skills – a list of your skills that are not covered by qualifications, such as a second language or computer skills
- notable achievement(s) – a list of any notable achievements you have, such as a Duke of Edinburgh Award
- hobbies and interests – a list of what you do in your free time
- references – names, titles and addresses of two referees. It is best if this is your current employer or tutor at college.

Application forms

Application forms are used by many organisations. They benefit the organisation as each candidate's information is in a standard format making it easier for the organisation to short-list candidates. There are two main formats for application forms:

1) Written – the traditional paper-based method of an application form. They are used by many companies in travel and tourism and tend to be generic

2) Online – job vacancies and applications for jobs are increasingly online. Online application forms are similar in structure to the paper-based version, except that you complete them online and then e-mail them to the company.

Key words

Generic – a general purpose rather than a specific use

Research tip

Most large travel and tourism organisations will have a career section on their website with information on jobs that are available.

Letter of application

A CV and an application form only tell the recruiter about the experience, attributes, skills and qualifications that you have. They do not tell the recruiter what your motivation is for applying for a new job or what you specifically have to offer the company to which you are applying. You should always include a letter of application when you return your CV or application form. If it is an online application form, most companies also give you the opportunity to include an e-mail of application with your application form.

Personal statements

Personal statements can be included in an application form or in the covering letter. However, people are now providing a personal statement within their CVs. This is a statement of what you are good at and what you have managed to achieve in your career and personal life. You should include many positive examples.

Example

Rather than saying "I am good at customer service," a statement about the numbers of letters of praise that you have received would give the argument more strength. Never say that you feel or think something as this introduces doubt into the mind of the person who is short-listing applications.

INTERVIEW SKILLS

If you have been successfully short-listed, then you are likely to be called for an interview. There are many skills that you need to prepare before the interview takes place.

Advance preparation

You must prepare in advance for an interview. You need to know where it will be held, how to get there and how long it will take to get there. You also need to prepare yourself for the types of questions you could expect to be asked. Although all interviews are different depending on the company, level of job and what the company wants to get out of the interview, there are some general questions that you can prepare. You could even organise a mock interview with a friend or member of the family to give yourself some practice.

Think How would you answer the following:

- What are your main strengths?
- What are your main weaknesses?
- Where do you see yourself in five years time?
- Why should I employ you rather than any of the other candidates?
- Tell me about the company.

Company knowledge

Many organisations will expect you to know about the organisation that you have applied to join. Using the Internet, it is quite easy to find out about a company and what they do. Some knowledge of turnover and the number of staff employed would also impress the interviewer. You should certainly know about the scale of the organisation's operations and the sectors of the industry in which the company works.

Telephone screening

Many companies use telephone screening as a stage in the short-listing process. This is a form of interview, but is not face-to-face. It provides a low-cost solution to having to interview a large number of potential candidates.

Attending interviews

This is a vital part of the recruitment and selection process. You need to be able to sell yourself in an interview. Most companies today will use a structured interviewing technique. This use of standardised questions helps prevent any issues of discrimination (see page 59).

Personal presentation

How you present yourself in an interview will create a first impression in the interviewer's mind. There is no standard way of dressing for an interview as it depends on the organisation and job that you are applying for. However, if you do not know what is expected of you, then a smart business suit is a safe option.

Example

If you are applying for the job of a team member at a theme park, you would dress differently than if you were applying for the job of the theme park's Managing Director.

Projecting a positive image

Your personal presentation does not only include how you dress but also how you act and behave.

An interviewer may have a large number of candidates to interview for any particular job. You need to project a positive image to be able to sell yourself. There are four main areas to consider.

Body language

The way in which you position yourself tells the interviewer a great deal about you. In Unit 4, Book 1, you considered your body language when looking after customers. The same basic principles apply in an interview scenario. Closed body language, such as covering your face and leaning back when sitting, gives the interviewer a negative impression. Open body language, such as good eye contact and leaning forward when sitting, provides a more positive image.

Figure 6.10 Body language at an interview affects a potential employer's perception of you

Responding to and asking questions

An interview is a two-way discussion for the company's representative to find out about you and for you to find out about the organisation. You should consider what questions you might be asked before the interview, so that you can prepare yourself. You also need to ask questions to find out the information that you need to decide whether you want to work for the company or not. Most interviewers will give you a chance to ask questions.

Attitude

Your attitude has a huge influence on whether you are offered the job. Attitude is a highly important consideration when companies are selecting staff to represent their organisation to customers. For most jobs, companies are looking for someone with a positive, willing attitude.

Time management

Time management is also important in an industry where a minute's delay can lead to expensive penalties and congestion for airlines. If you are late for an interview, it makes a bad impression even before the interview starts.

If you are going to be late, it is important to contact the interviewer and explain the situation. Checking where a building is located or finding out your route before an interview is a good idea. Check the timetable if you are using public transport. Leave enough time so that you will not be late even if you are delayed. Aim to arrive early.

EVALUATION

You need to evaluate your own skills as this could help you to choose a job that does not concentrate on your weaknesses and maximises your strengths. You can also develop strategies to overcome your weaknesses.

Strengths

Everyone has particular strengths. It may be that you are very good at administration or that you have the ability to empathise with others, which you could use to offer excellent customer service. To identify your strengths, you should think about what you are good at, but also ask people that know you well. A tutor or parent might identify things that you have never thought about.

Weaknesses

Just like strengths, everyone has particular weaknesses. In the work environment, you should obviously play on your strengths rather than doing a job that focuses on your weaknesses. However, in most jobs, you have a range of tasks that need to be completed. You need to improve your areas of personal weakness that affect your job.

Areas for improvement

Areas for improvement are those that you have identified as ones that would benefit from improvement. You might have identified these areas yourself or they might have been revealed as part of an appraisal system. Any areas that have been identified are in need of improvement.

EVIDENCE ACTIVITY

P3 – P4 – M2

When you have successfully completed your National Diploma course you will need to apply for a job within the travel and tourism industry. This activity is designed to help you develop both your knowledge and experience of the recruitment and selection process, by analysis of the recruitment and selection process and by role playing the process.

1. Describe the stages of the recruitment and selection process. (P3)

2. In preparation for your role play produce guidelines highlighting how to be successful in the different stages of the recruitment and selection process. (M2)

3. Using the job details in figure 6.10 (page 46) for the post of a UK Sales Consultant for a Flight Centre, produce a Curriculum Vitae and a covering letter to apply for this job. (P4)

Your tutor will organise a mock interview to test your interviewing skills.

4. Analyse how successful you were in your application for the post of a UK Sales Consultant for a Flight Centre. Use your guidelines from task 2 to help you. (M2)

6.4 Understanding the factors that contribute to an effective workplace

WORKING ENVIRONMENT

The working environment affects how effectively people work and even who you can recruit to work for an organisation.

Location

The location of the business will affect who is available to work. You cannot always control where you are located in the travel and tourism industry. For example, you cannot move Stonehenge closer to London to make it easier to recruit staff. You also need to consider the ease of getting to the location by public and private transport and car parking facilities.

Working conditions

When people have to work in noisy, dirty and inhospitable conditions, it will affect their effectiveness and your ability to recruit staff.

Hours of work

The hours of employment are important to staff. Flexibility with regard to working hours is being used increasingly to make an organisation more attractive to staff. Options include **flexi-time**, **parent friendly hours** and **job sharing**. Many jobs in the travel and tourism industry have hours of work that do not fit into the conventional 9am-5pm office hours.

> **Key words**
>
> **Flexi-time** – a working practice where staff must work a specific number of hours within a timeframe, for example, a week or month, but they can choose when to work
>
> **Parent friendly hours** – working hours that fit around the school day and school holidays
>
> **Job sharing** – where a job is done by more than one person sharing the work and sharing the salary

CASE STUDY: RYANAIR BANS STAFF'S 1/2P MOBILE CHARGING

In an effort to cut costs Ryanair has banned staff from charging their mobile phones at work. The seemingly drastic action is just one in a series of cuts made by the company after it was decided that the electricity used by an employee to charge a mobile phone was a cost they no longer wished to be burdened with.

The airline reasoned that saving money wherever possible enables them to continue lowering fares for customers. However, many, including the Transport and General Workers' Union, believe that the discontent amongst the workers caused by this rule will far outweigh the money saved.

Although this may seem a small amount of money to be concerned about, it is worth noting that it could still be interpreted as theft from the employer.

QUESTIONS

1. How would this make you feel if you worked for Ryanair?

2. Do you think this change in working conditions could affect the effectiveness of the staff?

Health and safety

The Health and Safety at Work Act states that health and safety is the responsibility of everyone, including staff, management and even customers and suppliers. No one wants to have an accident at work with the current trend of suing organisations who are deemed responsible for an accident. The resulting effect that this has had on organisations' insurance premiums has made health and safety a bigger priority than ever before in many managers' minds.

Another effect of poor health and safety is that staff may be off sick due to accidents. This leads to more pressure being put on other members of staff and affects the effectiveness of the workplace.

Equipment

The effectiveness of a workplace depends on the equipment that is provided to support the staff in their job roles. Equipment is increasingly important today, especially communication and information technology.

If the employees do not have the appropriate equipment to be able to do their jobs properly, then this will lead to poor service delivery. Equipment can also be used to give an organisation a competitive advantage.

Resources

It is also important that resources are effectively used. In the travel and tourism industry, information is a major resource that is used to increase effectiveness. A customer can be provided with better customer service and a holiday can be sold more effectively with further information about the resort.

Example

Travel agencies use Central Reservation Systems (CRS) and Global Distribution Systems (GDS). These pieces of software give a travel agency the ability to book flights and accommodation anywhere in the world. Computerisation has also reduced the cost and time of administration.

Theorists

There are a number of theorists who have focused on the effectiveness of the workplace and how to have an effective workforce. None of the theories provide a definitive solution on how to manage an effective workforce, but they each give different insights that help you to manage situations better.

Abraham Maslow's hierarchy of needs

In 1954, Maslow developed the hierarchy of needs model.

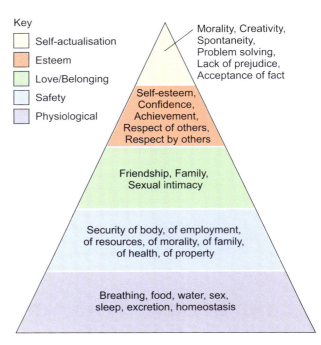

Figure 6.11 Maslow's hierarchy of needs

Maslow identified five different levels of needs that humans have. The bottom four levels are called 'D needs' or deficiency needs. These needs do not affect the person unless they are missing, but they will de-motivate the person if they are. Maslow called the top level of the pyramid 'B needs' or being values. When the B needs are fulfilled, the person is motivated.

The lower the level of need in the pyramid, the more basic the need is. The higher level needs will emerge only when lower level needs are satisfied. For example, you will not have a need for a car if you do not have food and water.

Frederick Herzberg's Motivation-Hygiene Theory (also known as Two Factor Theory)

In the 1950s, Herzberg investigated factors that motivate and de-motivate employees. He released his findings in his book in 1959, The Motivation of Work.

Herzberg stated that there were two types of factors. Those that satisfy, which he called motivators, and factors that prevent dissatisfaction, called hygiene factors.

Examples of motivators	Examples of hygiene factors
Advancement and promotion	Pay levels
Interesting work	Fringe benefits
Responsibility	Job security
Achievement	Company policy
Recognition	Supervision

Table 6.4 Motivators and Hygiene factors for employees

Social events

Social events help a team to form informal relationships that make a team work closer together. They can also be used as a reward. The **informal relationships** that people build at work help with staff retention. After all, people are more likely to remain working somewhere where they have friends than somewhere they don't. It is worth remembering that most full-time employees spend more time with their work colleagues than they do with their loved ones.

Key words

Informal relationships – relationships that do not fit within the organisational structure

Example

It is common practice on Christmas Day in hotels and restaurants for the employees who have worked at lunchtime to have a Christmas Dinner later on in the day, which is served by the hotel management.

Impact on motivation

All these factors are important to staff members and can be used by management to motivate people. These issues are very important to people and will affect how long a member of staff stays at the organisation.

WORKING RELATIONSHIPS

You will be expected to work with other people in most travel and tourism jobs. These could be other members of your organisation, suppliers or customers. The way in which you relate to these individuals and their relationships with you affects your work.

Management style

There are three main types of management styles, although no manager will only use one style. A manager is likely to use elements of each management style in different situations to obtain different results.

Democratic management

This is management through consensus, although the final decision and the responsibility for the decision remain with the manager. This style of management helps to make members of staff feel involved in the decision-making process.

Autocratic management

This is management through order. This style involves telling people what to do. Although this type of management does not let the staff feel involved in the decision-making process, it is very effective in dealing with crises or when there is a lot of work to be done.

Laissez-faire management

This is management through delegation. Employees have set objectives and targets and are left alone to achieve these goals. Laissez-faire management is sometimes mistaken for bad management and a lack of caring, but this is not the case. Laissez-faire management involves developing the employees' skills and **empowering** them to be able to achieve targets and giving them the space to do the tasks, although managerial support must be always available if required.

Teamwork

Teams are important in any workplace. Two people doing the same job separately are not as productive as two people working together. For a team to work effectively, it requires a number of different skills and abilities.

Dr R. Meredith Belbin developed a team inventory while studying at Henley Business College in the 1970s. In the team inventory, Belbin identified

nine roles that are required for a team to be effective. This does not mean that a team needs nine members as most people will have abilities in a number of these roles with one or two dominant roles and one or two weak roles.

Table 6.4 below shows Belbin's nine team roles and some of the main strengths and weaknesses of each role.

Research tip

To find out more about individual team roles, visit www.belbin.com.

Key words

Empowerment – giving individuals the power to be able to do their jobs independently

Belbin's team role	Strengths	Weaknesses
Plant	Comes up with original and sometimes unconventional solutions to problems	Finds explaining ideas difficult
Resource Investigator	Good at finding opportunities and contacts Not afraid to ask for directions	Loses momentum towards the end of projects
Coordinator	Good at seeing the 'big picture' Helps to stabilise the group	Spends too long managing and not enough time working
Shaper	Drives the team forward Tackles problems head-on	Can be insensitive to the needs of others and their feelings Can act without thinking
Monitor Evaluator	Brings fairness and a detached overview Sees all available solutions and judges on merit	Can seem robotic in their behaviour and finds motivating others and themselves difficult
Team worker	Maintains the team concerns with others and how the group is working together Talent for smoothing over conflict in the team	Unwilling to take sides Can be paralysed in decision-making process, due to their need not to offend
Implementer	Makes things happen Efficient and effective and can be relied on	Closed minded and inflexible when the plan is set
Completer Finisher	A perfectionist and will make sure everything is just right Very meticulous and strong sense of duty	Worries about the smallest detail Cannot delegate tasks they feel they can do and have tendencies not to trust other people's standards
Specialist	Brings a high level of skill in their specific area Good concentration and ability in their specialisation	Can only contribute in specific area Often loses others in the detail of their specialisation

Table 6.5 Belbin's nine team roles

Job roles and lines of responsibility

Job roles and defined lines of responsibility help a team to understand the responsibility of every individual. This is particularly the case when dealing with teams that are planned to be together over a long period of time.

Example

The travel agent will employ a number of holiday representatives to look after the customers in the resort. The agent also recruits a resort manager to coordinate the representatives. The job roles of the team are defined by their titles, for example, children's representative, transfer representative and resort representative.

Channels of communication

There are two channels of communication: formal and informal. Formal channels of communication go through the organisational structure. An operational member of staff communicates to their supervisor and so forth up and down the organisational structure. This channel is vital for the communication of information and instructions, especially with regard to the communication of corporate goals and team objectives. Informal channels of communication are also important to maintain the team and include any communication outside the formal structure. This sometimes occurs as team members have shared social interests.

Equal opportunities

All members of staff should have equal opportunities as it can seriously affect the operation of a team if individual members feel they are being treated less favourably than others. There is also a legal obligation not to discriminate. Discrimination under any of the following laws may result in legal action and the related costs in terms of time and money, and damage to the organisation's reputation, affecting sales and recruitment.

Equal Pay Act 1970 (EPA)

The Equal Pay Act states that men and women doing the same work or deemed to have the same value must be paid the same amount. You cannot pay a man more than a woman who is doing the same job with equal responsibility and experience.

Sex Discrimination Act 1975 (SDA)

The Sex Discrimination Act states that you cannot directly or **indirectly discriminate** against either gender when it comes to recruitment, employment, promotion and training.

Key words

Indirect discrimination – where terms or conditions are attached to employment, promotion or training that make it more difficult for one group to qualify

Race Relations Act 1976 (RRA)

The Race Relations Act is similar to the Sex Discrimination Act in that it prevents discrimination on the grounds of race or religion, either directly or indirectly.

Disability Discrimination Act 1995 (DDA)

The Disability Discrimination Act protects the rights of disabled employees. It states that an organisation must make reasonable adjustments to the working methods, equipment and buildings to facilitate the work of a disabled person. However, if there is a serious and clearly defined health and safety risk involved in employing a disabled person, then this has the upper hand.

Example

It is legal to discriminate against a wheelchair user who applies for the post of cabin crew due to the health and safety elements of the job.

Legislative requirements

There are a number of legislative requirements. These could be basic requirements that are required in most workplaces, including staff training in fire procedures, food handling certificates, Control of Substances Hazardous to Health (COSHH) training, and lifting and handling training. This also includes the legal requirement for a number of First Aid trained members of staff.

Other legislative requirements may be more specific to the type of business in which your organisation is involved, for example, licences for pilots and coach drivers.

Grievance and disciplinary procedures

There will be disagreements and problems from time to time. Most situations can be dealt with by a discussion between the parties involved. However, in some situations, a disciplinary process may have to be used. Organisations have a set procedure if the company has a problem with the behaviour or work of a member of staff. This is called the disciplinary system. This system normally has a number of steps, for example, verbal warning, written warning and dismissal.

If the employee has a problem with a senior member of staff or the company, they also need a method of recourse. This is called the grievance procedure. It includes who you should contact and how to lodge a grievance.

Investors in people

Investors in People is a quality standard that is awarded to businesses. It is concerned with the development of a business by the development of its people. This is accomplished through developing strategies to improve performance through training and development and also effective management and leadership.

INVESTORS IN PEOPLE

Figure 6.13 Investors in People logo

Research tip

For further information, visit www.investorsinpeople.co.uk.

Buddies and mentors

When you start work, you will have many questions and issues that will come up on a day-to-day basis. These tend not to be major issues, but little problems that you need to ask someone to help with, for example, 'where do I put my coat when I am working?'

Many travel and tourism organisations will pair you up with a mentor, who is sometimes known as a buddy. This is usually someone who does the same job as you or who works in the same department in the organisation, but has worked there for some time. The idea is that if you have someone to whom you can turn with your problems when you start work, you will become integrated quickly into the way in which the organisation works. This helps the new members of staff feel part of the organisation and that they belong there.

Job security

No job is completely secure in today's modern business environment. However, a job that can offer higher level security will help motivate staff as they feel that they are safe.

Impact on motivation

The way in which employees are treated and how they perceive that treatment affects their motivation. Making a member of staff feel part of a team and helping them to create informal relationships at work will affect how long they are likely to stay in the organisation.

INCENTIVES

Incentives are the rewards received that encourage an employee to work more effectively.

Remuneration

Remuneration is the pay received for the hours worked. This may be an hourly rate or an annual salary. Some organisations may ask their employees to work overtime. These are extra hours of work, which are above and beyond the contracted hours. Employees are sometimes remunerated at a better rate than the standard pay for doing overtime, for example, time and a half or even double time.

Performance-related pay

Performance-related pay is becoming increasingly popular. This is where an element of the pay, or maybe an annual pay rise, is related to how well an employee has performed in the previous year. Although this initially seems to be a good idea, it can be difficult to apply to some job roles.

Incentive schemes

Incentive schemes are designed to encourage staff to achieve a particular target.

Example

Royal Caribbean Cruises offer a free cruise to the member of sales staff who registers the most bookings in a specific time frame.

Commission

Commission is also used to encourage staff to achieve targets. These tend to be sales-related. The staff will receive a percentage or an amount of money for each sale, which is usually above their personal target.

Example

A travel agent offers staff 1% commission on every sale they make. This means that 1p in every pound of the holiday cost goes to the travel consultant.

Bonuses

Bonuses are financial rewards that are given for a number of reasons, including team performance, long service and Christmas. A bonus can be seen as a reward for long service or for a particular achievement.

Discounts

A number of travel and tourism organisations offer their staff discounts on the goods and services that the company offers. This is a relatively cheap way of rewarding staff as the perceived cost of the discount is considerably less than the cost to the company.

Example

Staff working for a Best Western Hotel can book any room in a Best Western hotel for half the advertised room rate.

Figure 6.12 Best Western employees can stay for half price

Holiday entitlement

Every employee in the European Union is entitled to four weeks holiday and bank holidays every year. As a reward for long service or as part of the contract of employment, some companies may offer staff a better holiday entitlement than this.

Pension schemes

Company pension schemes can also be part of the package that a member of staff receives. Most company pension schemes require that the employee makes a contribution to their pension and the company will also make a contribution.

A company pension scheme is designed to pay the member of staff an income when they retire.

Perks

Perks are not financial rewards, although they may reduce your personal expenses. They can include company cars, free meals and uniforms.

Opportunities for promotion and progression

Opportunities for promotion and progression can also be seen as a benefit of working for a particular organisation. A company with an internal promotion and transfer policy will retain staff members as they can see a career pathway within the organisation.

Impact on motivation

All these benefits and financial rewards motivate staff, but only in the short term as they are additional factors. Money and rewards are not the only reasons why people go to work. Bonuses, performance-related pay and commission schemes can also have a negative effect on motivation if they are seen as being imposed on the staff or if they are unfair.

TRAINING

All staff need to be trained, so that they understand the systems, policies and procedures that the organisation uses. Some training is required as it is needed to comply with current working regulations. Employees also require training to develop their skills in order to help their career progression.

Induction

Induction usually takes place when an employee first starts their employment. It is the process of introducing new staff members to the organisation and the ways in which the organisation works. Induction includes initial staff training with regard to fire procedures and health and safety.

In some sectors of the industry, induction can be a lengthy process and may include considerable training.

Example

Customer service staff induction for British Airways is an intensive training programme that lasts for four weeks, including a series of examinations and tests before they are allowed to have contact with a customer. This is followed by work shadowing an experienced member of the customer service team, before being allowed to work with customers under supervision.

Training opportunities

Throughout your employment, there will be a number of training opportunities offered to you in the workplace. These opportunities may be through training programmes, the development of new skills or related to new products, services or pieces of equipment.

Appraisal

An appraisal is a review of an employee's performance. It usually takes place once every six months or annually. An appraisal involves an employee and their direct supervisor sitting down and discussing the employee's performance. It is also a time to identify any training and development needs to improve the employee's performance and develop their skills base. Individual performance targets should be set during the appraisal, so that the employee knows what their targets are for the next six months or year. Performance-related pay can also be tied into appraisal, but there are issues regarding disclosure.

Impact on motivation

The impact of training on motivation can be positive as it makes the member of staff feel valued by the organisation as it is investing time and money in developing their skills. However, if the opportunities are not available for that person to use their newly acquired skills, this can have a negative impact on the individual. The same can be said for appraisals. If appraisals are well-structured and training needs are identified and addressed, this can have a positive impact on the individual's motivation. However, if the appraisal is just a process that has to be covered and nothing concrete comes out of it for the employee, it can be a de-motivating factor.

Induction is designed not only to cover the legal requirements, but also to make the new member of staff feel part of the organisation by explaining the corporate values to new employees. The more that a new member of staff feels part of the organisation, the more likely they are to stay working there.

EVIDENCE ACTIVITY

P5 – M3 – D2

Your local tourist board has asked you to produce a handbook that can be given to small local travel and tourism businesses to help them develop a more effective workplace.

The handbook needs to cover the following points:

1. You need to describe the factors that contribute to an effective workplace in travel and tourism organisations. (P5)

2. Explain how different travel and tourism organisations motivate staff in the workplace. (M3)

3. Analyse the factors that contribute to an effective workplace and highlight examples of best practice from different travel and tourism organisations. (D2)

Retail and business travel operations

unit 9

This unit looks at the key roles of the retail and business travel sector in the industry. It is a fast paced and highly competitive sector.
You will find out how different agents operate and the frameworks that they work within. You will also see how technology has changed their operations and how the agents have adopted strategies to retain and grow their market share. You will be able to gain knowledge of the range of products and services offered, how secondary sales are made and how, above all, the agents meet their customers' needs. You will also be introduced to the practical skills of creating itineraries.

By the end of this unit, you will:

9.1 Understand the retail and business travel environments
page 67

9.2 Understand how advances in technology have affected retail and business travel operations
page 77

9.3 Understand how retail travel organisations seek to gain a competitive advantage
page 82

9.4 Be able to produce complex itineraries for retail and business travel customers
page 86

So you want to be a...

Travel Agency Manager

My name Hakan Callow

Age 25

Income £25,000

If you are a confident sales person and leader of people, who enjoys the challenge of hitting targets, then keep reading...

Why did you decide to work in the travel and tourism industry?

I've always had a real passion for travel. After I left school, I did a BTEC National Diploma in Travel and Tourism. I got a chance to do several work experience placements in different parts of the industry. That's how I fixed on travel agency work.

What training did you have?

To begin with, I worked for a small agency for a couple of years. That's where I learned all the basics and I got my ABTAC certification. Most importantly, I learned how to be confident about talking to people and how to sell them our services.

What did you do then?

I moved on to work for one of the big multiples. It was hard, but there are plenty of opportunities if you have the ambition to get on. After a year, I applied to become an assistant manager in another branch, then a year or so later, I got my first branch manager's job.

> **"There are plenty of opportunities if you have the ambition to get on"**

What does the job involve?

It's a varied job. I have to make sure that everything is running smoothly, I supervise a lot and guide the staff. I have to make sure they are up to speed on training and specialist knowledge. We've got weekly and monthly targets to hit. It's not always easy, but you need to sell extras to make the targets.

How do you meet the targets?

I have regular meetings with the area sales manager and the bosses in head office. They're always talking about new targets and identifying new products and how to keep ahead of the competitors.

What advice would you offer?

Learn as much about destinations as possible and get in some sales experience, too. The upside is the thanks from customers for going that extra mile to sort things out for them. What's the downside? Well, that's got to be the complaints. Get it right the first time and you keep those down to a minimum.

Grading criteria

The table below shows what you need to do to gain a pass, merit or distinction in this part of the qualification. Make sure you refer back to it when you are completing work so you can judge whether you are meeting the criteria and what you need to do to fill in gaps in your knowledge or experience.

In this unit there are 4 evidence activities that give you an opportunity to demonstrate your achievement of the grading criteria:

page 76	**P1, M1, D1**
page 81	**P2**
page 85	**P3, M2, D2**
page 93	**P4, P5**

To achieve a pass grade the evidence must show that the learner is able to...	To achieve a merit grade the evidence must show that, in addition to the pass criteria, the learner is able to...	To achieve a distinction grade the evidence must show that, in addition to the pass and merit criteria, the learner is able to...
P1 Describe the retail and business travel environment, (including the relationship between retail and business travel agents and other sectors of the travel and tourism industry) using examples where appropriate	**M1** Explain how relationships operate in the retail and business travel environment and its impact on the travel industry as a whole	**D1** Evaluate the effectiveness of retail and business travel organisations and how they operate in the travel industry environment
P2 Describe how technological advances have affected retail and business operations	**M2** Compare the effectiveness of two retail travel organisations seeking to gain a competitive advantage	**D2** Recommend how two retail travel agents can gain a competitive advantage
P3 Explain how retail travel organisations seek to gain a competitive advantage		
P4 Use appropriate resources to produce two complex travel itineraries for retail travel customers to given client briefs		
P5 Use appropriate resources to produce two complex travel itineraries for business travel customers to given client briefs		

9.1 Understand the retail and business travel environments

TYPES AND ROLE OF RETAIL AGENCIES

There are approximately 6,500 travel agency shops in the UK alone. They range from multiples, which may have several hundred branches scattered around the country, to independent travel agents, with just a single shop. The vast majority of them, however, are members of chains, such as Thomas Cook, Going Places and Thomson.

The number of agencies has actually dropped in recent years as many more customers are purchasing their travel and tourism products and services using the telephone or the Internet.

The owner, backed up by a small team, usually runs **independent** travel agents. Some of the independents are in fact chains in themselves, such as the Co-op's Travelcare (www.travelcare.co.uk).

Figure 9.1 Travelcare has branches nationwide

Other types of retail travel agents are what are known as **miniples**, which are small chains of travel agencies that are located in a single regional area.

The top four travel agents in the UK can be described as **integrated** travel agencies. They own their own airlines, as well as travel agencies, which give them considerable control of both supplies and demand. They compete on price, which forces many smaller operators to specialise in niche markets in order to survive.

Key words

Niche market – a small, specialist market, such as bespoke, tailor-made holidays

An increasing trend in the retail travel agent sector is the e-agent. The e-travel agent does not have a high street presence and nor does it usually have brochures or sales literature. They rely completely on their websites to sell products and services. For example, Scotland has its own e-travel agent in www.visitscotland.com. Other more general e-travel agents include www.lastminute.com and www.expedia.com.

One other notable trend is the personal travel consultant. They are independent travel agents who are employed directly by the customer to put together specific travel and tourism requirements. They will liaise directly with travel and tourism providers and will aim to meet the specific needs of their customers.

Example

Some existing tour operators and travel agents, such as Hays Travel (www.haystravel.co.uk), use personal travel consultants in addition to their usual service. These individuals are home workers and they receive the full support of the business's head office. This extends to a business telephone line, appropriate computer hardware and software, online credit card authorisation, a personalised website and a range of other support. Both the travel consultants and the telesales home workers receive leads by teletext classified pages and advertising on several television channels.

TYPES AND ROLE OF BUSINESS AGENCIES

With some 3.8 million business travellers staying in hotels alone in the UK each year, the business travel sector has never been so buoyant. Technology has had a major impact on business travel and around 31% of business travellers book their hotels directly by using search engines. Only 6% use a travel agent.

The main purpose of business travel agents is to take away the stress from either the business traveller or the employer of organising flights, hotel accommodation, car hire, visas and a host of other requirements. They can identify the best flight routes, itineraries, fares and airlines.

Corporate hospitality is also a large part of the business travel agents' work. It can be divided into two main categories: client or customer-based and staff-based. The purpose of corporate hospitality is to retain and motivate clients or employees. Corporate hospitality usually involves the following:

- attendance at a major event (such as a football match)

- an appropriate location or venue for the event

- professional organisation of the event

- quality food and drink.

As far as employees are concerned, incentive travel is another major area for business travel agents. Incentive travel is a reward system offered by a business for top performers. The idea is that the reward system motivates employees by offering them a positive return for their efforts.

Not all business travel agents operate completely independently, with a sales force, separate offices and other traditional set ups. Another variation is known as an implant, which is a small travel agency set up within a larger business. Its main purpose is to provide the facility to book travel and tourism products and services by the main business and by its employees.

Research tip

For an example of the range of business travel services and corporate hospitality, visit the Advanced Travel Partner website at www.atpi.com.

THE LEISURE AND BUSINESS MARKETS

In the UK alone, the business travel market is worth £6.8 billion. Worldwide, online corporate travel sales are worth approaching £20 billion. Again worldwide, a medium to large-sized business will routinely spend up to £5 million on global travel.

For many years, businesses such as American Express (www.americanexpress.com) dominated the market, although new businesses with a purely online presence have begun to reduce their market share.

In the UK, the online leisure travel market accounts for about 17% of the total leisure UK travel market, which is valued at £28 billion. The numbers of people booking flights online grew by 400% in the four years up to 2006.

Research tip

Online business travel is now also provided by www.expedia.co.uk. Choose the corporate option to see their full range of services. www.travelocity.co.uk provides similar services.

Think   What services do you think that companies might need in the business travel sector?

PRODUCTS AND SERVICES

The travel and tourism business does not just restrict itself to selling flights, accommodation and holiday or business packages. It is far broader and it continues to widen its scope in search of additional sales and profits.

Broadly speaking, however, when you compare retail to business the range of products and services offered is rather similar. There are some notable exceptions to this.

For example, the majority of leisure air travel takes place using **chartered** flights, while business travellers tend to use **scheduled** flights.

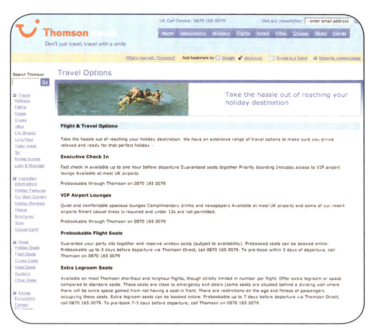

Figure 9.2 *Just some of the extras offered by Thomson*

> ### Key words
>
> **Chartered** – flights run on demand. Additional flights are laid on during the peak season, but these flights do not usually run out of season. Although it is possible to book direct seats, tour operators take most seats
>
> **Scheduled** – flights that operate throughout the year on set times of the day or week. Tickets can be purchased direct from the airline or travel agents. They are usually more expensive than chartered flight costs

Retail

Obviously the bulk of retail sales are package holidays, incorporating flights, transfers and accommodation. However, retail travel agents can offer an enormous range of other products and services, including:

- airport parking
- booking holiday excursions, events and theme park tickets
- foreign currency exchange
- car hire
- coach and taxi transfers
- executive check-in
- bookable seats
- excess baggage
- insurance
- passports and visas
- health advice.

> ### Research tip
>
> For an example of additional services offered by a tour operator, visit www.thomson.co.uk and click on the 'Extras' option.

> **Think** What extras does Thomson offer? Which do you think are the most popular with retail customers and why?

Business

Business travel agents are set up to handle the complete travel needs of their clients and have close relationships with airlines, hotel groups and other suppliers in order to obtain the best prices for their customers. They can offer a full range of additional services, including:

- booking accommodation
- insurance
- rooms for meetings
- conferences and seminars
- bulk air travel fares.

LEGAL AND REGULATORY FRAMEWORK

Retail and business travel agents do not work in isolation. They are members of trade associations, consortia and have memberships with various organisations. They are also controlled by licensing and must fulfil certain legal obligations.

Trade associations

ABTA (the Association of British Travel Agents) is one of the largest British organisations, representing over 6,000 travel agencies and 850 tour operators. Their members include specialist tour operators, independent travel agents, incorporating those using high street outlets, Internet booking services and call centres.

Figure 9.3 The ABTA logo reassures customers that standards will be met

As far as customers are concerned, the ABTA logo used by a travel agent signifies their membership of the association. It means that the member operates under ABTA's code of conduct and that the agency is required to give advice on insurance, visas, passports and health requirements. ABTA's members account for around 90% of package holidays sold and about 45% of independent travel arrangements bought.

Another example of a trade association is the Association of Train Operating Companies (ATOC). It was created in the 1990s and it aims to ensure that members comply with the conditions of agreements and operating licences. This extends to timetabling, fares and ticketing.

> **Research tip**
>
> For information about ABTA's code of conduct and member requirements, visit www.abta.com. Click on 'Holidaymakers' and scroll down to the 'Code of conduct' and 'protected' links.

> **Think** Why is it important to keep all paperwork if you have made a booking through a travel agent? What protection does ABTA offer if the travel agent stops trading?

> **Research tip**
>
> Visit the website of ATOC at www.atoc.org and click on the 'more' link on the welcome page to find out what the association does and the names of its full members.

Consortia

Consortia are organisations that have negotiated rates between accommodation providers and travel agency groups. The relationship is designed to ensure that the travel agent receives the best possible price, while the accommodation provider receives guaranteed business through the travel agency. Consortia are major players in the travel industry.

> **Example**
>
> ABC Corporate Services, based in Massachusetts, has deals with 15,000 hotels belonging to over 200 chains worldwide. They provide access to this arrangement to around 4,000 travel agencies, including Thomas Cook and Advantage Travel. 85% of ABC's business is corporate and the remaining 15% leisure.
>
> DerTours, a German tour operator, heads a consortium with a turnover of €37 billion. 60% of their work is for the leisure market and they represent 1,200 travel agents in Germany.

> **Think** Consortia offer at least 10% off the rack rate. What does this term mean? What other advantages could a relationship with a consortium offer a travel agency?

Memberships

We have already seen that the vast majority of travel agents belong to ABTA. Others belong to the International Air Transport Association (IATA) (www.iata.org). There are 270 airlines among its members. The major IATA departments can be seen in figure 9.4.

As far as customers are concerned, IATA aims to create a system by which people can move around the global airline network as if they were travelling on a single airline in a single country. This means that members have made steps to simplify the travel process.

IATA demands that its members operate safely, securely and efficiently under a series of rules.

Licensing

All travel agents must be licensed by the Civil Aviation Authority's Air Travel Organisers' Licensing Scheme (ATOL). It means that customers purchasing products or services through a travel agent or a tour operator are protected if the operator goes out of business.

The following travel and tourism organisations need to be licensed:

- those that offer packages based around either scheduled or charter flights

- flight-only sales on charter flights

- scheduled flight tickets where money is taken in advance and tickets are issued at a later date.

Research tip

To find out whether a business has an ATOL licence, visit www.caa.co.uk and choose 'Check an ATOL' from the menu. You only need to know the name of the business and not the ATOL number.

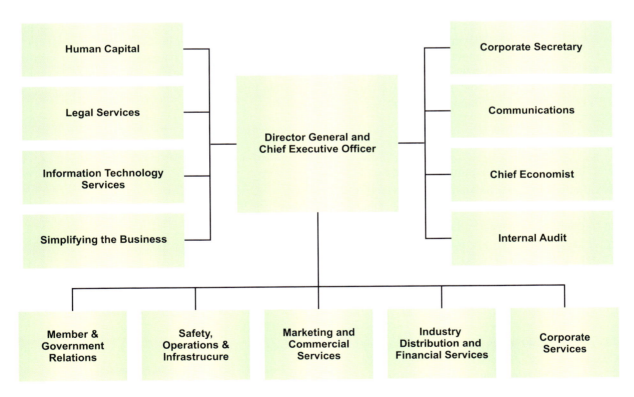

Figure 9.4 IATA organisational chart. 2007

Table 9.1 Legal considerations for the travel and tourism industry

Legal consideration	Explanation
Consumer protection	Membership with ABTA or ATOL actually provides consumers with a more in-depth level of protection than the basic requirements of consumer protection law. Relevant acts include: The Consumer Credit Act (1974) The Consumer Protection Act (1987) The Development of Tourism Act (1969) The Prices Act (1974 and 1975) The Trade Descriptions Act (1968) The Supply of Goods and Services Act (1982) The Sale of Goods Act (1979) The Sale and Supply of Goods Act (1994) The Sales of Goods (amendment) Act (1995).
Contract law	Whenever a customer purchases a product or service from an agent, they are entering into a contract. The contract sets out the terms under which the products or services are being supplied and the payment that the business expects to receive for them. Specific legislation includes: The Unfair Contract Terms Act (1977) The Misrepresentation Act (1967). Contract law is at the heart of all transactions. It is an agreement between two parties and can be recognised and enforced by law.
Financial Services Authority	This organisation regulates the financial services industry in the UK. It requires that businesses do not have unfair terms in their customer contracts that might limit the customer's legal rights. As far as the travel industry is concerned, it is largely involved in insurance and the selling of insurance (www.fsa.gov.uk)
EU package travel regulations	These regulations largely cover package holidays, defined as including at least two items of transport, accommodation or other tourist services. They require the business to provide correct and adequate information in brochures, information about how price changes are handled and what must happen if customers wish to make amendments or cancel their holidays. It also requires the agent to ensure that the holiday is covered by suitable financial protection if the business runs into financial difficulties.

Legal framework

Like all businesses, travel agents have to comply with a number of laws, particularly those relating to consumer protection and contract law. They also have to comply with specific laws relating to credit as travel agents tend to ask for a deposit, with the balance of payment made a certain number of weeks before departure. Finally, there are also European laws to consider.

Think In what ways do you think each legal consideration affects the behaviour and practices of travel and tour operators?

Research tip

Useful websites of trade associations and consumer protection include the following:

Foreign and Commonwealth Office – www.fco.gov.uk

Air Transport Users Council – www.auc.org.uk

Trading Standards Service – www.tradingstandards.gov.uk

Association of ATOL Companies – www.aac-uk.org

Association of Independent Tour Operators – www.aito.co.uk

Federation of Tour Operators – www.fto.co.uk.

RELATIONSHIPS

The travel and tourism industry has always had a degree of cooperation, partnerships and other business relationships. These have generally been between travel agents and tour operators, or tour operators and airlines. However, in recent years, this process has accelerated and there has been a great deal of merging of travel and tourism suppliers of products and services, creating large businesses that are able to provide not only the core packages, but also ancillary services.

Integration

Integration takes place when two or more businesses are joined together to create a single entity. This can be achieved in the following three ways:

1) By a merger – when both businesses become a single business, but they may retain their original name as this may be well-known to customers.

2) By a takeover – this is when one business acquires all of the assets and customer databases of another business. They will incorporate the business that they have acquired into their own business, perhaps still operating it as a separate entity.

3) Joint venture – when two or more businesses join together to create a third business, which provides different products and services or perhaps deals with a different market.

> **Think** Why might a tour operator seek to integrate with a chain of travel agents? What advantages might there be for both parties?

There are two basic forms of integration.

1) Vertical – when two businesses integrate while belonging to different parts of the supply chain. A prime example of this would be a tour operator acquiring a chain of travel agents.

2) Horizontal – when a business integrates with another business at the same level of the supply chain. An example of this would be two airlines merging together.

CASE STUDY: MYTRAVEL AND THOMAS COOK MERGER

After much speculation, the holiday companies MyTravel and Thomas Cook announced in February 2007 that they would be merging, with the merger plans to be completed by June. Thomas Cook will own 52% of the new group with the remaining 48% owned by MyTravel shareholders. According to the chairman of Thomas Cook, "The combined organisations will offer customers unrivalled choice". The total value of the new company is £8 billion with a combined customer base of 9 million.

QUESTIONS

1. Using the Internet, find out which other major tour operator had hoped to sell their package holiday business to either MyTravel or Thomas Cook.

2. Which business that owns Thomson is the group's major rival in the package holiday market?

3. What nationality is the company that actually owns Thomas Cook?

Agency agreements

An agency agreement is an agreement that allows one party (in this case, the travel agent) to sell the products or services of another party (in this case, an airline or tour operator), in return for commission payments.

The travel agent works as an agent on behalf of a travel and tourism supplier as the point of contact with the customer. There are three different types of agency agreements.

1) Exclusive – where only the agent represents the supplier and the supplier cannot enter into contracts with any other agent.

2) Sole agency – where the supplier cannot appoint other agents, but can deal with customers directly.

3) Non-exclusive – where the supplier can freely appoint other agents and deal with customers directly.

Commission levels

The usual arrangement with any kind of agency agreement is the payment of a commission, which is a fixed rate or percentage on sales generated by the travel agent on behalf of the supplier. There are clear guidelines as to how much should be paid and when it should be paid.

The standard travel agency commission is around 10%, although commission is beginning to disappear in the airline and car rental sectors. In the accommodation sector, travel agents that can generate bulk bookings can attract commission of between 7 and 10%, although the standard agency commission is around 5%.

As airlines have axed travel agency commission, this means that agents have to add their own **mark-up** if they are to make any profit on selling the airline's tickets.

Key words

Mark-up – a set amount of money added to the selling price to provide the agency with income for sales that have not generated a commission for them

Preferred operators and racking policies

As far as travel agents are concerned, these two considerations are effectively part of the same decision. Preferred operators will be tour operators and other suppliers that are either part of the travel agent's group or those that offer the best commission to the travel agency. It is obviously in the agency's interest to push the products and services of suppliers that belong to the same organisation, such as Lunn Poly and Thomson.

If there is no such close relationship, then the agency will adopt what is known as a **racking policy**. This is a decision made on how to display suppliers' brochures in the high street store. The agency may decide not to display the brochures of certain suppliers as they do not offer the agency the best commission levels or they will prominently display the brochures of those that pay them good commission.

Policies such as these extend across all of the multiples and many of the independents. It ultimately means that truly impartial advice is not necessarily assured to the customer. The racking policy has a drastic effect on particular destinations.

In Europe, more than 60% of integrated suppliers sell tour packages. Many of these are happy to de-rack brochures as a means to force larger commission payments from tour operators. At times, they have also pressurised the tour operators not to supply brochures to independent travel agencies.

Think Is it ethical for an agent to only offer products and services from tour operators and other suppliers that provide them with the best commission rates?

SECTORS

It is becoming very difficult to recognise discrete sectors in an increasingly integrated travel and tourism industry. However, they broadly fall into three categories: accommodation, transport and ancillary services. It is important to bear in mind that accommodation and transport providers are principles. They are called this as they provide the essential nuts and bolts of any holiday package. Anything beyond this, including services provided by travel agents, tour operators and insurance companies, are classified as ancillary services. This is despite the fact that the same business may provide all of them.

Accommodation providers

Travel agents can provide customers with the ability to book accommodation, but other ways in which accommodation can be reserved are:

- directly with the accommodation provider

- indirectly through a tour operator

- indirectly through a tailor-made package using an e-agent

- using accommodation-specific booking companies, such as www.roomcheck.co.uk.

Transport providers

Similar options are available for customers wishing to book transportation. This is regardless of whether the transport is restricted to domestic destinations or international destinations. It is also irrespective of whether the transport is by vehicle, rail, air or sea.

Figure 9.5 It is possible to book the Eurostar through several different providers

Ancillary providers

As we have already seen, ancillary providers include insurance, car hire and airport hotels. The following options are usually available.

- Insurance can be purchased either from an agency that receives a commission or from an airline or a tour operator, also in return for commission. The major alternative is to buy annual travel insurance from organisations such as the Post Office.

- Travel agencies and tour operators also offer car hire. For example, easyJet offers a free choice service incorporating airline flight, accommodation and car hire at the point of destination all through preferred operators.

- Airport hotels have financial or agency agreements with airlines and with tour operators. They generally incorporate an overnight stay with car parking for the duration of the holiday. This is usually a formal financial arrangement and each customer who books hotel accommodation at the departure airport generates a commission or a flat fee to be paid to the airline or to the tour operator.

Figure 9.6 Airport hotels usually have agreements with operators and airlines

Tour operators

Tour operators usually provide ready-made holiday packages that incorporate return flights, transfers and accommodation. The customer can purchase all other aspects of the package as ancillary services.

Some tour operators own airlines, while others block book charter flights. Tour operators also have preferred providers in the accommodation sector where they will grade, check and then block book a number of rooms or the entire premises.

They will also have their own staff and coaches available to transfer customers from the arrival airport to the resort, as well as the return trip. An integral part of generating additional sales and profit is to maintain a close relationship with customers in the resort. By deploying holiday representatives, the tour operator is able to sell additional services, such as excursions and car hire.

Research tip

For more information about holiday representatives, visit www.careerintravel.co.uk.

EVIDENCE ACTIVITY

P1 – M1 – D1

You work for a large department store in a major town. The family that owns the department store has been looking at different ways in which to diversify. One option is opening a travel agency on the top floor of the department store. The family and all of the management have no knowledge or experience of the travel agency business and they have asked you to prepare a comprehensive presentation, supported by any necessary visual aids, explaining the operations of the retail and business travel sector.

1. Describe at least three different types of retail and business agent. Make sure you mention the type of market each attracts and the products and services they sell. (P1)

2. Describe relevant trade associations, consortia, membership and licence organisations paying close attention to the key aspects of the legal framework. Remember to include information on the Package Travel Regulations and the role of the Financial Services Authority in ensuring compulsory insurance training for agents selling holiday insurance. (P1)

3. Describe the relationship between the different agents and other sectors of the industry. (Remember that all agents work closely with accommodation, transport, and ancillary service and operator providers.) (P1)

4. Explain more fully the relationships that operate in the retail and business travel environment, giving industry-specific examples, such as tour operators and airlines offering different commission levels. (M1)

5. Give industry examples of integration that has taken place. (M1)

6. Explain the current strengths and weaknesses in the industry. (You could focus on different booking systems, the abilities of agents to respond to changing needs and how their range of products or services are often affected by the commission that they receive.) (D1)

9.2 *Understand how advances in technology have affected retail and business travel operations*

ADVANCES IN TECHNOLOGY

With integrated databases accessible from remote locations by the use of passwords, integrated booking services have revolutionised the travel and tourism industry. It is now possible to search for a travel query, having established a customer's requirements and then to make a firm booking and receive confirmation. All of this has been integrated with secure payment systems, allowing either retail or business travel agencies to carry out the function on behalf of the customer or for the customer to use the agency's own website to search for an appropriate package by themselves.

Internet

The vast majority of airlines, tour operators, transport providers, ancillary businesses and other travel and tourism providers offer secure online purchasing. The principle requirement of a website is for the customer to be able to identify their specific requirements, such as date and destination, and then to be offered a series of choices from a list drawn from the database of available packages.

Many businesses have extended the basic search and selection function, so that customers can build their own bespoke packages, selecting specific flight times, connections and transfers and accommodation preferences.

Example

A prime example of a flexible website with a broad database is www.lastminute.com. Options include flight and hotels, package holidays, flight only or hotel only. The customer is able to select their departure point and date and time (if important), then make similar choices with regard to destinations. Further options include direct flight only, which narrows down the search.

Transport

With the exception of airlines, many transport providers have actually been quite slow in adapting to online booking services. However, it is now possible to do online bookings for coach travel (www.nationalexpress.com), rail travel (www.nationalrail.co.uk) and sea travel (by booking services, such as www.ferrysavers.com).

The greatest competition is in the area of air travel. Websites such as www.cheapflights.co.uk have massive databases, with over one million flight seats through 600 airlines and **flight brokers**.

Key words

Flight brokers – organisations that have relationships with many different airlines and can find the cheapest price available

All of these services rely on fully searchable databases, which contain up-to-the-minute information on issues such as availability and price changes. Many of these businesses still provide traditional telephone contact and booking for customers. They use the same database and booking system, inputting the information on behalf of the customer.

Figure 9.7 lastminute.com offers customers inspirational and unique leisure and travel ideas including flights, hotels, theatre and gigs

Reservation systems

There are many ready-made computerised reservation systems that can be adapted by the agent to match their specific needs. Larger businesses tend to employ software developers to build dedicated reservation systems. The systems require online booking and secure payment systems as integral elements.

The more sophisticated Internet-based reservation systems can cope with single or multiple locations of destinations, different types of package operator and travel and ancillary services.

Communication methods

There have been a number of advances in communications technology, all of which have been embraced by the travel and tourism industry to a greater or lesser extent. Broadband and e-mail are essential communication methods that have been enabled by improved telephone lines.

Direct connection between booking agents and principles is no longer necessary in the traditional sense. Previously secure cabling made the connection, but now digitally secure Internet connections serve the same purpose. They have the advantage of being more flexible as connections can be set up quickly without needing to install cabling infrastructure.

Another major advantage has been an improvement in telephone services. Booking can be made online using voice recognition systems (such as www.travelodge.co.uk). This voice recognition software enables full interaction between the computerised system and the customer, using necessary prompts and supported by the use of the telephone keypad. This is a similar system to those used by UCI cinemas and telephone banking systems.

> **Think** Voice recognition software is highly effective and sophisticated, but is it really an effective replacement for human operators? What impact might the use of this software have on customers' willingness to use telephone-booking services?

CASE STUDY: RESERVATIONS

In 2006, Thomas Cook announced a £67 million project to create a reservation system to cover its 34 tour operator brands and travel agencies. Prior to this, the business was using a number of different reservation systems; 11 had been inherited as the business gradually purchased other companies. Thomas Cook gave the code name 'globe' to the IT project and its primary aims were to improve efficiency and cut costs.

QUESTIONS

1. What possible disruptions could there be to the organisation as the new reservation system is adopted?

2. Find out which software company is providing the basic reservation system for Thomas Cook.

EFFECTS ON SALES

Providing the ability for customers to book at any time and in any place extends the period during which customers can make purchases. In the past, when companies relied purely on employees to process or facilitate the sale, businesses had to seriously consider shift work and weekend work in order to cope with peak period demand.

> **Key words**
>
> Shift work – working a standard number of hours per day, but perhaps starting work at 08:00, 14:00 or 22:00

Obviously, a traditional high street travel agent does not stay open for 24 hours a day, but after the store itself has closed, customers can still contact the organisation and make bookings or enquiries, either using telephone communications or the Internet through the business's website. This has given businesses far more capacity to deal with volume calls and contact by customers. This has meant that booking and reservation systems have to be robust and capable of dealing with multiple enquiries at the same time. Even now, however, some of the larger tour operator websites fail to respond at peak times and show a message to the user, requesting them to return to the website at another time.

EFFECTS ON TYPES OF PRODUCTS AND SERVICES SOLD

Assuming that a travel agent has established relationships with the broadest possible range of other organisations in the industry, it is possible for them to sell a far wider range of products and services than ever before. The travel agency effectively works as a sales point for additional services and principle services, receiving payment in the form of commission for every sale that is achieved by them.

When relationships such as these are developed, there is always the question of responsibility and division of work, as well as the question of who will handle the payment system. Once this has been established, it can then be decided how shares of payment are to be distributed. Most travel agents will opt to collect funds for the sale of products and services themselves and then pass on appropriate payment to the actual provider, minus their share of the transaction.

As technology has developed, it is now possible to make these bookings, sales and payments instantaneously. Electronic transfer of funds enables the free flow of payments that have been cleared by the customer's issuing bank.

```
************************************************************

YOUR CONFIRMATION NUMBER IS:            FOD9Q8

You will need this confirmation number and VALID ACCEPTED
FORM  OF PHOTO ID(as detailed below) at check-in to
receive your boarding card.

 ITINERARY/RECEIPT - All times are local.

 PASSENGERS
1. Phillip Jones     ADT  2. Claire MacDonald ADT

 GOING OUT
From London Stansted(STN) to Alghero(AHO)  Tue, 09Oct07
Flight PQ258 Depart STN at 09:15 and arrive AHO at 11:50

 COMING BACK
From Alghero(AHO) to London Stansted(STN) Tue,16Oct07
Flight PQ456 Depart AHO at 14:05 and arrive STN at 16:40

 PAYMENT DETAILS
********40.00 GBP     Adult
********79.30 GBP     Taxes, Fees & Charges
********15.20 GBP     Aviation / WCHR Levy
*********0.00 GBP     Car Rental
*********0.00 GBP     Insurance
*******134.50 GBP     Total Paid

************************************************************
```

Figure 9.8 Example of a flight confirmation e-mail

EFFECTS ON ADMINISTRATION SYSTEMS

This has streamlined the administrative systems as very few transactions are carried out manually or recorded solely on paper using traditional copies. All of the details of a product or service sale are dealt with electronically, with necessary copies or confirmations being automatically sent to relevant businesses, in the case of flight bookings or accommodation and summaries printed out for the customer along with booking reference numbers. An example of a confirmation email can be seen in figure 9.8 on the previous page.

Example

A customer decides to book a flight using easyJet's website. The customer selects the destination, date and time of flight, together with the departure airport. They complete online forms, including their name and address and then confirm the booking and make the payment. When easyJet's database has been used to check the availability of the flight and once the booking is confirmed (at the point when payment is approved by the issuing bank), a booking reference number appears on the screen and a confirmation e-mail is sent to the customer

Meanwhile, the database has reduced the number of available seats on that particular flight and entered the customer's details onto a checklist of customers. This can then be crosschecked with the booking reference number when the customer checks in at the departure airport. It isn't necessary for easyJet to print a copy of any of these documents at any stage in the process.

OPERATIONS

Advances in technology have had a major impact on the operations of all parts of the travel and tourism industry. This has affected the distribution (sales points for products and services), the booking process itself, how payment methods are used and overall security, in terms of payment security and transfer of funds.

Distribution

There are now effectively two differing types of distribution as a result of technology changes.

1) The direct sales of airlines, attractions, accommodation providers, insurance, car hire and other aspects of the industry. By establishing an online presence, these businesses are able to 'cut out the middlemen' and sell directly to customers. This provides the business with a number of key advantages. The first advantage is the receipt of the full sales price of the product or service without having to pay a fee or commission to an intermediate seller. The second major advantage is that the business has a stronger control over the sales process and can actively seek additional sales by responding to demand, without having the complication of others selling on their behalf.

2) Integrated agents are still very important in the industry as they offer the 'one stop shop' alternative for customers. The major advantage of agents such as these is that they can offer all key and peripheral products and services by talking to a single individual and processing a single payment.

Direct sales are particularly common when booking flight–only or when purchasing tickets to attractions or for travel only. Integrated agents tend to be used for more complex demands, which could incorporate transport, transfers and accommodation.

Booking process

Technology has driven down costs. Many businesses have automated the booking process from the actual booking through to actual ticket fulfilment. It is possible for agents to access travel data instantly and then to use a computer software system that takes them through both online and offline bookings. Further software captures the transaction data for billing and reporting purposes.

Systems such as Abacus can check the availability of air, car and hotel elements of a package and allow the travel agent to book the parts individually or as a group. It is then possible for the agent to follow up on the booking by verifying parts of the trip or all of the trip elements, price the trip and then issue the tickets. This can all be done using automated software, therefore reducing the demand for employees to man telephones or high street shops.

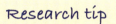

Research tip

To find out more about the Abacus system, visit www.sita.aero.

Payment methods used

The UK is Europe's largest e-commerce economy with over 60% of people making purchases online. Electronic payments offer the following advantages to businesses:

- convenience by removing the need to deal with invoices, cheques and cash

- immediacy by having credit and debit cards instantly approved and processed

- improved cash flow by receiving payment at the time of purchase

- **competitive advantage** by offering services that some competitors still resist.

Key words

Competitive advantage – gaining an advantage, either in the level of service, promotional activities, range of products and services or some other factor that the competition does not offer

Security

Protecting card details is crucial to attracting online sales. There are three main options for encryption and security of personal and card details:

1) Secure socket layer (SSL) – this allows scrambled or encrypted data and it can protect against basic attempts to decipher card details as it takes over an hour to break into one message.

2) Secure electronic transaction (SET) – this encrypts payment card transaction data and also verifies that both parties in the transaction are genuine. It is seen as being more secure than SSL.

3) Public key software infrastructure (PKI) – this works like a business's bank night safe. It allows the business to deposit money into the safe, but only the private key that belongs to the bank can make withdrawals.

EVIDENCE ACTIVITY

P2

The family and senior management have expressed some concerns about installing new technology and whether this is strictly necessary. You need to describe the importance of technological advances to the retail and business travel operations.

1. Describe how technological advances have had an impact on all types of travel agent. You must cover at least three methods of distribution and also mention the effect on the booking process. (P2)

2. Describe how technological advances have had an impact on the types of products and services sold. (P2)

9.3 *Understand how retail travel organisations seek to gain a competitive advantage*

TRAVEL ORGANISATIONS

Different types of agents are more or less able to gain a temporary competitive advantage over their closest competitors. If it is a large-sized business with a high **turnover** and profit level, then it has more funding and flexibility to invest in features that could give it a competitive advantage. It is more difficult for smaller or independent operators to gain a competitive advantage. For example, instead of competing on price, they will concentrate on their level of staff training, their personal service and, perhaps, their convenience as primary points of comparison with their competitors.

> **Key words**
>
> Turnover – the amount of money that comes into a business through sales or income over a period of time, usually a year

COMPETITIVE ADVANTAGES

A competitive advantage does not necessarily have to mean offering the lowest possible prices through discounting or indeed being able to afford far more advertising than other similar businesses. It also doesn't always mean having the most outlets or staff.

Competitive advantages tend to be temporary and there is a major reason for this. All businesses in the travel and tourism industry, like any other area of business, will keep a close eye on the activities of their competitors. If a business sees that a competitor has successfully used one of its features or a policy or approach, which has been seen to be effective, then they will inevitably copy it. This means that to have a true competitive advantage the business always needs to be ahead of its competitors and to be planning its next move, even when its current activities are showing a positive impact.

Level of service

Customers are far more discerning and demanding than ever before. What may have been considered as excellent customer service in the past is now expected as a minimum level of service. This means that businesses have to continually improve and maintain their level of service. This can be measured in the number of telephone rings before a call is answered, the responsiveness of a website or the mere fact that if an employee promises to carry out a particular task by a particular date, then this is always given priority.

Staff training

Although excellent customer service is at the heart of most staff training, the travel and tourism industry is not alone in having to ensure that their employees are fully orientated and conversant with the industry itself. Basic product and service knowledge is a minimum requirement. Customers rarely contact a travel and tourism organisation being completely confident of the products and services that they require; they always require a degree of advice and guidance. It is this aspect that often opens the door to a key staff training requirement of selling skills.

There are many opportunities to sell additional or enhanced products and services in the industry. Customers will often contact an agency with a vague idea of their requirements. It is the role of the employee to identify the customer's particular needs and to sell them a range of products and services, which not only match those needs, but also provide the agency with the greatest level of profit.

> **Think** Knowledge of the product or service range and appropriate selling skills require experience and training. At what point in an employee's career would this need to be introduced?

Promotional activities

Promotional activities are designed to arouse attention and interest in the business's products and services. Once the customer has made contact, promises made through promotional activities, combined with the selling skills of the employees, are designed to create a sale. Businesses will normally use three major promotional activities.

Discounting

Discounting is designed to sell excess products or services at a time when demand is comparatively low. Discounting is used in all areas of business to stimulate sales during low peak demand periods. The travel and tourism industry uses discounting to encourage early bookings. By securing early bookings, a certain level of sales can be achieved far earlier than would normally be the case if the products and services were sold at standard prices.

Example

easyJet uses discounting in order to encourage early sales of airline tickets. The first few seats on any flight are sold at under-cost price. The price increases gradually as the number of available seats on the flight is reduced. This process goes through to the very last seat on the flight, which is charged at a premium rate. Overall, the seat cost evens out by offering discounts, then standard prices, and finally high prices.

Low deposits

Low deposits are another promotional activity designed to encourage early bookings. By offering to secure a booking with a relatively low deposit made by the customer, the client is encouraged to make a commitment much earlier. Not all agencies offer low deposits and some still require full payment to be made at the time of booking. This does place them at a competitive disadvantage, but a full payment is necessary for nearly all agents if the departure is imminent and certainly if it is within eight weeks.

Advertising

Just like many other parts of the travel and tourism industry, agents routinely advertise using a variety of different media, including newspapers, magazines, radio and television. In order to identify the source of the advertisement that has prompted the customer to contact the organisation, a series of promotional codes are often printed or quoted during the advertisement. These have a dual purpose. Firstly, they are unique identification codes, so that the business can log the response rates of each advertisement. This will help them in future planning of advertising campaigns. The other advantage is that the customer can use the promotional code to secure a discount, offer or low deposit.

Figure 9.9 Customers are often instructed to quote the promotional code

Range of products and services

No business wants their customers to leave the premises needing to go to a competitor to secure part of a package that they cannot supply themselves. Therefore, agents offer the broadest possible range of products and services, which goes far beyond simply booking flights, accommodation or packages. This is seen as a process known as **diversification**.

Key words

Diversification – when a business expands its range of products and services beyond those usually offered, so that it can pick up additional sales from customers by selling ancillary products and services

As a business cannot easily predict trends and fashions in the travel and tourism industry, it must offer the broadest possible range, including destinations, travel options, grades of hotel and the widest range of ancillary products and services.

> **Think** Diversification not only broadens the range of products and services offered, but it also protects the business's sales. Why is this the case?

Add-on sales and ancillary products and services

Strictly speaking, most holiday packages include all or most of the customer's requirements. These would inevitably include a return flight, transfers and accommodation. However, there are still opportunities to sell additional products and services, including insurance, currency exchange, excursions, excess baggage, preferred seating, executive lounges and transport to and from the airport.

By offering some or all of these additional products and services, the business is able to:

- secure additional turnover in terms of income and profit

- ensure that there is no need for the customer to purchase products and services from a competitor

- offer the customer peace of mind and the convenience of being able to book all requirements in a single transaction.

Example

The integrated booking agent, Freedom Direct (www.freedomdirect.co.uk) offers package holidays, flight only, accommodation only and flight and accommodation options. When a customer's specific requirements involve the purchase of a separate flight and separate accommodation, the transfers to resort are not included in the package price. This is offered at a £50 per group return all-in price as an add-on sale. Freedom Direct Holidays also require customers not purchasing insurance through them to complete an indemnity form, which identifies their insurance provider.

Dynamic packaging

When package holidays were first introduced, they were rigid, ready-made flight, transfer and accommodation packages. While many holiday packages still retain this format, travel agents have realised that many customers want a greater choice of flight options, transfer and accommodation. This has coincided with more direct overseas flights from regional airports, which has further increased choice.

Dynamic packaging therefore involves giving the customer the opportunity to select the precise flight and carrier on a specified day to a specified destination. They can then choose the accommodation and their transfer preference.

CASE STUDY: GREEK SUN

Independent tour operator Greek Sun (www.greeksun.co.uk) offers packages to the lesser-known Greek islands. In addition to this, they also offer three other choices that demonstrate the dynamic packaging of their products and services.

• Tailor-made holidays – customers are able to specify their departure airport and identify the Greek islands that they wish to travel to and the number of days they want to spendon each island. The company then designs a tailor-made package to meet these requirements.

• Island hopping – although there are several ready-made island-hopping packages, customers are able to specify the precise order in which they wish to visit the islands and whether they wish extensions to be made beyond the normal seven or fifteen days.

• Two-centre holidays – the company lists popular two-centre holiday packages, although they can organise any two-centre holiday to meet the customer's requirements. The company will organise transfer between centres as part of the pricing.

Integrated organisations

As with many other industries, there has been a trend towards larger businesses buying up smaller, specialised businesses and competitors. This has allowed the larger organisations to bring many of the ancillary products and services and add-on sales in-house, which they would previously only earn a commission from selling.

A prime example is the way that airport transfers are arranged in the Balearic Islands. In the past, many of the major tour operators used Spanish coach companies to facilitate the transfer of passengers from the airports to the resorts. Now the drivers and the coaches are owned by the tour operators, rather than being contracted by them. This means that the tour operator can control the costs and availability of the coaches more closely. The staff can be trained and given uniforms to reinforce the image of the business.

Market share

Market share can be measured in various ways. It is the proportion of a market that is controlled by a particular travel company. The actual term 'market' can refer to the value of sales or the number of customers purchasing a particular product or service. There are many different markets in the travel and tourism industry, although these are not usually country-specific, but specific to the customer's country of origin. In other words, one market could be the number of British tourists buying package holidays in Spain. A sub-market could be those people travelling to the Balearic Islands.

As many agents offer the broadest possible range of products and services, they are, in fact, competing in several different markets at the same time. This means that the general measurement can be the total spent on travel-related products, either for leisure or business reasons.

The market itself incorporates the full value of all sales in terms of money. The market share of an individual business is how much of a slice of that market it controls.

> **Think** There are now three major players in the tour operator market. What kind of market share do you think each one has? Have recent purchases of other businesses affected this market share?

EVIDENCE ACTIVITY

P3 – M2 – D2

The family and the senior management are still unconvinced and fear that there is already a great deal of competition in the local area and that the company would struggle to make any kind of impact on the local market. They need some reassurance, assuming that they are prepared to invest heavily enough. As a retail operation the managers would understand far more if you focused on retail travel agents.

1. Explain how the level of service and staff training provides a competitive advantage. (P3)

2. Describe how promotional activities and a range of different products and services can provide a competitive advantage. (P3)

3. Explain how add-on sales, and ancillary products and services can provide a competitive advantage. (P3)

4. Explain the importance of dynamic packaging and explain how it can provide a competitive advantage. (P3)

5. Describe how dynamic packaging has been used to offset the activities of integrated agents. (P3)

The family are coming round to the idea, but they want tangible examples of retail travel agents and how they are faring in the competitive marketplace.

6. Compare the effectiveness of two named retail travel agents in their attempts to gain a competitive advantage. (M2)

7. Recommend what the two named travel agents could also do in order to improve their competitive advantage. (D2)

8. Justify your recommendations by giving evidence to support your suggestions. (D2)

9.4 *Be able to produce complex itineraries for retail and business travel customers*

COMPLEX ITINERARIES

An itinerary is essentially a comprehensive and organised listing of a trip. It contains information on when, where and how the traveller will be travelling. Sometimes draft itineraries are prepared before final itineraries are completed.

The complexity of the itinerary will depend on a number of factors, including:

- client details
- flight or service numbers and operators
- departure and arrival in local time
- relevant transfers
- accommodation details
- any passport, visa or health requirements
- whether any intermediate stops are being made
- the confirmed booking or availability of additional services, such as car hire or excursions.

Meeting a range of different needs

For both retail and business travel agents, it is not simply a question of booking appropriate transport and accommodation. For both types of agents, it is becoming an increasing trend to specifically produce packages and associated itineraries that match particular customer needs. Examples include flight and accommodation to Italy with a cookery course or a business traveller who is visiting Germany and having to attend meetings in three or four different German cities over the course of a week. In both cases, not only are flights and accommodation required, but also transfers from the airport to accommodation or from accommodation to accommodation.

Example

An unusual example of sightseeing and a skiing itinerary is provided by www.skilebanon.co.uk.

Day 1: Sunday
Depart London Heathrow arriving into Beirut in time for dinner. Transfer to 4-star hotel in Beirut. Overnight in Beirut City.

Day 2: Monday
After breakfast, transfer to the ski resort. The ski resort of Faraya Mazaar is only an hour from Beirut. Collect skis from the slope ski hire shop, then enjoy a day's skiing. Night in 5-star hotel located on the ski slopes.

Day 3: Tuesday
Qalaat Fakra and the natural stone bridge at Kferdiban (near Faraya resort). Full day to ski or sightsee. In the afternoon if the snow is not too deep, it is then possible to walk around the Roman temple ruins. Night in the resort in 5-star hotel.

Figure 9.10 The Lebanon offers visitors the chance to ski and sightsee

Day 4: Wednesday

Full day to ski or sightsee. Overnight in the resort in 5-star hotel.

Day 5: Thursday

After breakfast, check out and transfer to Beirut visiting the Jeita Grotto, Harrisa and Our Lady of Lebanon and the ancient city of Byblos. Lunch is near the port, overlooking the sea. The port itself is very pretty and the shops behind it are interesting. Overnight at 4-star hotel in Beirut City.

Day 6: Friday

Full day to ski or sightsee at the Cedars. After breakfast, head out on a full day tour to Baalbeck and visit the famous wine caves of Ksara. (There may also be time to visit Anjar.) Return to Beirut for dinner and overnight in 4-star hotel.

Day 7: Saturday

After breakfast, head out on a full day tour of Besharreh and the Maronite chapels in the Kadisha Gorge. There will also be time to see the Kadisha Grotto and Malil Gibran Museum and also Der Mar Antonio Quozhave, the largest hermitage in the valley. Overnight in 4-star hotel in Beirut.

Day 8: Sunday

After breakfast, take a full day tour of Tyre and Sidon. Overnight in Beirut in 4-star hotel.

Day 9: Monday

Depart for London Heathrow in the morning. If travelling directly to London on British Mediterranean or on MEA, this will be around 07.40. Arrive London at 10.45 (MEA times and BM are similar).

Think Itineraries such as the one shown are common for sightseeing tours. Suggest two other types of packages that would require similar detail.

RETAIL ITINERARIES

Many retail itineraries are standard packages, particularly for family holiday products. The itineraries are already determined by the tour operator and include the following:

- departure airport

- departure time, airline and flight number

- arrival at destination in local time

- transfer arrangements

- name of accommodation, number of nights and the basis (self-catering, bed and breakfast, half board, full board or all-inclusive)

- transfer to airport arrangements

- departure airport

- airline operator

- flight number

- check-in and departure in local time

- arrival time in **GMT**.

Tailor-made packages

Tailor-made packages are becoming increasingly common, requiring the agent to produce a specific itinerary that incorporates all of the details listed above, but usually on a one-off basis. Rather like ready-made holidays, tailor-made holidays have all accommodation, transfer and travel booked in advance. They must take domestic transport schedules into account and will usually employ the services of local agents and/or accommodation owners.

The other key advantage of tailor-made packages is that departures can be organised on a daily basis, rather than the standard **changeover day** for a particular resort.

> **Key words**
>
> **GMT (Greenwich Mean Time)** – the time in the UK
> **Changeover day** – the day when the bulk of incoming and outgoing tourists from a particular country or a particular tour operator arrives and departs

Example

14-night "Cycladic Adventure"

Day 1	Fly to Athens and continue by air to Santorini for a stay of 3 nights at the King Thiras Hotel in Thira
Day 4	By ferry to Naxos (3 hours) for a stay of 2 nights at the Hotel Coronis in Naxos Town
Day 6	By ferry to Paros (1 hour) for a stay of 2 nights at the Parian Village in Parikia
Day 8	By ferry to Antiparos (10 minutes) for a stay of 2 nights at the Artemis Hotel
Day 10	By ferry to Tinos (1 hour) for a stay of 2 nights at the Leandros Hotel in Tinos Town
Day 12	By ferry to Mykonos (30 minutes) for a stay of 3 nights at the Hotel Ilio Maris in Mykonos Town
Day 15	Flight home from Mykonos via Athens

Depending on air schedules, this itinerary may have to be reversed.

Source: www.greeksun.co.uk

Additional services

Agents will often take the opportunity to sell ancillary products and services at the same time as the main travel arrangements are booked. These can include reserved seats. This allows the customer to specify where they wish to sit when they travel, particularly if they have special requirements such as a window seat or additional legroom.

Details of any additional services purchased will be included on the itinerary, as well as booking, reservation and confirmation details of the transport provider. For example, for a tailor-made holiday, any details of car hire at the destination airport will also be included on the detailed itinerary.

BUSINESS ITINERARIES

Business itineraries may be even more complex than tailor-made retail itineraries. This is due to the requirement for other specific elements to be included in the itinerary, such as:

- the type of aircraft being used for transportation

- the class of travel and whether any seats have been reserved

- any intermediate stops and the duration of those stops

- the address and room type of any accommodation

- specific arrangements regarding transfers to locations of meetings or conferences

- any other specific entertainment-based arrangements, including restaurant bookings and the theatre

- advice on getting around in a particular destination is also useful, particularly if there are periods of congestion that might affect travel

- some indication as to the weather conditions at the time of travel could also be advisable.

Multi-sector

Business travellers are more likely to need multi-sector journeys. These are tickets or flight coupons that include more flights than a simple return journey. The ticket will include flight details for each leg of the journey, which could, for example, appear as:

Sector 1: 14 April 20. London (LHR) to Johannesburg (JNB) on British Airways (BA)

Sector 2: 16 April 20. Johannesburg (JNB) to Durban (DUR) on South African Airways (SA)

Sector 3: 23 April 20. Durban (DUR) to Johannesburg (JNB) on South African Airways (SA)

Sector 4: 24 April 20. Johannesburg (JNB) to Paris (PAR) on Air France (AF)

Sector 5: 26 April 20. Paris (PAR) to London (LHR) on British Airways (BA)

The flight number would be identified for each of the journeys, as well as the following:

- class of travel

- departure date and time

- whether the seat is guaranteed

- the validity of the ticket (the last day for use)

- basic fare for the flight and taxes on each ticket

- payment method

- baggage allowance.

Components

Think How might the tickets or flight coupons differ if individual flights were booked directly through each of the three airlines?

Again, just like a retail itinerary, the key components of a business itinerary will tend to focus on transport, departure points and time, as well as arrival points and time (in local time).

Business travel is likely to incorporate various transport types. Accommodation details would also indicate board type and there may be suggestions as to where meals can be taken if the stay is not on a half-board basis.

RETAIL AND BUSINESS ITINERARY CONTENT

Many of the features of retail and business itineraries are very similar. Where appropriate, differences between the two are highlighted in this section. Regardless of the purpose or content of the actual travel itinerary, it needs to incorporate all of the major headings included in this section as a minimum. It also needs to be in a clear and logical format.

There is no specific industry standard for itineraries as they can be produced either as word-processed documents, pro-forma documents that have been completed or brief details incorporated into an e-mail or as an attachment to an e-mail.

Client details

The individual who has made the booking or the group leader is referred to as the lead passenger. The lead passenger's details always appear first in the client details section. The client details will include:

- surname, then forenames
- age, if relevant
- address
- nationality.

Check-in details

Although the departure time will be included in the itinerary, it is important to include the necessary check-in time, which may differ from airport to airport and from location to location.

Example

www.flybmi.com has several different types of check-in procedures:

- their online check-in opens 24 hours before departure and closes 30 minutes before departure
- self check-in machines allow check-in up to 40 minutes before departure
- priority check-in requires the customer to present themselves at a check-in desk.

Usually check-in desks open up to four hours before departure. The departure gates normally close around 40 minutes before the flight is due to depart. International flights usually require longer check-in times than domestic flights. Even ferry terminals require between one and two hours check-in prior to departure.

Flight or service numbers

It is important that the itinerary specifically identifies the flight or service number. A specified departure time may be known at the time of booking and when the itinerary is created. However, situations may arise that affect the departure time and the customer needs to be able to identify their specific flight or service number, so that they can make enquiries at the departure point.

Think Suggest three ways in which a customer with a flight number could check the intended departure time prior to leaving for the airport.

Transport operator

For retail itineraries, the airline and the tour operator are normally only required in this section of the itinerary. The airline named must match the flight number and the tour operator named should concord with details relating to the transfer and the accommodation.

For business itineraries, customers will usually only need the airline name as other parts of the itinerary are unlikely to be part of an overall package.

The transport type also needs to be incorporated for business travel itineraries. Identification of the type of aircraft used, such as a Boeing 737, and the class of travel that the customer has booked (First Class, Business Class or Economy Class) achieves this.

Departure and arrival in local time and intermediate stops

Tour operator packages will show departure and arrival in local time. It is important to remember that there are time zones and that this will affect the times quoted in the itinerary. If there is any doubt about the local time given, this can be checked using Internet services, such as www.timeanddate.com, which provides the world clock and time zones. Approximate arrival time in local time can also be calculated if the duration of the flight is known.

Business travel customers may also need to have details in their itinerary relating to intermediate stops.

Example

A business traveller flying from London to Australia cannot fly there directly. An intermediate stop will have to be made, regardless of whether the customer is travelling west (with an intermediate stop in the USA) or east (with an intermediate stop in Hong Kong or Singapore). This means that local time arrivals, duration of stay and, if relevant, overnight accommodation need to be incorporated into the business itinerary.

Transfer details

Most tour operator holiday packages will include the transfer from the arrival airport to the resort or accommodation. The itinerary needs to identify what or who the customer needs to look for at the airport. Larger resorts will tend to use tour operator representatives and coaches, whereas independent operators may use local taxis, minibuses or even accommodation providers for transfers.

Business travellers will tend to have booked taxi or cab services, which will wait for them at the arrivals gate. These services transfer the traveller from the airport to the accommodation or to their first destination on the itinerary.

Additional services

The itinerary for retail customers will tend to revolve around in-flight meals, reserved seats and whether car hire has been arranged at the arrivals airport. Accommodation may be an additional service if either a retail or business customer needs to stay over on an intermediate stop before flying on to their final destination.

Accommodation details

The name of the hotel, the resort and room type are normally sufficient in a retail holiday package.

Contact details are necessary for a business traveller, particularly if they are making their own way to the accommodation, including an address, a contact name, telephone numbers (bearing in mind that prefixes may be necessary if the business customer is using a UK mobile phone). The accommodation details will also identify room type and on what basis the customer is staying in the accommodation (such as whether it incorporates use of facilities and breakfast).

Passport, visa and health requirements

Theoretically, travel within the European Union does not require the use of a passport. An acceptable alternative is an identity card. However, at the time of writing, identity cards have not yet been adopted as an alternative to passports in the UK.

Travel outside the UK and most of Europe does require a passport. It is important for the agent to check that the passport is valid and will remain valid for the duration of any overseas visit.

Visas can be rather more complex and these may require organisation well in advance of the departure date. For British citizens, it is important to check with the British Foreign and Commonwealth Office. They advise that all travellers must hold a full ten-year passport and must check that it is still valid for at least six months from the return date. In addition, a visa may be necessary. The website, www.fco.gov.uk, contains a comprehensive list of all visa requirements around the world.

Example

A British national visiting Algeria is required to obtain a visa from the Algerian Embassy before travelling. The Foreign and Commonwealth Office also strongly recommends comprehensive travel and medical insurance, including medical evacuation.

The Foreign and Commonwealth Office is also useful for checking on health and safety issues related to particular countries. For example, their advice regarding the Maldives states that there are only two hospitals and that some of the islands are at threat from mosquito-borne diseases.

Procedure and terms for alterations to booking

Although booking conditions may have been clearly explained to the traveller at the time of confirmation, specific conditions are often incorporated into the small print as part of the booking conditions guidelines, as laid down by ABTA and ATOL. Usually administrative charges are levied if changes have to be made to the booking. This is particularly the case if the changes are made very close to the departure date. Customers need to be alerted to the fact that changes must be made at the earliest possible opportunity in order to ensure that any alterations can be incorporated into their new and amended itinerary.

Research tip

For information on amending a booking as handled by an airline, visit www.easyjet.com and select the 'Contact us' link at the top of the page.

RESEARCH TIPS

Although there may be existing itineraries that almost meet the requirements of a customer, these may only be of particular use if all of the needs and requirements of the customer are matched. Elements such as departure dates and duration of stay may not necessarily match the precise needs.

For retail itineraries, many have already been created and incorporated into brochures, websites of tour operators, for example, and more special–interest based itineraries can be found in travel guides and on the websites of independent tour operators. It is important to ensure that the latest data is being used and that current passport, visa and health checks are made if the destination is outside Europe before presenting a proposed itinerary to a customer. Current difficulties in particular countries may make travel to the area unduly hazardous and alternative suggestions could be made to avoid areas that are problematic.

CLIENT BRIEF

You will be given several client briefs in order to practise your skills at being able to identify the key features, requirements, needs or special requests of customers. Bear in mind that these will inevitably be complex and cannot be solved immediately without a degree of research. It is important to make sure that you attempt to match the relevant aspects in the brief against the itinerary that you are preparing, regardless of the type of client brief you are given.

Broadly speaking, you will be offered three different types of client brief:

1) The pen portrait – this is the simplest form of client brief and will only include the basic details and requirements of the customer. There may be one or two specific requirements within the pen portrait, such as a travel restriction, travelling with young children or a requirement not to travel during the night.

2) Case study – the purpose of the case study is to essentially hide or scramble information that you will need in order to create an itinerary. Read the case study thoroughly. Create a basic checklist of what you feel you may need to know about the client. As you read through the case study, identify the relevant information and write it alongside your headings as notes. You can always refer back to the case study to clarify information.

3) Real customers – you will hopefully be given the opportunity to carry out some work experience, which will give you the chance to match the real needs of a particular customer against your ability to create or design a tailor-made itinerary. Just as you will have paid specific attention to the requirements included in a pen portrait or a case study, ensure that you listen for key requirements and needs from the customer.

EVIDENCE ACTIVITY

P4 – P5

You have been requested by the family to organise the holiday of managing director and a holiday package for a nephew's family. They also want you to book their next two business trips.

> **Director's holiday (for 12 month's time)**
> Bertram is 74 and wants to fly to Australia around this time next year. He wants the cheapest possible fare with a night's stopover in Singapore. He wants to spend three weeks in Australia, beginning in Perth. Bertram wants to see as much of the countryside as possible and wants you to organise the hire of a motorbike. He definitely wants to go to Alice Springs, Melbourne, Sydney and Adelaide and would like to fly back from Brisbane, preferably stopping over in Hong Kong on the way home.

> **Nephew's holiday (within the next six months)**
> Rick, his wife and three children (all under ten) want to go on a fly-drive holiday to Florida. They want a large, air-conditioned car and a villa with a pool. They also want six-day passes to all of the major theme parks in Florida.

> **Business Trip 1 (within the next month)**
> Roland and Trevor want to fly to Greece to find suppliers. Ideally they would like a direct flight to Athens, arriving no later than 13.00. They want two double rooms with views of the Acropolis and a car to drive them from the airport to the hotel. They have a meeting in Piraeus at 12.30 and then they want you to book a table for 20.00 in a restaurant in the Plaka. They want to fly back to England the following morning.

> **Business Trip 2 (within the next fortnight)**
> Jocelyn is the fashion buyer and has a fear of flying. She needs to spend two nights in a 4-star, centrally located hotel in Venice. On day one she needs a car with air conditioning so that she can visit a factory. On day two she needs four opera tickets with good seats and a table reservation for 23.00 at a restaurant in Venice that specialises in fish. On the final day she wants an afternoon guided tour of Venice and will return home the following morning.

Use appropriate resources to produce complex travel itineraries for the two retail travel customers and the two business travel customers. (P4 + P5)

Sustainable tourism development

unit 11

Following the increase in environmental awareness in the early 1980s, the recent trends for recycling and the measurement and offsetting of carbon footprints, the issue of sustainable tourism has become increasingly important in the tourism industry. Tourists' understanding of sustainable destinations and the role of tour operators has increased over recent years and these factors are often considered by tourists when choosing their destination and the tour operator they travel with. Many tourists now want to ensure that they do not damage the local environment when travelling and the feeling of treating both the environment and local population with respect has recently become known as sustainable tourism.

The World Tourism Organisation defines sustainable tourism as a set of 'principles referring to the environmental, economic and socio-cultural aspects of tourism development', which then goes on to say that a 'suitable balance must be established between these three dimensions in order to guarantee a destination's long-term sustainability'.

Sustainable tourism is all about limiting the negative impacts of tourism, enhancing its positive impacts and ensuring that individual destinations will continue to attract tourists for many years.

By the end of this unit, you will:

So you want to be a...
Tourism Officer

My name Amy Wooster
Age 24
Income £24,000

If you are a keen researcher who is interested in regional, national and international tourism then take a look...

What do you do?
I work for the County Council, within a small team who are implementing the tourism policy across the county.

What responsibilities do you have?
I visit local tourism providers, for example hotels and visitor attractions and explain the current tourism policy to them. I organise meetings with tourism providers so that we can try to implement the tourism policy together. I monitor and report on the benefits that tourism brings, whilst limiting any of the apparent negative impacts. I also attend conferences and exhibitions to promote the region as a tourist destination.

How did you get into the job?
I did a BTEC National whilst at college, during the BTEC course I became increasingly interested in sustainable tourism and tourism development and so choose this kind of specialist qualification for my university degree. The degree was important as this kind of job involves lots of research and report writing and I also need to be able to manage my time well.

How did you find your current job?
The Guardian website, but most government jobs are advertised in both local and national newspapers.

> **"I get to work from home regularly"**

What training did you get?
I attended the county's induction course, however the majority of my training came from my colleagues. I was given a mentor who helped me through my first few months but as we are a small team I found that everybody was willing to help.

What are the hours like?
I normally work 36 hours a week and I get to work from home regularly. However, I sometimes work weekends and evenings if attending conferences.

What skills do you need?
Project management skills and the ability to multi-task are important. I have to keep up to date with all of the international, national and regional tourism policies so this involves lots of reading; I have to be able to explain these policies to tourism providers so communication skills are important. Some knowledge of marketing is useful, especially when I am involved in writing promotional material.

How good is the pay?
I get paid £24,000, Government salaries go up each year in line with inflation so I get a small pay rise each year. I get expenses when I travel.

What about the future?
I would like to work for VisitBritian writing and researching tourism policies across the UK.

Grading criteria

The table below shows what you need to do to gain a pass, merit or distinction in this part of the qualification. Make sure you refer back to it when you are completing work so you can judge whether you are meeting the criteria and what you need to do to fill in gaps in your knowledge or experience.

In this unit there are 3 evidence activities that give you an opportunity to demonstrate your achievement of the grading criteria:

page 103   P1, M1, D1

page 113   P2, P3, M2

page 117   P4, M3, D2

To achieve a pass grade the evidence must show that the learner is able to...	To achieve a merit grade the evidence must show that, in addition to the pass criteria, the learner is able to...	To achieve a distinction grade the evidence must show that, in addition to the pass and merit criteria, the learner is able to...
P1 Describe the impacts of tourism development in one specific short-haul and one specific long-haul destination	**M1** Explain how the positive impacts have been maximised and the negative impacts minimised at a selected destination	**D1** Assess the effectiveness of measures taken in a destination to put the objectives of sustainable tourism development into practice
P2 Describe the roles of agents involved in sustainable tourism development at a selected destination	**M2** Explain how the agents involved in sustainable tourism development have conflicting objectives in a selected destination	**D2** Recommend how the travel and tourism industry could adapt to support sustainable tourism development in a selected destination, justifying recommendations by drawing on examples of good practice
P3 Explain how the objectives for sustainable tourism development are put into practice at a selected destination	**M3** Analyse how effectively the industry is supporting sustainable tourism development in two destinations	
P4 Describe how the travel and tourism industry supports the development of sustainable tourism at one specific short-haul and one specific long-haul destination		

11.1 *Understand the impacts of tourism development at selected destinations*

ECONOMIC IMPACTS

One of the main reasons for the development of a tourist destination is the perceived economic benefits that tourists and tourism will bring to the region and the local people. The economic impacts of tourism are the easiest to measure and also the easiest to observe. These impacts can be direct, where the host community receives money from direct contact with the tourists or indirectly with additional income generated from the knock-on effect of the tourists being present.

Example

A tourist tipping their waiter would be a direct economic benefit to the waiter, but the profit made by the local orange supplier from the sale of oranges to a hotel for use in the kitchens or for breakfast would be an indirect profit with money being paid to the local supplier by the hotel.

Positive economic impacts

The economic impacts of tourism are normally seen by a destination as being positive impacts. These could include the following:

- the creation of jobs directly related to the tourism industry, for example, work in hotels, as tour guides or in airports. These jobs create more money in the local economy, therefore the local population has a greater disposable income and tourists' money is indirectly spread throughout the local community.

- money paid by tourists in tax can be used by the government to improve the local infrastructure

- the purchase of locally produced souvenirs by tourists

- tourists eating and drinking in local restaurants and bars can increase profits.

Negative economic impacts

The negative economic impacts of tourism are less obvious and are harder to measure. The negative economic impacts of tourism start to be seen by the local community when not all of the money spent by tourists stays in the local economy. Some of it may be paid to hotel owners and workers who are not from the local community or it is paid to suppliers from overseas or cities outside the local tourist area. This is called leakage as money leaks away from the local economy to outside stakeholders. Other negative economic impacts include an increase in the basic cost of living – for example the price of gas and electricity could go up and the cost of food and drink may increase to prices that are only affordable by tourists.

> **Think** Can you think of any other negative economic impacts of tourism?

Key words

Host community – the people who live in the destination visited by tourists

Infrastructure – basic physical and organisational structures needed for the operation of a tourist destination. For example, roads, public transport, electricity and water supply

Leakage – when the economic benefits of tourism do not remain in the host community and tourist destination, but are beneficial to outside stakeholders

Local people may choose to work in the tourism industry as they think that tourism industry workers are well-paid and working with tourists offers them a type of status symbol. This can lead to a decline in the number of people willing to work in other more traditional industries such as fishing and eventually leads to an economic decline in other industries.

People working in the tourism industry may be employed on a seasonal basis and they will try to make as much money as possible during the summer months or high season. If the season is not successful, they may not have enough money to survive the winter or low season months when they are unemployed.

There is also a major concern about ensuring the destination's continued long-term popularity, especially when a destination becomes dependent on tourism and the local economy becomes overly focused on the industry. If a destination becomes unpopular, fewer people will be employed in the industry and unemployment will increase. Potentially, this can have many more negative impacts on the community. (For further information on this cycle, please see Butler's Destination Product Life Cycle in Unit 7, Book 1.)

Figure 11.1 Locals in Fiji teach tourists how to make their own jewellery

ENVIRONMENTAL IMPACTS

It is often the natural environment, such as an unspoilt beach or beautiful lake, which attracts a tourist to visit a destination. Therefore, the environmental impacts of tourism are particularly important.

Positive environmental impacts

Overall, the positive environmental impacts of tourism are limited and not always obvious. However, if tourism development is controlled at the destination, the main positive impact would be the conservation of the local area. This could be by the creation of national parks, official conservation areas or the preservation of historic buildings or areas of importance. Money gained from tourism could be used to monitor the environmental impacts of tourism and also to sustain any local plant or wildlife.

Some destinations use their natural resources to aid their infrastructure by using wind turbines, solar energy or water power to provide electricity for tourist facilities. However, these renewable forms of energy and their visual impacts need to be weighed up against the economic gain and are not always in the best interests of the destination.

> ***Think*** Why might renewable forms of energy not always be in the best interests of the destination?

Negative environmental impacts

The negative environmental impacts of tourism are extremely obvious and are often among the first signs that tourism development at a destination is proceeding too quickly. Some of the negative environmental impacts could include the following:

- Overbuilding in the destination, for example, the building of high tower blocks that are not traditional structures and do not fit in with the local landscape.

- Natural resources, for example beaches, being polluted by tourists. These resources may become overcrowded or dirty. Hotels may be built on or near beaches causing pollution of the natural resources by sewage.

- Local facilities, such as narrow streets and public transport, may become crowded and parking may be difficult. The infrastructure may become overused and local people may be left without water or electricity as these essential services are diverted to tourist facilities like large hotels.

- Historic tourist attractions may become damaged by visitors, either by deliberate damage like graffiti or by unintentional damage caused by the large numbers of visitors walking around the attraction, causing general wear and tear.

Figure 11.2 The development of multi-storey hotels can ruin the surrounding landscape

SOCIAL IMPACTS

The social impact of tourism refers to the impact of tourism development on the local people who live in the destination. These impacts can be both positive and negative. However, the combination of many large negative impacts can lead to the host community becoming disillusioned with tourists and tourism and may eventually cause an anti-tourist feeling in the local community. The social impacts of tourism are linked to both its environmental and economic impacts.

Positive social impacts

When a destination starts to develop as a tourist destination, the positive social impacts are seen very quickly by the local population. They may include:

- an improvement in the local community facilities, such as sport and leisure centres or an increase in the number of flights to other major airports

- better opportunities for local people with regards to training and education

- improved social status for local people who are involved in the tourism industry

- job creation and the renovation or building of local facilities and changes in the resort's infrastructure can lead to an improvement in the local population's **quality of life**.

> **Think** Can you think of any other positive social impacts of tourism on a destination?

> **Key words**
> **Quality of life** – the traditional values and way of life held by the original host population

Negative social impacts

The negative social impacts of tourism can only be observed after a period of time, if the host community gradually realises that not all the effects of tourism are good and that tourism can have a direct impact on their quality of life.

Like the environmental impacts of tourism, social impacts are hard to measure and can vary from destination to destination, depending on the local way of life, the religion and the general state of development when tourism arrived there. The main negative social impacts of tourism are:

- An increase in the number of people working in the tourist industry and the high social status of these jobs may lead to a large number of people leaving their traditional villages and moving into tourist destinations in the hope of employment. Firstly, this leaves local villages with a smaller working-age population and secondly, there may not be sufficient work at the tourist destination, so some people may turn to prostitution or crime in order to survive.

- An increase in the destination's crime levels. This may be tourist against tourist or the local population against the tourists.

- Tourists arriving in the destination may have different values and a more relaxed approach towards dress, drink and drugs, and this may offend local people who have a more traditional way of life.

- Local people may be forcibly removed from their land by local developers or the government in order to make way for the development of tourist facilities.

- An increase in sex tourism or prostitution. This may be due to high unemployment rates, tourist demand or the **tourist receiving area's** advertised policy or reputation for relaxed attitudes towards sex tourists. In turn, this may lead to an increase in the number of the local population that are infected with AIDS or other sexually transmitted diseases.

- A local population that is unhappy with the behaviour of tourists or feels that the tourists have taken over their hometown may become violent or hostile towards them. This can take a variety of different forms, from general rudeness to protests and violence.

Key words

Tourist receiving area – an area that receives tourists, such as a tourist destination or resort

CULTURAL IMPACTS

The cultural impacts of tourism refer to its impacts on the host community's traditional way of life. It is important to consider the cultural impacts of tourism as many destinations are visited by tourists who wish to meet and interact with the local culture. This is a major factor in destination selection.

Example

The majority of tourists who visit Australia wish to experience the local Aboriginal culture and those who do not meet or see Aborigines can leave feeling disappointed. In some cases, this can cause the local population to feel exploited by tourism officials and tribal leaders to seek to limit the impact of tourism on their people.

Figure 11.3 Ayers Rock is significant in Aboriginal culture and is also a popular tourist attraction

Positive cultural impacts

One of the main positive cultural impacts of tourism is the maintenance of local traditions, crafts and customs. Tourists want to observe these customs and possibly buy locally produced traditional souvenirs such as wooden carvings. As a result, these traditions are maintained as attractions and are often funded by the sale of goods or entrance charges. Interest from tourists in the local culture and traditions often means that the local people become prouder and more aware of their heritage and are more likely to pass traditions, such as language and dances, on to their children.

Think Can you think of any souvenirs that you have bought yourself or received as a present from people who have been on holiday? Is the souvenir traditional to the country it came from? Does it have religious or cultural significance?

Negative cultural impacts

Negative cultural impacts can be directly linked to the positive impacts. For example, traditions may be amended and altered to suit the tastes of tourists or their perceived images. This could mean that dances are shortened to fit into tourist itineraries or that dress or costumes are changed in order to make the tourists feel more comfortable. Local people and events can become staged with houses and traditional events put on display especially for the visiting tourists.

Local people may observe tourists' clothes, jewellery or way of life and seek to behave or dress like them. This is called the **demonstration effect** and can be observed in local people wearing western clothes and finding social status in western objects like iPods and expensive watches. More dramatic forms of the demonstration effect can be seen in the host population's changing attitude towards alcohol and drugs.

Key words

Demonstration effect – the exposure of local people to tourist lifestyles has a direct impact on the expectations and lifestyles of local people who seek to act and dress like the tourists

CASE STUDY: THE IMPACTS OF TOURISM IN GOA, INDIA

In the 1960s, hippies and backpackers were attracted to the former Portuguese colony thanks to its long sandy beaches and relaxed lifestyle. This colony has since become the Indian resort of Goa. These hippies and backpackers were the first tourists to the region and since then Goa has expanded quickly as a tourist destination, attracting specialist and mass market tour operators as well as a large number of independent travellers.

Accommodation at the destination varies from luxury five-star complexes, which offer such a wide range of facilities and private beaches that the tourist has no need to leave the hotel, to simpler luxury niche hotels, numerous apartment blocks and many cheaper hostels that appeal to the original, independent, hippy backpacker market.

Tourism development in Goa was unplanned, and this has left the destination with many observable negative impacts of tourism and little evidence of the positive benefits that tourism can bring to a destination.

Figure 11.4a Luxury hotels have sprung up all over Goa

Due to its monsoon season, Goa has a defined tourist season. Making money during the high season from November to March is important for the local community, which is largely dependent on the tourist industry to earn enough money to survive the wet summer months when there are very limited tourist numbers. While backpackers are seen by the government as giving the destination a bad name, they do stay in local accommodation and eat at local restaurants. Therefore the host population regards them as good tourists because they obtain direct financial benefit from them.

Throughout the resort, there are a number of large hotel chains like the Taj Group, Radisson Hotels and The Four Seasons. Leakage is therefore high with western products being flown in to satisfy guests' requirements and the hotels' profits being transferred back to each hotel chain's head office around the world. These large hotels are often built on the seafronts and have private beaches, reducing the number of beaches that can be used by the local population. In addition to this, hotels are being given preference over local residents for scarce resources like water and electricity. This has left several villages without water supplies and is being used to encourage or force local people to leave their villages, so the land can be developed for tourism.

Figure 11.4b Many backpackers stay in the locally run huts along the beach

Although the beaches are one of the main attractions, tourists also visit because of Goa's reputation for nightlife and its relaxed attitude towards drink, drugs and wild parties. Led by the hippy and backpacker communities, but also attended by other tourists, these inappropriate parties that are often held on the beach offend the local population that is mainly Christian but also Hindu and Muslim.

Many social and cultural impacts can be observed. When talking to the Goan people, many of them use phrases that can only have been learnt from western tourists, such as 'I give you Asda price' and many have western names.

Western dress has become more common than the traditional sari and the Goan people often take tourists home to meet their families. The homes that are shown to the tourists have often been staged to show poverty, in the hope of receiving money or presents from the visitors.

In an attempt to move the image of Goa away from its wild party reputation, the Goan government is pitching their market towards luxury tourists. However, the plans for golf courses and casinos may not fit with a sustainable tourism policy any more than the existing market. The government has made some recent attempts to police the parties and local markets where drugs are being sold and has made efforts to stop the recent increases in child sex tourism.

There is growing discontent within the Goan population over the way income from tourism is being distributed amongst the large operators and several protests have been staged over the large number of mass market tour operators. This included a dispute over the use of coach companies instead of local taxis, the use of resort representatives from overseas instead of using local staff and protests against attempts by the government to insist that the local population shut down their small shacks, bars and restaurants along the seafront. These seafront shacks are seen by the local population as one of the few ways they can still benefit directly from tourism.

The government, mass market tour operators, hotel owners and the local population remain divided over Goa's future as a tourist destination.

QUESTIONS

1. Consider the economic, social, cultural and environmental impacts of tourism in Goa and suggest ways in which these negative impacts of tourism could be minimised.

2. Use brochures and the Internet to examine the current direction of tourism in Goa and decide how you think tourism should be developed.

SELECTED DESTINATIONS

Although the impacts of tourism are evident at all tourist destinations, it is easier to observe the impacts of tourism at destinations that are older or those which have very distinctive local populations. In recent times, several studies have been carried out to try to measure both the positive and negative impacts of tourism.

Short-haul

A short-haul destination is one that is in Europe and under six hours flying time from the UK. More information about European destinations can be found in Unit 7, Book 1.

Long-haul

Long-haul destinations are places that are over six hours flying time from the UK. Often the social and cultural impacts of tourism are more evident at these destinations due to their very different cultures and ways of life. More information about long-haul destinations can be found in Unit 8, Book 1.

EVIDENCE ACTIVITY

P1 – M1 – D1

You are currently working for a voluntary organisation called TourismAid whose aims are to promote sustainable tourism throughout the world. TourismAid are planning to run a stand at the World Travel Market next year in order to promote sustainable tourism to the many visitors who attend the exhibition. You have been asked to develop a range of different materials to use on the stand. These materials will highlight many of the important issues of sustainability. In order to create these materials you will need to research and explore sustainable tourism within two different destinations, one long-haul and one short haul. Take care to choose your two destinations carefully. The long–haul destination should be a destination which is experiencing tourist growth, possibly in a developing country. The short-haul destination should be a European resort which has been established for many years. This will enable you to easily compare the different impacts of tourism and make it easier for people visiting your trade stand to understand the issues involved in sustainable tourism.

1. Using one long-haul (over 6 hours flight time from the UK) and one short-haul European destination create two leaflets (one for each destination) which describe both the positive and negative impacts of tourism within each destination. Make certain you consider a range of social, cultural, economic and environmental impacts. (P1)

2. One of these leaflets should be more detailed and longer than the other (you can choose which one). In the longer leaflet explain how the positive impacts of tourism have been maximised and give examples of how the destination has attempted to minimise the negative impacts of tourism. (M1)

3. As an additional handout to go with the leaflets, create one handout on the destination used for the expanded leaflet in task 2. In this handout you should assess how effective the measures taken to implement sustainable tourism have been in the destination and how they put the objectives of sustainable tourism into practice. For example, consider the ways that the destination has attempted to maximise the positive impacts of tourism and minimise the negative impacts and assess how effective these measures have been. If the implemented measures have not been effective consider reasons why you think they have not been successful. (D1)

11.2 Know the roles of the agents involved in sustainable tourism development

SUSTAINABLE TOURISM

Sustainable tourism is considered to be tourism that ensures the long-term future of the destination. It is tourism that uses the local resources in a way that ensures they will be intact and in a good condition for tourists to use in the future. Sustainable tourism also tries to limit the negative impacts of tourism on the local population and to maximise its positive impacts. It also aims to involve the host community in tourism development and in the decisions made throughout the destination or resort.

A number of other names are used to describe different types of tourism that are similar to the characteristics of sustainable tourism. However, each term has a slightly different meaning.

- Eco-tourism – the forerunner of sustainable tourism, eco-tourism concentrates on visitors who want to visit wildlife and local populations in their original ecosystem or location.

- Alternative tourism – this is seen as tourism that isn't mass market and therefore covers many of the specialist niche market tour operators who may or may not practise sustainable tourism.

- Nature or green tourism – this mainly concentrates on the use of local natural resources for tourism, for example, hill-walking, kayaking or cross-country skiing.

- Community tourism – this concentrates on involving the local community in tourism for example by promoting accommodation run by local people, using local tour guides and encouraging the development and ownership of tourism organisations by local people.

Although a considerable amount of adventure tourism relies on the use of natural resources and is often run by small specialist tour operators or excursion owners, adventure tourism itself is not considered to be a variety of sustainable tourism, although, like other forms of tourism, it can be implemented in a sustainable way.

ROLES

Many different organisations are involved in the development of a sustainable tourism destination. These include public, private and voluntary sector organisations, working together for the benefit of the destination. Together with other interested parties, these organisations will create a **destination management organisation** that will develop, plan and implement a **tourism policy** for the destination.

Each different organisation within the destination management organisation has a different role to play at the destination. While trying to promote sustainable tourism, they will also be trying to meet their own individual organisational goals. These goals may sometimes be in conflict with other organisations within the destination management organisation or occasionally against the principles of sustainable tourism.

Key words
Destination management organisation – the group of people that will plan and coordinate the development of tourism within a resort or destination
Tourism policy – a plan of how tourism will be developed and controlled within the destination

Funding

One of the main roles of the destination management organisation is to obtain the funding required for the development of the tourism destination.

A wide range of different funding opportunities will need to be explored. These might include the following options.

- Donations from charitable trusts that assist destinations with regeneration or provide grants for the development of heritage visitor attractions.

- A range of government grants – these could be as part of a national tourism development programme or money provided to specific areas that are regarded by the government as needing regeneration or requiring assistance with a specific tourist development programme.

- Worldwide funds – European destinations can apply to the European Union for grants from a range of Structural Funds. These funds offer money to destinations for different activities, which can include money for staff training and the redevelopment of fishing and rural communities. Destinations can also apply to both the World Tourism Organisation and the United Nations for funding.

Figure 11.5 The European Union provides funding to European travel destinations

- Private organisations may provide funding or sponsorship for a specific development or attraction, although they may limit the activities or development that can be undertaken with their money.

Think Can you think of any other types of funding that might be available for tourism development?

Destination marketing

Once a destination has developed or has decided to develop itself as a tourist destination, it will need to attract tourists. The destination will need to decide on its target audience. This could be mass market tourists like families or a specific type of tourist who has a particular interest in the local wildlife, history or culture. Once the destination has identified its target market, it will have to implement a marketing campaign aimed at attracting them. It also needs to advertise to the travel and tourism industry by contacting tour operators, airlines and travel agents through a trade marketing campaign. More information about marketing campaigns can be found in Unit 5.

Promoting sustainability

One of the keys to developing a sustainable tourism destination is to make sure that all of the organisations involved and the local population understand the importance of sustainable tourism. They need to be clearly aware of both the long and short-term benefits that sustainable tourism can bring to a destination and host community.

Explaining the concepts of sustainable tourism to organisations and the local community can be done in a number of different ways. These include exhibitions, road shows and the implementation of a series of awards and rewards for organisations and businesses that follow the sustainable agenda. These awards are often given annually, such as the World Legacy Awards presented by the National Geographic Magazine.

Research tip

Use the Internet to find out about the promotion of tourism at www.wtmlondon.com.

Figure 11.6 *www.wtmlondon.com has information on all different kinds of travel and tourism promotion, including World Responsible Tourism Day*

Facilitating partnerships

Many organisations and businesses cannot become sustainable by themselves. They often need assistance with implementing and understanding the objectives of sustainable tourism. In addition to these challenges, many organisations work with each other at a destination and must therefore rely on each other to ensure their sustainable goals are met.

One of the roles that the destination management organisation should carry out is introducing different organisations to each other and helping the different organisations, which may all have slightly different aims, to work together for the good of the destination.

PRIVATE SECTOR AGENTS

Landowners/property development

Once a location has decided to develop itself as a tourist destination, the resort needs to be developed and a range of facilities built. One of the first activities carried out is the planning of a destination. There is a temptation for local landowners to immediately develop their land into tourist facilities, making large amounts of money in the process.

This could mean that areas attractive to tourists, like natural attractions such as forests, are destroyed in order to make way for hotels and man-made visitor attractions. Access to the beach or beautiful views can be spoilt by the development of high-rise housing and apartment blocks. Property development should be controlled and buildings and attractions should merge into the existing environment.

Example

Lanzarote has banned the building of any structures over three storeys high in a bid to stop the natural landscape being spoilt by high-rise hotels.

Government planning regulations need to be strictly implemented in order to ensure a sustainable, environmentally friendly resort is created by developers and landowners.

Tour operators

There are two different types of tour operators that are important when considering sustainable tourism: mass market and specialists. Mass market tour operators concentrate on selling their holidays to a large number of people. Many mass market tour operators are less involved in sustainable tourism than specialist or niche market tour operators, which attract a smaller number of tourists who are interested in a particular activity, region or culture. Further information regarding tour operators can be found in Unit 12. Further information about specialist holidays can be found in Unit 13, Book 3.

Destinations that are already developed will generally attract mass market tour operators and, as a result, there is less opportunity to implement a sustainable tourism policy. It becomes the responsibility of the destination management organisation to ensure that the existing tour operators try to implement sustainable policies in their programmes.

When a sustainable destination develops, the tour operators that are involved in its development will be specialist tour operators. In this case, there is an opportunity to ensure that the tour operators work with the local community and local businesses to implement a sustainable agenda by using local tour guides, coach companies and accommodation.

Hotel chains

Once a destination begins to become popular with tourists, hotel chains want to open accommodation in order to ensure that they make a profit from the developing destination. In other destinations, which are already popular with tourists, hotel chains will already be established and receiving bookings and tourists.

Many large hotel chains are not good for sustainable tourism. Firstly, they often import their own managerial staff, promoting them from existing hotels elsewhere in the world. Therefore, the number of employment opportunities for local people is reduced and leakage is increased. Hotel chains are mainly large four or five-star hotels and use extensive amounts of water and electricity, which has many environmental effects. Some hotel chains are becoming more sustainable, implementing training programmes for local people and attempting to be more environmentally friendly by encouraging their guests to re-use towels. However, these projects do not make a huge difference to the overall negative impacts of large hotels. To have any lasting effect smaller local accommodation providers will need to be encouraged and the number of hotel chains limited.

Airlines

The number of flights that arrive at a destination directly relates to the number of tourists who are arriving. Limiting the number of tourists arriving is an easy way to limit tourist numbers, which can therefore cut down the negative impacts of tourism. However, this needs to be balanced with the resort's desire to make money.

The environmental impact of airlines arriving and departing from a destination also needs to be taken into consideration. Airlines can cause noise and environmental pollution. This needs to be carefully controlled by both the airport authorities and individual airlines.

Research tip

Further information on the environmental impacts of airlines and the methods used to control these impacts can be found at www.caa.co.uk.

Entertainment companies/excursion organisers

Tourists who are visiting resorts will want to visit the local area and therefore entertainment and excursion organisers will start operating in order to meet this need. These organisers often have large impacts on the local community and environment. As a result of this, they need to be made aware of the different ways in which they can limit the potential negative impacts they may have on the various resources used for their excursions.

Most destinations offer a range of different entertainment and leisure activities. When planning these activities, the local community needs to be considered, their way of life and religion needs to be respected and appropriate facilities and excursions offered.

Example

Destinations with Muslim populations generally choose not to develop casinos and several destinations like Brunei will only allow the consumption of alcohol in authorised hotels.

Evening excursions offering local entertainment often provide an opportunity to educate the tourists about the local culture, dancing, music and traditional entertainment. These evenings are often popular with tourists. Local people should be consulted to ensure that authenticity is maintained and the local population do not feel that their culture has been modified in order to meet tourist requirements.

Day excursions, for example jeep safaris that visit villages away from the tourist area, should take care to ensure that tourists are aware of the local culture that they are visiting and their impact on the people they see. Excursion operators might want to implement a dress code or give tourists a short talk on appropriate behaviour while visiting sites or local villages.

Travel publishers

Many tourists will read a guidebook before their departure and some tour operators send small guidebooks to their customers with their flight tickets. Travel writers and the publishers of these guidebooks should include sections on the host community's local customs, religion and way of life. Several publishers have recently also included a code of conduct, which offers suggestions to tourists on how they can cut down on the negative impacts that they have on a destination.

Figure 11.7 Guide books

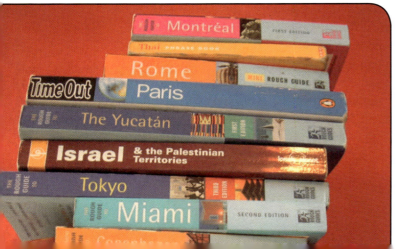

PUBLIC SECTOR AGENTS

National tourist offices/ tourist boards

The local and national tourist office and tourist boards normally have several main functions, apart from providing information to visiting tourists. With regard to the implementation of sustainable tourism, these can include:

- working together with the government to develop the national, local and regional tourism development plans and policies

- the worldwide promotion of the destination as a sustainable tourism destination. This could include attendance at exhibitions like the annual World Travel Market

- organising, funding and running educational trips to the destination for specially selected travel agents and tour operators

- encouraging tour operators to include the destination in their brochures

- ensuring that the different agencies and organisations involved in tourism development are working together to achieve a sustainable tourism destination

- running and funding smaller tourist offices in major destinations and resorts. These small offices might deal with the promotion of local attractions and the booking of excursions and accommodation, and offer the opportunity for tourists to ask questions about the implementation of different sustainable tourism policies

- meeting local people and visiting schools, colleges and universities to improve the overall understanding of sustainable tourism.

Research tip

Look at next year's World Travel Market and research several different destinations that are promoting themselves as sustainable tourist destinations. www.wtmlondon.co.uk.

Regional development agencies (RDAs)

Regional development agencies are very active in tourism development in the UK. They may be called something different in other countries, for example, Regional Assemblies or the Department for Development.

These regional agencies are government organisations that are responsible for the coordination of tourism facilities across their region. The regions are generally large areas, such as the east of England. The regional development agencies try to make sure that different tourist resorts that are close together do not develop the same facilities and try to compete for the same target market. They will try to encourage different resorts to target different types of customers, making one resort into an activity centre and another into a business or conference location. This ensures that all of the area's resorts have the potential to become sustainable.

The regional development agencies also provide funding for different tourism projects and are actively involved in introducing different companies and organisations to each other in the hope of creating partnerships or dialogue between organisations with similar or conflicting views.

Research tip

Use the Internet to find your local Regional Development Agency.

Think What tourism-related activities are your local regional development agency involved with?

Local authorities

Local authorities are often responsible for the implementation of sustainable tourism development plans in the local area. Local authorities approve or decline planning applications and therefore have direct control over property development with regards to the building or extension of visitor attractions and hotels.

Some local authorities also monitor the various impacts of tourism and publish these results in the hope of encouraging a more sustainable approach throughout the destination. They also provide and fund the local infrastructure, including transportation and the essential resources like water and electricity, which are used for both tourism and the local population. This can often cause conflict, regarding the use and distribution of these resources.

Some local authorities collect income directly from tourists and therefore have access to funds that can be used for tourism development. They can often approve the use of tourist revenue for investment into the local community's facilities that are unrelated to tourism.

VOLUNTARY SECTOR AGENTS

Voluntary non-government organisations are often very active in promoting and attempting to limit the environmental and socio-cultural impacts of tourism. Organisations may be specific to the destination or resort or they may work across many different destinations in raising issues that are causes of concern throughout the tourism industry. Some organisations concentrate on a particular aspect of tourism such as the environment, while others have wider concerns and try to highlight many different areas or issues of concern to the potential tourists and destination.

Tourism Concern is an organisation that works on many different levels throughout the tourism community. It runs specific campaigns that aim to improve the conditions of tourism workers, such as the working conditions of porters in Nepal. It promotes the general principles of sustainable tourism.

Figure 11.8 The Tourism Concern homepage highlights issues the organisation is currently tackling

Some destinations will have local community groups that focus on the specific impacts of tourism locally. These groups may be part of larger countrywide organisations or many have a very detailed focus with the aim of protecting a specific aspect of the community or environment from tourism development.

In addition to organisations that concentrate on tourism-related issues, there are a number of organisations that promote sustainability in a more general context. These include Fairtrade organisations that try to ensure that local people are paid reasonable amounts of money for the goods they produce and environmental groups, such as Greenpeace, that work to protect the environment.

Research tip

Research the current campaigns that Tourism Concern is currently working on at: www.tourismconcern.org.uk.

11.3 Understand how objectives for sustainable tourism development are put into practice

Sustainable tourism is not just about the environment or local people. The different organisations involved in implementing sustainable tourism will all have slightly different aims and objectives, and sustainable tourism can help these organisations meet their goals.

These different aims can vary from meeting political goals to protecting a specific type of animal or wildlife or ensuring that the money generated from tourism is used to benefit the local community.

POLITICAL OBJECTIVES

Governments become involved in sustainable tourism for a number of different reasons. Tourism often generates income for a destination and the government will be interested in ensuring that this money is collected, used and spent well. Governments become involved in the planning stages of tourism as they have the ability to make sure that the different facilities and the required tourism infrastructure are in place. Governments also offer training programmes and influence what is taught in schools. In doing this, they can ensure that future workers in the tourism industry have the right skills and qualifications to work and lead the industry. Governments also set out the legislation, rules and regulations that govern the industry.

The government can also benefit by using tourism to raise the overall profile of a country. This could be done by staging a major event, which is seen on television throughout the world, or by hosting annual festivals. Other ways in which the government can promote its destination is by authorising films to be made, using the destination's scenery as a backdrop, which results in film-induced tourism.

> **Think** Can you think of some destinations that have recently become popular because they have featured in films or on the television?

Destinations that have not had a particularly good reputation or destination image in the past can use tourism and the presence of tourists to show themselves in a better light. The images of tourists appearing in brochures or on television can change people's perception of a destination and therefore encourage more people to visit.

Figure 11.9 South Africa is hoping to boost its tourism numbers by hosting the 2010 World Cup

ENVIRONMENTAL OBJECTIVES

The main environmental objective for sustainable tourism is to ensure that the destination will not be damaged by a large number of visitors. Sustainable tourism also aims to raise people's awareness of the environment, conservation issues and to influence both the tourists and the people living in the surrounding area in a positive way.

The environment does not just mean the natural environment, but can also mean the built environment, including built heritage visitor attractions, heritage cities and monuments. Money from visiting tourists should be used to ensure the preservation of both the built and natural environment.

Funds can be used to create natural areas of beauty, national parks or wildlife conservation areas and to replant trees and maintain natural habitats. Other preservation that is carried out can include the repair and restoration of historic houses, gardens or antiques.

Built visitor attractions that have historical importance should be maintained for future generations of visitors and plans made to ensure their long-term future. Often the surrounding area itself, such as the university buildings and colleges in Oxford, are considered to be a built visitor attraction. Therefore, sustainable tourism plans should consider this and use money and tourism development plans to preserve these areas.

One of the ways in which organisations raise tourist awareness of the natural beauty and importance of the local area or environmental visitor attraction is by educating the tourists who are visiting the destination. This can be done in a number of different ways. Notices at the entrance to attractions may advise the customers of the importance of following footpaths. These notices can be used to inform visitors of the historical importance of the attraction they are visiting. Educational leaflets and exhibits can also be used. Often a range of educational quizzes and competitions are used to help children and families engage and learn about an exhibition or attraction.

THE ZIG-ZAG PATH WAS CUT BY GILBERT WHITE AND HIS BROTHER IN THE YEAR 1753. PLEASE HELP TO PRESERVE IT BY KEEPING TO THE PATH AND NOT CUTTING THE CORNERS OR SLIDING DOWN THE BANKS.

Figure 11.10: The National Trust puts up notices in order to both educate and instruct visitors

SOCIO-CULTURAL OBJECTIVES

One of the other main aims of sustainable tourism is to improve the lives of the local population. This can be done many different ways.

Money generated by tourists from purchasing souvenirs or from entrance fees to local attractions can be used to improve the facilities used by the local population. This could be a direct investment into parts of the infrastructure that are shared with the tourists, such as improving the roads or a sewage water purifying plant. Other investments could be made that are unconnected with tourist resources. These could vary from building a new school or sports centre to funding a health centre or paying the salary of a visiting community doctor or nurse.

Tourism that is good for the local community can also promote cultural understanding. The local population have the opportunity to learn about the tourist's culture in the same way that the visiting tourists learn about the host population. Obviously these exchanges need to be managed in order to avoid the demonstration effect and negative social or cultural impacts on the host community.

Sustainable tourism can also be used to ensure that local traditions and the traditional way of life of the host community or indigenous population are maintained. Their unique way of life is often one of the main reasons that the tourists enjoy visiting and it is therefore important that this is maintained and not affected negatively by tourism.

Overall, well-managed sustainable tourism has a very positive impact on the local community and can improve its quality of life. In sustainable tourism, the income that tourists generate is well spent and the local population can see that the benefits of tourism are spread throughout the community. The negative impacts of tourism are controlled and the positive impacts like the continuation of the traditional way of life are maintained.

ECONOMIC OBJECTIVES

Many destinations decide to develop themselves as tourist resorts as they want to benefit from the financial opportunities that tourism provides. One of the main ways that tourism is seen to generate income for the local community is by increasing the number of jobs available. With well-implemented sustainable tourism, there should be a range of jobs available to the local community that do not just include the lower level jobs, such as waiters and maids. The local community should also be given the opportunity to work in high levels of many different types of organisations, including hotels, tour operators and excursion organisers. It may be that the government insists that a range of different training programmes or the joint ownership of businesses is implemented within the resort.

Figure 11.11 Local tour guides talk to tourists at Tortuguero National Park, Costa Rica

Example

Following the government regulations and contractual terms, the European company that provides diving instructors in the Maldives also trains a number of Maldivian dive instructors free of charge and the Canadian Sea Plane company that operates there has trained several Maldivian pilots and crew members. These programmes encourage local people to get involved in the organisation of sustainable tourism and also provide other members of the community with positive role models.

Sustainable tourism aims to ensure that income is generated by tourism. This could be directly from the tourists by charging them with an eco-tourism tax or by charging entrance fees to natural and man-made visitor attractions. Alternatively, money can be generated by the knock-on effect of tourists who spend money in the resort. This is called the **multiplier effect** as the indirect impact of tourists' spending money filters down throughout the destination and benefits local suppliers and companies who do not have direct contact with tourists.

In order to buy souvenirs or spend money in the destination, the tourists will generally need to exchange money. Some destinations, such as Morocco, choose not to allow their currency to be purchased outside their own country. This increases the amount of money that the government earns on money exchange and can provide the government with cash in other currencies like US dollars or the Euro to use for international purchases or debt repayments.

Destinations that have not previously been tourist resorts may have generated their income through another activity, such as logging in the rainforests or fishing. As these activities no longer generate income, the villagers are unable to earn a living. Changing the main income generation activity of the village from a previously loss-making activity into a sustainable tourism project offers the villagers an opportunity for economic regeneration.

Key words

Multiplier effect – sales to tourists from one company normally require purchases from another company and therefore suppliers who do not have direct contact with tourists can benefit indirectly from tourist sales

EVIDENCE ACTIVITY

P2 – P3 – M2

Your boss at TourismAid would like some detailed information for visitors to the stand to take away and read after the travel show. You have been asked to write a report on some of the issues surrounding sustainable tourism. Although this is a report, your boss would like it to be easy to read and of interest to the people visiting the stand and so, if you like, you can use some pictures and logos. The report covers three separate topics and must focus on one of the destinations you have examined in the leaflets and handout you have already created.

1. For the first part of the report choose one of the destinations that you used in the earlier assessment activity and describe the roles of the public, private and voluntary sector agents who are involved in implementing sustainable tourism. Name specific organisations which are active in the destination and make sure you consider at least one public, private and voluntary organisation. (P2)

2. The second part of the report is going to contain more detail on the issues surrounding the different organisations that work in a destination, and so you should investigate some of these organisations in greater detail and explain and identify the different conflicting objectives and goals that these organisations have with regard to implementing sustainable tourism. (M2)

3. As you identified the different objectives and roles of the organisations involved in sustainable tourism in the first part of the report, the last section should explain how the objectives of sustainable tourism are implemented in this particular destination. Try to give specific examples for the destination you have chosen. (P3)

11.4 Understand how the travel and tourism industry supports sustainable tourism development

TRAVEL AND TOURISM INDUSTRY

Tour operators

Although not normally associated with sustainable tourism in a positive way, large mass market tour operators can provide reliable information in an easily accessible format to their customers. This can help a destination to educate its tourists about the possible impacts that they may be having on the destination and will hopefully lead to the tourists changing their behaviour in order to minimise their negative impacts.

Large tour operators can also assist smaller destinations with resources, possibly providing computers, IT systems and marketing expertise that is lacking in the destination. These resources are often expensive and beyond the budget of developing or smaller destinations or resorts. Therefore, joint ventures between tour operators and local suppliers benefit both parties and also ensure that different companies are working together to implement sustainable tourism.

Smaller specialist tour operators are generally considered to be better placed to support and implement sustainable tourism. However, they do not normally have the large resources or financial backing of the larger mass market tour operators. Specialist tour operators normally operate in less developed or specialist destinations and therefore established destinations will be reliant on working with the mass market tour operators. When considering sustainable tourism, customers who are travelling with a specialist tour operator are often considered more attractive to a sustainable tourist destination for the following reasons:

- they pay more for their holiday and therefore there is the possibility of greater economic benefit for the destination

- they are better educated and therefore the social and cultural impacts are limited as these tourists often have a better understanding of different cultures and are keen to learn about the places they visit

- they are often repeat purchasers. This means that the destination can create a relationship with the customers.

Example

Tour Operators Initiative for Sustainable Tourism Development is a voluntary initiative established by a number of large tour operators, including Thomas Cook, Tui and First Choice. The initiative dims to encourage tour operators to work together to promote and spread good practice in developing sustainable tourism.

Hotels

There are many different types of hotel accommodation and this is explored in greater depth in Unit 19, Book 3. Established destinations will have a range of accommodation that probably includes several large five-star hotels and possibly a few hotel chains. Smaller and developing destinations will have fewer accommodation choices. These may vary from lodges and traditional hostels to established hotels and luxury accommodation such as spa hotels.

Many of the negative impacts of tourism are evident in hotels, although the size and location of the hotel means that their impacts vary. Most hotels now have an environmental policy in place, which aims to conserve water and electricity. Evidence of the implementation of these policies can be seen in the requests to customers to turn down the air conditioning. Hotels are also encouraged to use local suppliers for their food and the recent trends to use locally grown organic produce has led to many seasonal hotel menus.

Hotels that are particularly supportive of sustainable tourism may offer management training courses to the local population or fund community projects, such as English language classes or schools. Sometimes hotels will join together to form a pressure group, which works together for sustainable tourism.

Airlines

Generally, there is a considerable amount of negative publicity about the effects that the airline industry and air travel have on the environment. This focuses on greenhouse gas emissions, carbon footprints and the negative impacts that airlines and air travellers have on the environment. Despite this negative image, the airline industry is very active in trying to minimise its impact on the environment. Airlines mainly concentrate on two main impact areas:

1) Their impact on the local environment around the airport, concentrating on noise and fuel emissions

2) Their impact on global climate change.

In addition to trying to cut down on the impact of aircraft, many airlines also sponsor responsible tourism projects or awards.

Charitable foundations

Many of the organisations in the tourism industry support a particular charity or charitable organisations. Smaller specialist tour operators who only offer tours to a small number of destinations normally form links with local resort or country specific charities. These are often nearby orphanages or schools in order to appeal to tourists who want to donate to the local children. Large tour operators and airlines that operate across a wider range of countries and destinations will often link with a large recognised aid agency. For example, Kuoni sponsors the work of The Born Free Foundation.

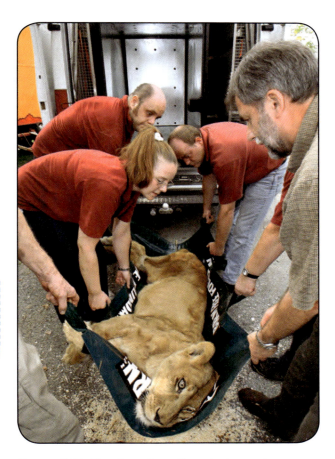

Figure 11.12 The Born Free Foundation strives to prevent animal suffering across the globe

CASE STUDY: CODE OF CONDUCT

This is an example of a code of conduct.

Whilst visiting our country, in order to make your stay enjoyable for both you and the local population and in order to maintain our beautiful country, please consider and follow these simple guidelines:

Show respect for natural and local heritage. Follow any instructions given by your tour guide and also observe the written instructions for visitors at local attractions.

Respect the local traditions and customs. This may mean observing dress codes and appropriate behaviour in certain locations. Think about what sort of clothing is appropriate for both men and women. If the locals are covered up, what sort of messages may you be sending out by exposing acres of flesh?

It is good manners to always ask before you take someone's photograph, even children. Please respect their wishes if they do not want to be photographed.

Try to put money into local hands. If you haggle for the lowest price, your bargain may be at the seller's expense. What may be a small sum to you might be a significant sum to the dealer. Even if you pay a little over the odds, does it really matter?

Resist giving money to begging children. Giving to children encourages begging. A donation to a project, health centre or school is more constructive.

If you buy local products and services, your money helps the local economy.

Avoid buying products that exploit animals and nature. For example, coral, ivory, turtle shell or sponges. Some of these products may be illegal, either to buy or import into the UK. Reduce your use of natural resources. To save energy, always switch off lights and electrical appliances when not in use. Conserve water by having a shower instead of a bath and do not insist that your towels are changed everyday.

Do not trample on vegetation, do not pick any flowers or plants and do not disturb local wildlife.

Do not light picnic fires and please ensure that cigarettes are properly extinguished.

SUPPORT

When developing tourism products, all the different organisations involved in tourism development should participate in the tourism planning process. Although tourism products are often seen as the complete package tour, there are many different components of each tour and the use of sustainable resources should be considered when creating a tour or package holiday. Further information about the different parts of a package holiday can be found in Unit 12.

Guidance in the form of a code of conduct should be given to arriving tourists and promoted by tour operators as beneficial to both the tourist and local community. Each code of conduct should be specific to the individual destination and should address the issues and challenges faced in controlling the negative impacts of tourism. Resort representatives, tour guides, excursion operators and excursion guides should all work together to ensure that the code is followed by tourists and they should be able to answer general questions about the resort's code of conduct.

Destinations, hotels and tour operators should also follow sustainable policies or codes of conduct. These will offer general guidelines and modes of operating, which will promote sustainability throughout the resort and can also be advertised as positive steps to potential tourists and other trade organisations.

The destination management organisation should work towards a sustainable tourism plan or tourism policy. This policy provides guidelines for tourism development over a number of years and also highlights the destination's mission statement and its main objectives for tourism development. These objectives will have been developed with the local community and will hopefully promote sustainability.

As a tourist destination develops and the tourism development plan is implemented, the destination management organisation should monitor the implementation of the sustainable tourism plan and try to measure the impacts of tourism. These results should be reviewed regularly and the destination's tourism plan and priorities amended accordingly. This will avoid sudden impacts becoming apparent and offers the destination the opportunity to correct negative impacts before they become too large and difficult to manage. This ensures the longevity of a sustainable tourism destination.

EVIDENCE ACTIVITY

P4 – M3 – D2

The last piece of material you have been asked to produce for the stand is a series of posters that visitors to the stand can take away with them to use in their own offices and show to their staff whom they employ in their own organisations.

Use your two destinations as case studies to provide named examples and possibly tourism statistics for your posters (you should consider using charts and graphs to display your statistics). One way of presenting the posters might be to use a question and answer format, maybe creating two sets of posters which interview the Head of Tourism for each of the two destinations you have chosen. The poster should consider the following topics.

1. A description of how the travel and tourism industry supports the development of sustainable tourism in both your long haul and short haul destination. Use the destinations you have already chosen for P1 to give specific examples of the tourism policies, aims and objectives which are being implemented in each destination. (P4)

2. Analyse whether the support provided by the industry for the implementation of sustainable tourism in each destination is effective. Give some reasons as to why you feel the support is good or bad. (M3)

3. For one destination recommend a number of ways in which sustainable tourism can be improved. In order to do this you should research and consider other destinations that are considered to be good practice in their implementation of sustainable tourism and use these destinations, organisations and partnerships as examples. (D2)

Tour operations

unit 12

Tour operations lie at the heart of the travel and tourism industry. Working hand-in-hand with other sectors of the industry, tour operators put together holidays, tours and cruises, as well as publishing holiday brochures that sell package holidays to the general public. The creation and selling of package holidays and the operations aspects of the industry in the UK and overseas make it one of the most exciting areas to work in. Although the industry is constantly changing and growing in order to reflect current trends, the demand for package holidays remains constant. According to the Association of British Travel Agents, the tour operator industry in the UK was valued at £26.2 billion in 2005 and 19 million people booked a package holiday in 2007. The industry continues to grow.

By the end of this unit, you will:

So you want to be an...

Overseas Contractor

My name Tony Cho

Age 38

Income £35,000 + expenses

Fancy travelling the world, staying in five star hotels and getting paid for it? Who doesn't!

What do you do?

I am responsible for setting up the contracts between the tour operator and the suppliers. This means that I have to negotiate the best deals for the tour operator. I am responsible for India, Sri Lanka and The Maldives.

What responsibilities do you have?

I travel overseas to find accommodation which is suitable for the holidays and tours we offer - checking that the facilities are up to the required standard. If I think that they are I meet with the hotel manager and negotiate how much the tour operator will pay per night.

The UK side of my job involves checking and writing the brochure descriptions and following up on any quality issues that were identified whilst I was overseas.

How did you get into the job?

I did a BTEC National whilst at college, followed by a degree in travel and tourism management. I spent some time working overseas for tour operators, learning how the overseas part of a tour operator's programme works. I then returned to the UK to work in the product department as an administrative assistant to a contractor and then when he left I applied for his position.

> **"I think this is one of the best jobs in the world!"**

How did you find your current job?

Most people get their first contracting job by internal promotion, but once you have some experience you can apply to other companies for similar positions. Often it's best to specialise in one area of the world and learn the language, but this can limit your opportunities.

What training did you get?

I did accompany a contractor on a visit to Egypt so I could see them in action. However it was very much a case of learning the job as I went along.

What skills do you need?

You need to be able to communicate with many different people, some of whom do not speak English very well. You need lots of patience but also need to be firm and not easily intimidated. Its important to be able to think on your feet and make decisions quickly.

Apart from the salary, any perks?

I normally travel business or first class and stay in 4 or 5 star hotels. When I travel all of my meals are paid for.

What about the future?

The next natural step would be to move into senior management and product development, but I have no plans to. I think this is one of the best jobs in the world!

Grading criteria

The table below shows what you need to do to gain a pass, merit or distinction in this part of the qualification. Make sure you refer back to it when you are completing work so you can judge whether you are meeting the criteria and what you need to do to fill in gaps in your knowledge or experience.

In this unit there are 4 evidence activities that give you an opportunity to demonstrate your achievement of the grading criteria:

page 129   **P1, M1, D1**

page 133   **P2, M2, D2**

page 140   **P3, P4**

page 143   **P5, M3**

To achieve a pass grade the evidence must show that the learner is able to...	To achieve a merit grade the evidence must show that, in addition to the pass criteria, the learner is able to...	To achieve a distinction grade the evidence must show that, in addition to the pass and merit criteria, the learner is able to...
P1 Describe the tour operations environment	**M1** Explain the challenges facing the tour operator sector	**D1** Evaluate the effectiveness of tour operators in responding to the challenges facing the sector
P2 Describe the products and services provided by different categories of tour operator for different travel markets	**M2** Analyse how a selected tour operator's portfolio of products and services meets the needs of its target market(s)	**D2** Recommend, with justification, how a selected tour operator could expand its range of products and services for its current target market or adapt its range of products and services to appeal to a new market
P3 Describe how tour operators plan, sell and administer a package holiday programme	**M3** Identify and explain the ways of maximising the profitability of the planned package holiday	
P4 Describe how tour operators operate a package holiday programme		
P5 Plan and cost a package for inclusion in a tour operator's programme		

12.1 *Understand the tour operations environment*

Tour operators plan, arrange and operate package holidays. A package holiday is defined as a pre-established combination of no fewer than two of the following elements, which are sold or offered for sale at an inclusive price.

- transport
- accommodation
- ancillary service.

A tour operator cannot work alone to produce and sell its holidays to the general public. It must work together with other sectors of the industry. A tour operator combines a number of different principals in a package holiday and this is then sold to the public, often through a travel agent.

LINKS WITH OTHER SECTORS

The way in which a tour operator sells its holidays to the public is called the chain of distribution. It can either sell directly to the customer using the Internet, telephone or post or it can sell indirectly through a travel agent. Further information about the chain of distribution can be found in Unit 1, Book 1.

Travel agents

Tour operators use travel agents to sell their holidays. In exchange for stocking their brochures and taking bookings and reservations, the tour operator will pay the travel agent commission for each sale made. Mass market tour operators who make their money from selling a large number of holidays are particularly reliant on travel agents selling their holidays. Smaller independent or specialist tour operators often sell directly to the public without the use of a travel agent.

Further information about the role of travel agents can be found in Unit 9.

Transport providers

When putting a package holiday together the tour operator must consider both transport to the destination and transport within the resort. Therefore, when planning the holiday they will contact airlines and airports about the availability of planes, routes and flight seats. They will also work together with overseas coach companies and car hire operators to provide in-resort transportation for their arriving guests. Tour operators in the UK often own their own coach company.

Key words

Ancillary service – additional services that tourists on package holidays may require either before their departure or while they are at the resort

Principals – organisations providing the individual products and services that a tour operator requires in order to create package holidays

Chain of distribution – the way in which a package holiday or the principal's product is sold to the public

Figure 12.1 Many tour operators have their own coaches

Accommodation providers

Most tour operators aim to offer their customers a choice of accommodation. This may range from luxury five-star hotels to self-catering apartments and campsites. Tour operators that specialise in a particular market, for example, luxury holidays, may offer less choice with regard to different standards of accommodation and will only offer accommodation that appeals to their target market. Tour operators need to ensure that the number of hotel rooms they have reserved in each destination matches the number of flight seats arranged with the airlines. They also need to guarantee that the standard of accommodation meets customer requirements and that health and safety regulations are observed.

More information about accommodation providers can be found in Unit 19, Book 3.

Ancillary products and services

Ancillary products and services are the additional services that tourists on package holidays may wish to purchase either before they leave or at the resort. These include insurance, car hire and excursions, as well as services that are not directly purchased by the customer, such as airport agents, excursion guides and local office staff.

Integration

In order to reduce the commission paid to travel agents and gain better deals with airlines and ancillary service providers, some tour operators began to buy existing travel agencies or principals such as airlines. This guaranteed them airline seats when required, gave them a direct outlet to customers through their own travel agencies and guaranteed the quality of the accommodation and ancillary services. This is called **integration**. When a tour operator buys another tour operator on the same level in the chain of distribution, it is called horizontal integration. When a tour operator buys a company on a different level in the chain of distribution (for example, a travel agent or airline), it is called vertical integration. Some tour operators have integrated extensively with other

companies and now own a range of different tour operators, travel agencies and principals. This allows them to target several different types of customers and it also gives customers different ways in which to purchase their products.

Example

Before its name change to MyTravel, the tour operator Airtours bought a number of different travel agencies and tour operators by both vertical and horizontal integration. They also expanded to create their own cruise company and airline.

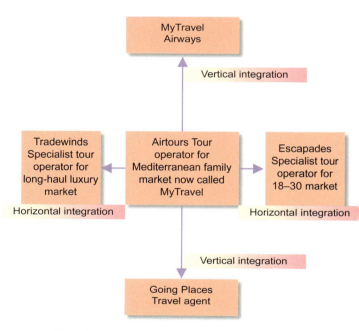

Figure 12.2 *The verical and horizontal integration of MyTravel*

Research tip

Use the Internet to research another large tour operator and discover how many different tour operators, principals and travel agencies they own.

LINKS WITH TRADE AND REGULATORY BODIES

Over the years, the tour operations industry has developed links with a number of different trade and regulatory bodies. These organisations vary from self-regulatory bodies, where the tour operators work together, to organisations that regulate the tour operations industry. Tour operators do not have to join any of these organisations, but membership does have many benefits.

ABTA

The Association of British Travel Agents works closely with all tour operators to regulate the way in which package holidays are sold to the general public. Tour operators who are members or approved by ABTA will conform to ABTA's regulations about the layout and content of their brochures. Their customer complaints procedures will follow ABTA's guidelines and any customer complaints that cannot be resolved can be referred to the ABTA arbitration body. The role of ABTA is explored in more depth in Unit 9, Retail and business travel operations.

Federation of Tour Operators

Figure 12.3a Logo for the Federation of Tour Operators

The Federation of Tour Operators is a group of tour operators that work together to directly improve arrangements for customers in the resorts. By influencing hoteliers, government bodies and resort authorities work together to improve resort health and safety, airport and tourist facilities. Tour operators work together within this organisation and are not in competition with each other.

Association of Independent Tour Operators

All members of the AITO are independent tour operators. They work together to promote the benefits of independent operators over mass market integrated tour operators. Their website promotes their individual products and provides direct links to individual tour operators' web pages and contact details. They also perform a similar role to ABTA, offering bonding, implementing a strict quality control charter and offering a Dispute Settlement Service for their customers.

Figure 12.3b Logo for the Association of Independent Tour Operators

Key words

Bonding – the process by which an organisation guarantees to repay customers after financial failure

UKInbound

Figure 12.3c Logo for the UKInbound

UKInbound used to be known as BITOA, the British Incoming Tour Operators Association. However, it changed its name as not all of its members were tour operators. A wide range of different organisations and companies are now members and all are connected in some way with inbound or domestic tourism. They include visitor attractions, hotels, excursion organisations, coach companies and tour operators. Members meet regularly and try to work with each other in order to maximise the amount of revenue that member organisations gain from inbound tourists.

Civil Aviation Authority

The Civil Aviation Authority regulates the airline industry and therefore tour operators who also own airlines work closely with them. They are responsible for ensuring the safety of aircraft, the training of air crew and ensuring that airlines are financially secure. By issuing ATOL licences, they also make certain that tour operators that use air travel within their holidays are financially secure.

LEGAL FRAMEWORK

Over the years, a number of different regulations have become important in the tour operations industry. As customers become more aware of their rights and the compensation culture grows, claims are increasing. Tour operators now have to adhere to a number of different legal requirements. Several of these regulations overlap and cover similar areas, but a tour operator must be aware of all of them when creating, selling and operating their holidays. Specific departments within a tour operator have detailed knowledge of regulations that apply to their area.

European Package Travel Regulations

In 1992, the European Union created the Package Travel Regulations. The purpose of these regulations was to create one set of legislation to be used by all European Union members. One of the aims was to ensure that customers received a fair deal and that their claims for compensation were dealt with fairly. The regulations also aimed to make it easier for customers to claim compensation and clarified the responsibilities of the tour operators. Under the EU Package Travel Regulations, the tour operator is responsible for all aspects of the holidays they sell to customers, unless the incident is classified as unforeseen or an **act of God**. Since these regulations have been implemented, tour operators have placed greater emphasis on quality and delivering the advertised product. Specific regulations within the Package Travel Regulations deal with individual areas of selling package holidays, for example, pricing and brochure descriptions.

Trades Description Act

The Trades Description Act covers how holidays are described to customers, especially the descriptions used in brochures, detailing the resorts and hotels available. Under the Trades Description Act, a tour operator must provide accurate information about the resort and the location of hotels and their facilities. They must also clearly state what is included in the hotel and board basis. If a hotel or resort facility is described incorrectly, then the tour operator is responsible for the error. They must try to inform the customers before departure that there is a mistake in the brochure. This is normally done by issuing brochure errata. The Trades Description Act also applies to descriptions given to customers over the Internet or telephone.

Consumer Protection Act

The Consumer Protection Act focuses on the way in which holidays are advertised to customers. This act particularly covers the discounts offered by tour operators and regulates the use of the words 'discounted' and 'free', as well as covering the issue of **value for money** and quality. Travel agents and tour operators cannot advertise a product as discounted when it actually is not the case. They must also advertise the full price of the holiday on offer to their customers, including any hidden extras and surcharges.

> ### Key words
> ---
> **Act of God** – an event cannot be foreseen or controlled by the tour operator, for example, a hurricane, earthquake or a terrorist attack
> **Value for money** – paying a reasonable price for a delivered service

Disability Discrimination Act

Under the Disability Discrimination Act, tour operators must try to ensure that the holidays they offer are accessible to disabled people. This act has a number of different implications that cover two main areas: the way in which holidays are sold and the provisions made for disabled customers in the resort while they are on holiday. A tour operator should be able to provide copies of their brochures in large print or Braille. If this is not possible, they should have experienced staff who are able to help a disabled person to choose their holiday. Hotels and visitor attractions that are used by tour operators should make reasonable adjustments, so that their facilities are available to all tourists. It is the tour operator's responsibility to ensure that hotels comply with these regulations. Long-haul tour operators often face challenges implementing this legislation within their programmes as different countries have different attitudes towards disabled people.

Contract law

When a customer books their holiday with a tour operator, they are taking out a contract. There are three different types of contracts in the tour operations industry: written, verbal and implied.

- A written contract contains all the details of the package holiday in writing. This includes the holiday described in the brochure and the terms and conditions printed at the back of the holiday brochure. This is the standard contract that covers both customers booking through a travel agency and customers who book directly with the tour operator over the Internet.

- A verbal contract is used when a customer makes a booking over the telephone and covers all items and terms discussed during the conversation.

- An implied contract covers the items that can be expected to naturally form part of the holiday.

Example

As part of the implied contract, a booking in a self-catering apartment would include saucepans, plates and cutlery that can be used for catering.

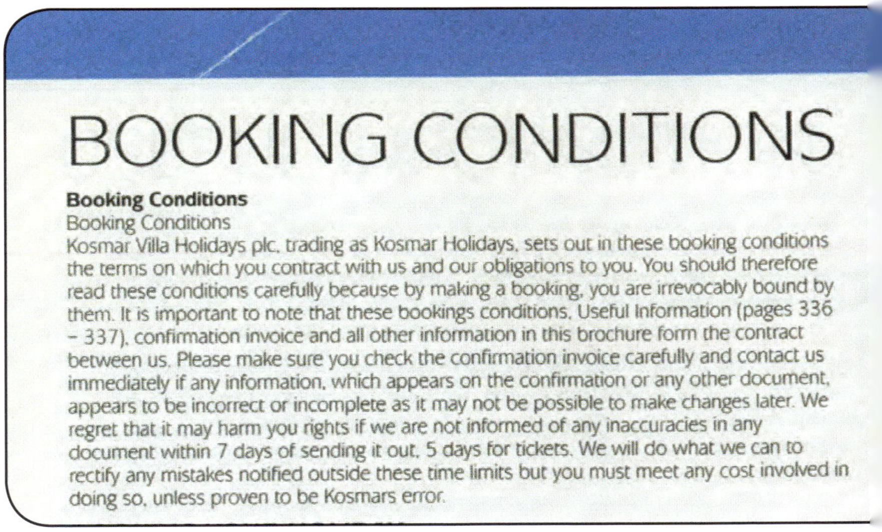

BOOKING CONDITIONS

Booking Conditions

Booking Conditions

Kosmar Villa Holidays plc, trading as Kosmar Holidays, sets out in these booking conditions the terms on which you contract with us and our obligations to you. You should therefore read these conditions carefully because by making a booking, you are irrevocably bound by them. It is important to note that these bookings conditions, Useful Information (pages 336 – 337), confirmation invoice and all other information in this brochure form the contract between us. Please make sure you check the confirmation invoice carefully and contact us immediately if any information, which appears on the confirmation or any other document, appears to be incorrect or incomplete as it may not be possible to make changes later. We regret that it may harm you rights if we are not informed of any inaccuracies in any document within 7 days of sending it out, 5 days for tickets. We will do what we can to rectify any mistakes notified outside these time limits but you must meet any cost involved in doing so, unless proven to be Kosmars error.

Figure 12.4 A copy of the terms and conditions can be found at the back of all holiday brochures
Source: Kosmar villa holidays

Think Why do you think contracts are important?

Licensing

Customers should be confident that, once they have paid their money, the tour operator is not going to go bankrupt or disappear before or while they are on holiday. In order to avoid this kind of situation, customers should only used licensed or bonded tour operators.

A bonded tour operator has lodged money with a bonding organisation as a form of guarantee. If the tour operator does go bankrupt, then the bonding organisation can use the money to assist the tour operator's customers in two different ways. Customers who have yet to go on holiday will receive a refund and assistance in booking their holiday again with another tour operator. Customers on holiday will be able to continue and will be flown home at no additional expense.

Figure 12.5

There are three main organisations that bond tour operators: ABTA, ATOL and AITO. However, tour operators that use air travel should hold an ATOL licence. Tour operators that are bonded by one of these organisations show a seal of approval on their brochures and websites. Tour operators that only operate coach holidays can be bonded by ABTA. Independent tour operators can choose to be AITO bonded. Tour operators that use any form of air travel in their holidays need to obtain an ATOL licence (Air Travel Organisers Licence), which can be obtained from the Civil Aviation Authority.

EXTERNAL INFLUENCES

While people always want to go on holiday, there are many different factors that influence where they choose to go, who they travel with, how much they spend and how they book their holiday. The resorts and destinations that tour operators are able to put into their brochures also depend on a range of external factors, which cannot be easily controlled by the tour operator.

Environmental factors

Many long-haul resorts are affected by extremes of temperature, such as monsoon seasons. This can be built into a tour operator's programme in advance by reducing the number of flights to the destination or closing the destination to tourists during the rainy season. However, natural disasters like hurricanes, tsunamis or floods can have an immediate impact on the availability of a destination. When this happens, tour operators may decide to pull out of the destination and offer customers the opportunity to transfer their bookings to other places.

Figure 12.6 Hurricanes often cause terrible damage to property, which can take many months to fix

Political factors

Often the destinations where tour operators travel to are not as politically stable as the UK. Therefore, a number of different political factors may affect the tour operator's ability to offer their customers a full range of services or products. This is particularly evident in the long-haul market. Political unrest and the continued threat of terrorism might influence a tour operator to stop offering holidays to a particular destination. For example, the political regime in Burma has led to a number of tour operators deciding to stop offering holidays to the destination. By doing this, the tour operators hope to influence the government into improving conditions for the local population.

Other factors that may have a direct influence on a customer's enjoyment of a holiday are the local working conditions and strikes. Strikes by airlines, baggage handlers or local protests may cause discomfort or distress to customers. These factors may increase the number of complaints received by tour operators. Over time if it becomes a regular occurrence, the tour operator may decide to withdraw from the destination or limit the number of holidays sold.

> **Think** Can you think of any other reasons why you might decide not to travel to a certain destination?

Economic factors

Tour operators cost their holidays several months in advance of their customers arriving in the selected destination. Tour operators try to consider currency and exchange rates when working out the costs of their holidays. They often build money into the price, which can be used to pay for additional unforeseen costs. However, large changes in the exchange rate, additional taxes or the cost of oil will directly affect a tour operator's profits and a customer's willingness to book.

Social factors

Social trends can have both short and long-term impacts on the tour operations industry. Over the last ten years, people have become more concerned about their impact on the planet. As a direct result of this, the industry has seen a growth in sustainable tourism. This can be observed in the increase in the number of smaller independent tour operators that market themselves as responsible or eco-tourism organisations. Further information about sustainable tourism can be found in Unit 11.

The changing demographic profile of the UK's population makes an impact on the range of products that tour operators offer for sale. An increase in the number of single parents has led to tour operators offering special offers for parents, which are different from the traditional one free child place with two paying adults. Other demographic influences can be seen as the ageing population is slowly changing the number of winter sun holidays on offer, and longer working hours are increasing the number of short breaks offered to customers.

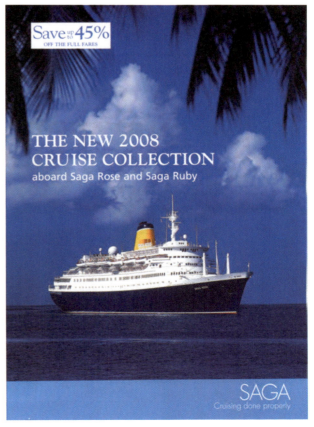

Figure 12.7 Saga specialise in holidays for the over 50's

Technological factors

As the number of homes with computers and Internet access grows, the use of the Internet is changing the way in which people book their holidays and the number of bookings made directly with tour operators is increasing. Even customers who do not want to book over the Internet may use it to research and check the availability and costs of their planned holiday or to compare different tour operators' products and prices. Tour operators have reacted to this change in different ways. Some of the larger tour operators have closed several of their high street travel agents and now rely on their websites. The smaller independent tour operators have gained from the growth of Internet sales as their products are now advertised and available to a larger market.

CHALLENGES

Changes in technology are not the only challenge facing the industry and forcing change. The Internet offers customers the opportunity to create their own package, using a range of different websites or by using a low-cost airline's gateway site. This is known as dynamic packaging. It allows the customer to create their own flexible itinerary. By purchasing different components of the holiday from different companies, the customers are not buying a package holiday. Therefore, there is less financial security and there are fewer options with regards to unhappy customers being able to claim compensation.

> ### Key words
> Dynamic packaging – the use of the Internet to sell customers individual components of a package holiday

In order to meet the challenge of the Internet and dynamic packaging, traditional tour operators now offer customers more choices about their holiday, as well as offering their customers non-traditional packages or unpackaged versions of their brochure holidays in a way that is similar to dynamic packaging. Customers are offered a choice of departure dates, flight times and airports, accommodation upgrades and a range of optional extras. As a result, traditional holidays are now sold in a number of different ways.

Tour operators have tried to meet the challenge of online booking by closing traditional high street travel agents and opening out-of-town travel hypermarkets instead. Some also offer price matches to Internet special offers and have invested money into advancing their online presence.

> ### Research tip
> Use a search engine to find some examples of dynamic packaging of tour operators on the Internet.

> **Think** Would you prefer to book a holiday or flight online or through a travel agent? What are the pros and cons for each method?

Integration

The integration of tour operators continues with what was known as the Big 4 (Tui/Thomson, First Choice, MyTravel and Thomas Cook), starting to join with each other to form increasingly larger companies. This has had an impact on the industry and customers in a positive and negative way. Travel and tourism workers may lose their jobs as the companies are streamlined. Customers will have less choice over who they travel with and these large tour operators can force low prices on the principals they do business with, such as hotels and excursion operators. Positive impacts may include the lowering of the costs of package holidays and a rise in standards.

These changes and the number of tour operators that are integrating with each other are constantly changing the industry's market share. It may appear that the market is shared by many different tour operators. However, many of these tour operators are integrated with each other. Therefore, the number of individual tour operators is actually very limited.

The tour operations industry has recently started competing with online budget airlines, selling spare seats on their charter flights. Some tour operators have also launched their own low-cost budget airlines, competing directly with the low-cost airlines on the summer sun routes. The rise in the number of tourists who are booking flight only is also affecting the number of tourists who book package holidays. This decrease in demand has resulted in some tour operators cutting down on the number of overseas resort staff they employ.

EVIDENCE ACTIVITY

P1 – M1 – D1

New owners have bought the tour company for which you work. To improve their understanding of the business you have been asked to create a 15 minute presentation on the tour operations industry. This presentation is in three sections (5 minutes per section, including an introduction and conclusion)

1. Fully describe the tour operations industry, including:

a) A description of how tour operators work with other sectors of the industry including their links with principals, travel agents and a range of trade organisations and regulatory bodies.

b) A diagram of the vertical and horizontal integration of a large tour operator and a brief definition, giving named examples, of both horizontal and vertical integration.

c) Examples of how different legislation affects the tourism industry. You might like to research and use recent news stories as examples. (P1)

2. Explain some of the current challenges facing the tour operations industry, covering one key environmental, political, economic, social or technological factor. (M1)

3. Using three of the challenges identified in the previous task and evaluate how effective tour operators currently are in meeting these challenges. Use examples to show how named tour operators have responded to a specific challenge that they have recently faced. (D1)

12.2 Know the range of products and services offered by tour operators for different target markets

TOUR OPERATOR CATEGORIES

Tour operators can be divided into five different categories. Although some tour operators could be categorised as more than one type, the majority fall into one category only.

Outbound

Outbound tour operators are companies that sell holidays to destinations outside the UK. These may be small specialist companies or larger mass market tour operators. Mass market tour operators concentrate their efforts on selling general holidays to many people. There is often limited choice with regard to upgrades and special advice. These tour operators focus on selling 7, 10 or 14-day holidays to major European destinations and resorts, running a summer brochure that concentrates on Mediterranean beach resorts with free child places and special offers. They also have a winter brochure offering winter sun holidays and ski resorts. These holidays are often competitively priced and appeal to families and couples who want to book a summer beach holiday. Some mass market tour operators include Tui/Thomson, My Travel, First Choice and Cosmos.

Inbound

Inbound tour operators are mainly companies based overseas. They sell holidays to tourists who want to visit the UK. They organise their incoming flights, accommodation and travel arrangements. The holidays they sell can vary and often include accommodation, tours and airport transfers. The majority of their staff are based overseas, but they have resort staff to look after their customers. Some English speaking nations like the USA, Australia and Canada will use British residents. However, others will recruit and employ their own staff. Some examples of inbound tour operators are Kuoni Travel Incoming, Trafalgar Tours, Sovereign, China Holidays and Euro Asia Travel Limited. Further information on the UK as a tourist destination can be found in Unit 3, Book 1.

Domestic

Domestic tour operators are companies that sell and run package holidays within the UK. These holidays are often by coach, but may also include internal flights. Tours may be for a single day to visit a particular event, destination, festival or visitor attraction that is of interest to the UK market. The tours may include overnight or a longer stay in a hotel or resort accommodation. For many domestic tour operators, the coach driver also acts as the tour guide or resort representative, dealing with customer enquiries and providing information and a commentary during the journey. Many domestic tour operators also have European programmes. The names of two domestic tour operators are WA Shearings and Johnsons. Many domestic tour operators are coach companies that have expanded into the domestic package travel market.

Independent

Independent tour operators are companies that are not owned by a larger integrated organisation. They are often small specialist tour operators that have not been bought by one of the larger mass market tour operators. Independent tour operators often offer customers more choice, but they are generally more expensive than mass market tour operators or specialist tour operators that are owned by larger companies. They often have many repeat customers who enjoy the individualised attention that the staff offer.

Specialist

Specialist tour operators are companies specialising in selling holidays that focus on a particular destination, activity or target market. Specialist tour operators provide customers with advice focused on their particular interest. More

detailed information on the holiday is provided in the brochure and by staff. Some specialist tour operators are owned and operated by larger companies, but others remain as smaller independent tour operators. The names of some specialist tour operators are Saga (over 50's) Escapades and Club 18–30 (young people), and Gold Par Excellence (golfing holidays).

Figure 12.8 Club 18–30 specialise in holidays for young people

Think Out of the five categories covered, which tour operator group do you think generates the least money? Explain your reasoning.

PRODUCTS

Most holidays are bought using a tour operator's brochure or website. There is a wide range of types of package holidays on sale.

Standard package holiday

This is the most common type of package holiday and it is bought directly from the tour operator's brochure and sold by mass market and outbound tour operators. It is normally a 7, 10 or 14-night holiday in a European resort. Flights, return transfers from the airport to accommodation, accommodation and the services of a **resort representative** are included in the price.

Depending on the type of hotel booked, a children's club that is run by the tour operator's staff may be included in the price. Most customers will also expect their transfer to the resort to be accompanied by a member of the tour operator's staff. On arrival in the resort, the resort representative will hold a welcome meeting or welcome party where they provide information about the resort, hotel and also offer customers the opportunity to buy excursions. Throughout the holiday, the resort representative provides customers with advice and assistance and deals with any complaints.

Tailor-made

Tailor-made holidays are those which do not follow the package holiday shown in the tour operator's brochure. Customers have the opportunity to change details of the holiday, creating their own personalised itinerary. These holidays are generally more expensive than standard package holidays, but they offer customers great flexibility in terms of their travel arrangements. Private guides, transfers and flights can all be costed into the holiday and the customers can choose their own accommodation and create their own individual itinerary.

Specialist holiday

A specialist holiday is one which is targeted at a particular market. The hotels, excursions and resort staff are all carefully selected to appeal to that particular market.

Example

Saga is a tour operator that specialises in holidays for the over 50s. There is less emphasis on Internet bookings and reservations can be made by telephone or through travel agents. Saga's resort staff are all older and hotels have good accessibility for disabled and elderly guests. The resorts are chosen on the basis of good medical facilities and the tour operator uses mainly daytime flights, which will not tire their older customers.

Think Consider some of the other specialist tour operators that you know about. What kinds of adjustments do they make for their customers?

Figure 12.9 Children's clubs are popular with holidaying families

Customer choice

Customers are offered a wide range of products and services to choose from in the holiday brochure. Some of these are included in the cost of the holiday, but tour operators will charge the customer a supplement for many of the additional services that are available. Some examples of the products and services that a customer can choose to pay extra for are:

- holiday insurance

- paying a supplement for a daytime flight or departure from a regional airport

- paying a supplement in order to guarantee a seat on the plane with extra legroom, a window seat or seats together. Late check-in and upgrades are also sometimes offered

- additional costs for meals onboard the plane

- private transfers on arrival and departure in/ from the resort

- car hire

- room upgrades, either to suites, rooms with a pool or sea view or speciality rooms like water bungalows or private villas

- a system of supplements and discounts for children sharing adults' rooms. This could be three people sharing a twin room or free child places

- a choice of board basis – half-board, full-board or all-inclusive

- pre-bookable excursions, **excursion packages** and car hire. These items can normally also be booked in the resort, although they may be cheaper in advance

- late check-out from the hotel room.

> **Key words**
>
> **Excursion package** – a group of excursions sold together at a discounted price

Figure 12.10 There are a number of different car hire companies to choose from when travelling abroad

TARGET MARKET

Tour operators target different markets and alter the holidays they offer accordingly. Many mass market tour operators target the large family market by offering children's clubs, free child places and special offers for early bookings.

Different couples are attracted to different types of package holidays, ranging from beach holidays to cultural or activity breaks. Tour operators normally offer a range of holidays to suit different budgets.

The increase in the number of single people travelling alone has seen a number of tour operators move into this specialist market. Other tour operators have increased the number of holidays that do not have large single supplements.

Special interest holidays have also been on the increase, attracting couples, single travellers and occasionally families. Many independent tour operators find it easier to target a particular segment of the market, avoiding direct competition with the integrated mass market tour operators.

Customers with disabilities are becoming a specific segment of the market. Many travel with existing tour operators and therefore reasonable adjustments must be made. These customers often require detailed information about hotels, transport and resort facilities before booking. For this reason, many tour operators have a dedicated team of customer service advisers to research this information and provide guidance to customers.

EVIDENCE ACTIVITY

P2 – M2 – D2

1. The new owners publish an inhouse magazine every month for their employees. In next month's magazine they would like to feature an article about the tour operations industry. You have been asked to write this article and can use pictures, logos and brochures (or brochure sections) to make it more interesting. The article will need to cover the following five areas:

a) Categories of tour operators

Describe the different categories of tour operators listed below and name three different tour operators who operate within each category:
Outbound
Inbound
Domestic
Independent
Specialist. (P2)

b) Target markets, products and services

Select one tour operator for each of the above categories and identify their target market or markets, then review the products and services that they offer. (P2)

c) Meeting the needs of the target market

Choose one of the tour operators you have identified in task b) and analyse how this tour operator meets the needs of their target market, consider both the products they sell and the range of services they offer to their customers. (M2)

d) Improving the products and services

Now you have reviewed the products and services offered and have identified the target market of one tour operator. Next suggest specific ways in which this tour operator could improve the range of products and services that it offers to its existing market. (D2)

e) Expanding into new markets

Suggest ways in which this one tour operator could expand into other target markets or destinations and make suggestions on the way their products and services could be expanded. Give reasons for your suggestions. (D2)

12.3 *Know how tour operators plan, sell, administer and operate a package holiday programme*

TIMESCALES

There are many things to consider when planning a package holiday, therefore tour operators plan their package holidays several years in advance. A package holiday for sale in 2009 will initially have been planned in 2007.

Table 12.1 A tour operator's year planner for a holiday in August 2009

October/November 2007	Planning which countries and resorts to use and how many holidays to offer
January/February 2008	Contracting hotel accommodation and airline seats
May/April 2008	Preparing brochures, confirming prices, finalising brochure descriptions and photographs
May 2008	Brochure launch, publicity and marketing
October 2008	Recruit overseas staff
November 2008	Airline scheduling to avoid congested flight times
February 2009	Bookings received and forecasts are considered for each destination. Adjustments and consolidations with regard to flights and accommodation are made, if necessary
March/April 2009	Train overseas staff. Finalise resort arrangements with accommodation and ancillary service providers
May 2009	Issue tickets and final invoices to customers
July 2009	Confirm names of customers to airline, accommodation providers and resort office
August 2009	Welcome holiday-makers to resort

PLANNING

When a tour operator carries out market research when it plans its programme, not only does the operator assess the success of its current programme, it also considers any new resorts that may be popular with customers and tries to identify resorts that might decline in popularity. Questionnaires are often used to identify trends in resorts and market research companies may be employed to provide a more detailed picture. Further information about market research can be found in Unit 5. The factors that lead to a resort's rise or decline in popularity are identified in Unit 7, Book 1.

Having carried out the market research, the tour operator then undertakes other marketing activities to identify the target market, to match the product and price in order to meet the market and to consider the viability of new products. As soon as a new product area or a gap in the market is identified, the marketing department tries to develop a product to match the gap. A **contractor** or product specialist is normally sent to the resort to locate new hotels, excursion providers and transport operators, which are suitable for the newly proposed package holiday.

Figure 12.11 Tour operators often have an agreement with large hotels or resorts

1) Guarantee – when the tour operator pays in advance to secure the use of a certain number of rooms in a hotel, the operator pays the hotelier regardless of whether the rooms in the hotel are used or not. This often offers the cheapest price per night for the tour operator.

2) Allocation and release – the tour operator and hotelier agree a date, for example, two weeks before each arrival date, when the tour operator has to state whether it will be using the rooms or not. The tour operator only pays for the rooms it uses and the unused rooms return to the hotel, which can sell them on to other tour operators or to the general public.

3) Ad hoc – this is a Latin term and means 'on demand'. Every time the tour operator wants to put together a package for a customer, the hotel must be contacted and availability checked. This is the most expensive way of contracting and is often used for tailor-made or individual specialist packages.

> **Key words**
>
> **Contractor** – the person who goes out to holiday destinations and negotiates the prices of all the services that a tour operator requires

Contracting

Once the desired components of the package holiday have been decided, the tour operator contracts the supplier. Contracting involves negotiating and agreeing the costs, terms and conditions with which the service will be supplied to the tour operator. These are legally binding agreements and the tour operator will seek to obtain the best deal from the supplier with regard to costs, rooms and special offers. When contracting a hotel, there are three different types of contract that can be used.

> **Think** Consider the three different ways of contracting and think about the benefits and drawbacks for both the hotel and tour operator.

Contractors will also contract airline seats, transport providers, cruise companies, car hire companies and a range of excursion providers. They put together a range of different products and services that form the basis of the package holiday and brochure choices.

Brochure production

Brochure production can begin as soon as the products to be offered by the tour operator have been confirmed. There are three main aims of a holiday brochure:

1) to sell holidays

2) to provide sufficient information about resorts and accommodation to encourage people to book

3) to project and reinforce the tour operator's image

In order to produce an accurate brochure, the tour operator begins by collecting the relevant information. This includes resort and hotel descriptions, photographs, sample prices and details of excursions. These details are then used to create mock-up pages of the brochure and the mock-ups are sent to the hotels, resort offices, the contractor and the ancillary service providers in order for them to check that the details are correct. Once the details have been approved, pricing information is added, everything is checked again and the brochure is sent to the printers for printing.

> **Think** Obtain a number of different tour operators' brochures. Consider the different approaches they have used, explore their use of colour, the quality of paper used and how they have presented the information provided. What kinds of pictures have been used throughout the brochures and how do these portray the tour operators's image?

Figure 12.12 Tour operators' publish many different brochures, catering to all possible customer requirements

SELL

Once the components of the package holiday have been contracted, the price of selling the holiday can be costed. Some flexibility is added into the prices in order to cover possible changes in exchange rates, taxes and administration costs. Availability is entered into the company database, so that travel agents and customers can check availability and make reservations. However, before the holiday can be sold, the holiday brochure must be created and the product details entered into the tour operator's website.

Brochure distribution

Tour operators choose to distribute their brochures in different ways, depending on their size and target market. Large tour operators tend to send their brochures to all travel agents and retail outlets. This is called intensive distribution. Tour operators that specialise in a particular market often choose to send their brochures to travel agents that have sold their holidays in the past or that specialise in this area. This method is called selective distribution.

Customers who have booked holidays in the past are often contacted directly by the tour operator with details of their new products and copies of their brochures. This can be done by post, but it is also being carried out increasingly by e-mail. Tour operators sometimes also send supporting promotional material like posters and details about late or early offers.

Pricing

Tour operators use different pricing strategies in their brochures and throughout the year to ensure that sales are good.

Market penetration pricing

Low-cost holidays and special offers are evident in brochures, highlighting the tour operator's use of market penetration pricing. These holidays might make a loss or only just cover their costs, but they attract new customers, switch sales and can be used to promote new destinations.

Cost plus pricing

Cost plus pricing is the standard costs of the holiday plus profits. This is the most common type of pricing found in brochures.

Competitive pricing

During the year, tour operators often compete to sell holidays and fill any empty hotel rooms and seats on planes. Competitive pricing involves selling holidays that match competitors' prices - they often have very small profit margins.

Market skimming pricing

Specialist tour operators and tour operators whose market segment involves luxury holidays may choose to limit the types of people who book with them in an effort to remain exclusive. For these companies, their name and reputation for quality is very important so prices are kept high to ensure quality and to provide customers with a personalised service.

Promotional activities

In addition to sending out brochures and contacting previous customers, tour operators may undertake a number of promotional activities. To advertise their name and products, some tour operators sponsor television programmes, events or sports teams. To ensure that the target market is aware of the company, sponsored activities are carefully selected to gain the maximum possible amount of publicity.

To encourage greater sales compared to competitors, tour operators offer special deals and incentives to travel agents. These include increased commission paid for sales, opportunities for staff to go on educational visits overseas or staff discounts on holidays booked with the tour operator.

ADMINISTRATION

Reservations, confirmations, amendments and cancellations

Once a customer has made a reservation the information is processed and held by the tour operator's reservations department in a database. Close to the date of departure and often coinciding with the accommodation release date contracted by the tour operator with the hotel, the database will confirm the reservation by issuing a **rooming list**.

> **Key words**
>
> **Rooming list** – the written details of the customer's booking, which are forwarded to the accommodation provider and resort staff

A rooming list provides the hotelier and resort staff with the customer's details, including the type of room booked, flight details, passenger names and any additional details or special requests such as pre-booked private transfers or requests for sea view rooms. This rooming list is used by the resort office to confirm accommodation with the hotel and also to organise airport transfers.

In addition to creating the rooming list, the database will also forward the passengers' names to the airline for inclusion on the passenger **flight manifest**. This manifest is used by the airline for check-in and is also passed on to the departing and arriving airport authorities.

After booking the holiday, any changes that the customer wishes to make are called **amendments**. The rooming list and passenger manifest reflect these amendments. Tour operators often charge customers to make changes to their original bookings, to cover the administration costs. The pricing details of making any changes are shown in the terms and conditions at the back of each tour operator's brochure.

Key words

Flight manifest – the official list of passengers being carried on a plane
Amendment – a change made to a booking once the deposit has been paid

Tour operators also charge customers to cancel their holiday if the cancellation is made at a certain time before departure. The costs of cancelling a holiday are also listed in the back of the tour operator's brochure.

Due to circumstances beyond their control, tour operators may be obliged to make amendments or cancel customers' holidays. This could be due to environmental or political factors or an incident in a hotel, for example, a fire that renders the hotel unusable for the foreseeable future. In most cases, if a tour operator has to make changes to a customer's reservation, they have to pay the customer the amount of compensation listed in the brochure.

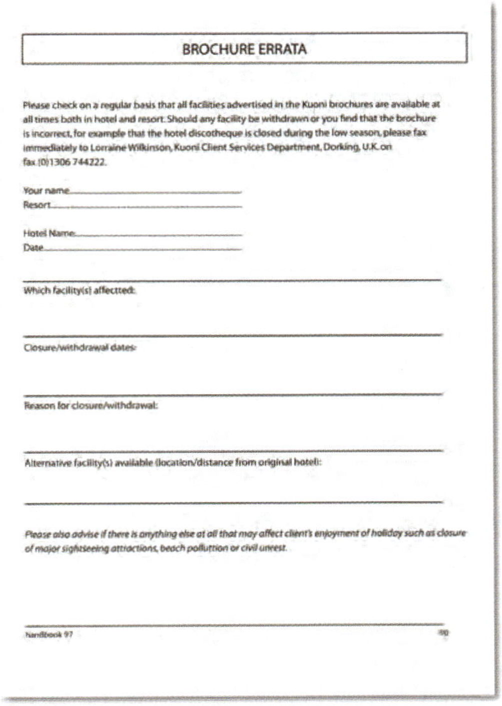

BROCHURE ERRATA

Please check on a regular basis that all facilities advertised in the Kuoni brochures are available at all times both in hotel and resort. Should any facility be withdrawn or you find that the brochure is incorrect, for example that the hotel discotheque is closed during the low season, please fax immediately to Lorraine Wilkinson, Kuoni Client Services Department, Dorking, U.K. on fax (0)1306 744222.

Your name__________
Resort__________

Hotel Name__________
Date__________

Which facility(s) affected:

Closure/withdrawal dates:

Reason for closure/withdrawal:

Alternative facility(s) available (location/distance from original hotel):

Please also advise if there is anything else at all that may affect client's enjoyment of holiday such as closure of major sightseeing attractions, beach pollution or civil unrest.

Handbook 97

Figure 12.13 Brouchure errata details any facilities that are not currently avaiable

If a tour operator is aware of a long-term change in a resort facility or an error in the brochure, it issues a brochure errata. It provides details of the facility that is no longer available and is logged on the tour operator's reservation system, so that reservations staff and travel agents can advise customers of the change before confirming the booking. If an errata is issued and plenty of notice of the change is given to the customer, then the tour operator might not need to pay any compensation.

Research tip

Use a tour operator's brochure to research the fees that a customer would have to pay to make changes to their bookings.

Think Looking at the same brochure, how much compensation would the tour operator have to pay if it has to cancel or amend a customer's holiday?

The tour operator sends an itinerary to the customer around the same time as the rooming list is issued. This contains detailed information about the holiday, including any upgrades and special requests. If the customer's journey requires flight tickets, these are also issued and sent to the customer.

OPERATIONS

A tour operator's operations department is the division that is actually involved in providing the holiday that the customer has booked. An operations department often has three sections — pre-departure, duty office and post-departure. The duty office works with the resort office and staff in dealing with any issues that arise when the customer is on holiday, which includes the departing and arriving flights. Pre-departure operations include organising any changes that have to be made to a customer's holiday prior to departure.

Consolidations

One of the main changes that tour operators regularly have to make to a customer's holiday is an alteration to the departing or arriving flight times. This is normally because the tour operator wants to make changes in the flight schedules. It is done in order to save costs on flights that have not sold well, for example, regional flights. When the tour operator decides not to operate a particular flight, they will consolidate it by moving the passengers from the cancelled flight on to another flight, therefore merging the two flights together. This is called consolidating a flight. The customers are sometimes entitled to compensation, but this often depends on the amount of notice given to the customer and the terms and conditions in the brochure.

Over-bookings

An over-booking is when a customer arrives at the resort and the accommodation booked is not available. Over-bookings are normally the fault of the hotel. They accepted too many reservations for their hotel, either on purpose to make money or due to an administrative error. The hotel, together with the tour operator, is responsible for finding the customer alternative accommodation of a similar level and paying the customer compensation for the inconvenience of the change. Most customers are upset about over-bookings and this is one of the main complaints that a tour operator and its resort staff deal with.

Transport operations

The resort office is responsible for organising airport transfers for all of its arriving and departing customers. They use passenger manifests and rooming lists to book the appropriate number of coaches and private transfers. They also pass on details of pre-booked car hire to the car hire companies. In addition to organising transport, the resort office also books excursions.

Duty office/UK and overseas resort liaison

The duty office is located in the UK and deals with all issues relating to the customer's holiday while overseas. The duty office, airport staff and resort offices work closely together. Although the duty office does not deal with the day-to-day running of the resort and any complaints in the resort, it is involved in more serious issues such as long flight delays, customers who are in hospital or who have been involved in incidents or emergencies.

Health and safety

Under the Package Travel Regulations, the tour operator is responsible for health and safety issues in the resort. This includes hygiene standards in hotels, the use of warning signs around swimming pools and lifts and the correct maintenance of children's facilities. Resort staff and resort representatives carry out health and safety audits and pass this information through the resort office to the tour operator's head office. If there are health and safety concerns, the head office contacts the hotel directly to request action.

Figure 12.14 Hotel pools display warning signs in order to comply with health and safety guidelines

Emergency situations and crisis management

Every resort has one person who is in charge. This is often the Area Manager, but the title can vary depending on the tour operator's resort structure. The Area Manager is responsible for the well-being of all of the customers and staff in the resort and is therefore the first person who is called in the event of an emergency.

Resort emergencies include hotel fires, coach crashes, accidents during excursions and natural disasters. Tour operators have procedures in place to cope with emergencies and the Area Manager, together with the duty office, is the person who implements them in the resort. The procedures include guidelines on dealing with the press, sending bilingual staff to hospitals and advising next-of-kin. The Area Manager and duty office also work together to deal with other less immediate crises, such as customers who have been arrested and the repatriation of the body if a customer dies.

Quality control

Tour operators normally have a quality control department, which monitors the post-holiday questionnaires and tries to identify areas in which the tour operator can improve its services. It considers all aspects of the customer's holiday, from the original booking to the flight home. The quality control department also measures the number of complaints received and takes measures to minimise them in the future.

Customer service

A tour operator's customer service department is normally divided into two sections – pre-departure and post-departure.

Pre-holiday

Pre-departure or pre-holiday customer services deal with customers who have not yet been on holiday. The customer often wants to make amendments to their holiday and the customer services department is responsible for carrying out these changes, processing the correct paperwork and advising customers of the relevant charges.

Atol Number 59763

28/06/2007

Holiday Reference Number   1703-0810

Departing   05/08/2008

London Gatwick
Estimated Departure Time 17.00
Flight Number SQ251

Destination   The Maldives (14 nights Kurumba Island)

Dear Mrs Jones,

We are writing with reference to your holiday listed above. We regret to inform you that we have had to adjust the flight time for your departing flight. This flight will now be departing at 11.15 am on the 5th August 2008.

We would like to apologise for any inconvenience that this amendment may cause you. We are sure that you are aware, as mentioned in our terms and conditions, that the flight times published in our brochures are often not confirmed with the airlines until nearer the departure date and therefore are subject to change once the airline schedules have been confirmed.

If you would like to discuss the matter further please don't hesitate to contact our customer services department.

Yours sincerely,

Figure 12.15 It is the responsibility of the tour operator to inform the customer of any changes to their travel itinerary

The pre-departure customer services department also advise customers about changes to their holiday, including advising them of consolidated flights, issuing brochure errata when a hotel or resort facility becomes unavailable and advising customers that they have been over-booked.

Post-holiday

The post-holiday customer services department deals with customer complaints when they have returned from their holiday. It investigates and answers complaint letters and offers compensation for incidents that occurred during their holidays when appropriate. In order to investigate complaints, the post-departure customer services department reads reports written by resort staff and may also contact individual resorts or staff members for further details.

Further information about health and safety, resort operations and in-resort customer service is available in Unit 13, Book 3.

EVIDENCE ACTIVITY

P3 – P4

1. The main job of a tour operator is to create package holidays and so the new company owners must understand the different stages involved in making a package holiday. To help them understand the process of creating a package holiday you have been asked to create a leaflet which outlines the different stages and departments involved in arranging a holiday. This leaflet must:

a) Describe the functions of a tour operator. You might like to concentrate on the activities of one particular tour operator.

b) Include a timescale for the creation of a package holiday and use examples to describe how each department's main functions are carried out. Within the leaflet make certain that you cover the five main areas of a tour operator:
Planning
Selling
Administration
In Resort Operations
(P3+P4)

12.4 *Be able to plan and cost a package holiday*

PLANNING

Accommodation

The type of accommodation booked and the method used by the tour operator to contract the hotel has a direct impact on the cost of the holiday. Although guaranteed contracting obtains the cheapest price per night, tour operators who use it for many of their holidays will seek to cover the costs of empty rooms and may not pass on all of the savings made to the customers. Accommodation upgrades, sea or pool views and the board basis chosen by the customer will also affect the price of the holiday. These additional charges will be listed in the brochure.

Excursions – included and optional

Excursions are not normally included in the cost of a standard brochure package holiday. They are sold to customers by resort representatives on arrival in the resort. If the customer is booking a tour, for example, a long-haul coach trip, then some excursions may be included in the price.

Additional services

A tour operator offers a range of different services to their customers. These services can be either booked in the resort or they can be booked before departure. Pre-bookable pre-departure additional services include offering customers the option to pay an additional fee to ensure seats together on the plane, pre-bookable excursions, private transfers, car hire and travel insurance. In-resort additional services mainly include booking excursions and car hire.

COSTING A PACKAGE HOLIDAY

Load factors

Not all aircraft used by the tour operator will be full to capacity on every flight. Therefore, a tour operator weighs up the cost of the seats that it expects to sell in order to cover the potential losses incurred from any empty seats and any empty journeys that the plane is required to make in order to re-position the planes at the start and end of the season. This is called load factor and involves calculating the percentage of seats that have to be sold in order for the tour operator to break even over the season.

Mark-up and profit margins

To stay in business, a tour operator must make a profit from its holidays. For this reason, the company adds a profit margin to the costs of the packages and also includes a 10% commission payable to the travel agents. The standard mark-up is around 35%, although this is sometimes raised during high season and might be lowered for new destinations and during low season. Tour operators that participate in market skimming pricing may have a substantially larger mark-up.

Currency conversion

The costs of exchanging currency and changes in exchange rates also need to be considered when costing the holiday. Some tour operators agree a fixed exchange rate that is valid for all payments throughout the season to their overseas suppliers. Other companies buy large amounts of currency when the exchange rate is good for use when the exchange rate is bad. This is called hedging.

Fixed costs

Tour operators' annual fixed costs are covered by the mark-up and holiday price. Costs include regular bills such as council tax, electricity and water bills, permanent staff salaries, the costs of bonding and the rent or mortgage on the offices.

Variable costs

Variable costs also need to be covered, although these are harder to predict and change depending on the size of the tour operator. Variable costs that require payment include resort staff, telephone charges and the costs of brochure production, advertising and promotion. In order to cost the holiday, the tour operator has to estimate their variable costs in advance.

PROFITABILITY

A tour operator aims to make the greatest possible amount of money from each holiday that it sells. It tries to do this in a number of different ways:

- using the correct contracting method for each hotel. This minimises both the amount of compensation paid for over-bookings and also tries to cut down on the number of empty rooms if a guaranteed property is not popular

- consolidating flights in order to cut down on the costs of flying empty planes

- hedging currencies or fixing exchange rates

- giving customers notice of planned changes to their holidays. The more notice given, the less compensation the tour operator has to pay the customer.

- owning their own travel agent in order to cut down on the amount of commission paid

- offering late deals that include guaranteed accommodation and existing flights, although these holidays may not make much profit, the tour operator can try to maximise sales elsewhere

- selling pre-departure services, such as flight upgrades, private transfers, excursions and car hire

- selling additional in-resort services, such as excursions and car hire.

CASE STUDY: COSTING A PACKAGE HOLIDAY TO CYPRUS

Based on a charter flight and basic 7 nights' holiday costing for 2 adults sharing.

Flight

The tour operator has paid £12,240 for 120 seats to Larnaca. This works out at £102.00 per seat if all seats are sold. However, the tour operator anticipates that only 90% of the seats will be sold, so it has to sell 108 seats in order to breakeven (90% of 120 is 108), therefore the cost per seat is £113.33 (£12,240 ÷ 108). The 109th seat onwards makes a profit for the tour operator.

Accommodation

Allocation and release contract at 40.00 Cypriot pounds per person per night on bed and breakfast basis, based on two people sharing. A fixed exchange rate was agreed at the start of the season. 0.85 Cypriot pounds = 1.00 Stirling, so the per night cost is £47.10, based on two people sharing a twin room.

Transfer cost

The cost of hiring a coach from the airport to the resort for return transfer is 250.00 Cypriot pounds per airport to resort. There are 54 seats on the coach, therefore the cost is 4.65 Cypriot pounds per person. Converted at the fixed exchange rate, this is £5.45 per person.

Tour Holidays

Cost per flight seat	113.33
Airport taxes	10.00
Accommodation 7 nights RB (7 × 47.10)	329.70
Transfer coach	5.45
Net cost of holiday	458.48
Travel agent commission 10%	45.85
Profit mark-up 35%	160.47
Total brochure price of basic holiday	664.80

Figure 12.16

CASE STUDY: COSTING A GROUP PACKAGE HOLIDAY TO PRAGUE

Based on a low-cost budget flight and 24 students in twin rooms on half-board basis for four nights.

Tour Holidays

Exchange rate Czech Republic Koruny to Pound Sterling: 43.00	
Flights inclusive of airport tax: £126.00 × 24	£3,024.00
Coach transfer from airport:	
CZK 5250.00 = £122.00 (one way)	£244.00 (return)

Accommodation

4 nights at 1560.00 CZK per room night (half-board)	
Per room per night:	£36.28
12 rooms = £435.35 × 4	£1741.39
Grand City Guided walking city tour	
890 CZK per person = £20.70 per person × 24	£496.80
Coach tour and entrance to Terazin concentration camp	
1000 CZK per person = £23.26 × 24	£558.24
River boat cruise	
750 CZK per person = £17.44 × 24	£418.56
Evening ghost tour	
130 CZK per person = £3.02 × 24	£72.48
Jewish Cemetery and tour of Jewish Quarter	
750 CZK per person = £17.44 × 24	£418.56
Net total 7,010.31	
Mark-up 35% (includes fixed and variable costs)	£2,453.61
Total cost	£9,464.22
Price per person	£394.35

Figure 12.16

EVIDENCE ACTIVITY

P5 – M3

1. Now you have explained to the new company owners how a holiday is made, you must next provide them with an example. You need to create a specific package holiday, for example an educational residential visit or a holiday that could be published in a holiday brochure. You should include:

a) a description of the planned holiday

b) the costings of your package holiday identifying where you have added mark ups, load factors and commission payments. (P5)

2. The new company are very keen to make a profit and so in order to complete this example you must identify specific ways that the tour operator could maximise their profits on the tour that you have created, for example currency exchange and cancellation charges. (M3)

Work experience in the travel and tourism industry

unit 21

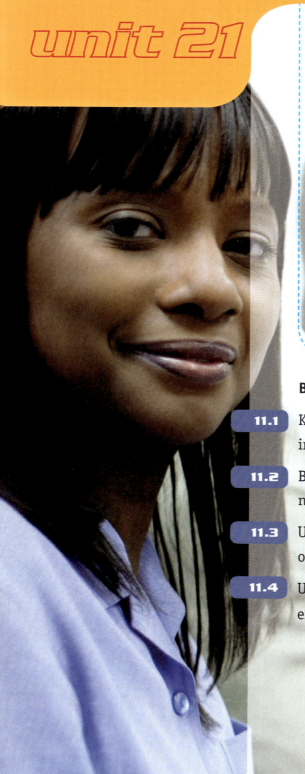

During this course you will have the opportunity to experience working in the travel and tourism industry. Ideally, you will have at least 60 hours of work experience. This should help you to see how suitable your skills and personality are to the industry and give you a chance to make contacts for your future career.

You will need to carry out your own research to find potential placements. This may even include attending an interview. Before starting work experience, you will have to set your own objectives and find out as much about the organisation as possible while working there. You need to keep a log during the work experience as you will have to present your experiences after the placement period. You will also need to evaluate your own performance and any benefits that you have obtained.

By the end of this unit, you will:

11.1 Know how to prepare for a work experience placement in the travel and tourism industry — page 147

11.2 Be able to demonstrate your skills, qualities and behaviour needed for effective performance in the workplace — page 155

11.3 Understand the nature of the chosen work experience organisation — page 159

11.4 Understand the factors contributing to an effective work experience placement. — page 167

So you want to be a...

Human Resource Manager

My name Luisa Nadal

Age 26

Income £28,000

If you are an organised and approachable people-person then Human Resources could be the career for you...

What do you do?

I need to ensure that the company employs the right balance of staff in terms of skills and experience and that training and development opportunities are available to employees to enhance their performance while achieving the organisation's objectives. In reality, it's a lot more than that. I deal with problems, disputes, angry managers and even angrier staff. It makes me want to smile, but I can't. It wouldn't be professional!

How did you get the job?

I was already a member of the Chartered Institute of Personnel and Development when I studied for my first professional qualification alongside my degree in Travel and Tourism. I was lucky enough to see a great job in my final year at university and the company was happy to wait for me to join after my finals. I was ideally suited, I guess, with a degree in travel and tourism, a CIPD qualification and I picked all of the human resource course options I could in my second and third year of the degree.

How did you find your current job?

The People Management magazine is a great place to look for full-time jobs. You can search the jobs database, just like other online job search websites and even look for jobs in the ideal pay ranges, too.

What training did you get?

Not much yet, as I'm more qualified than a couple of people who work with me. I'm hoping to study some more with the CIPD and maybe do a part-time or an open learning Master's Degree at some point. I had two weeks of induction training when I started and there are regular day and half-day in-house training programs to keep you up-to-date on stuff like employment law.

What about the perks?

The big perks are the cheap, often free, holidays. You get to try out new resorts and hotels. You have to fill in lots of forms and questionnaires, but its great going to a five-star, all-inclusive resort in Jamaica for the cost of a cheap flight to Paris.

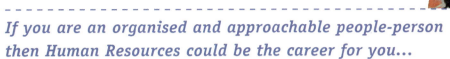 **"The big perks are the cheap, often free, holidays"**

What about the future?

I like the company, my boss and the people I work for, so I suppose I'm here for the long haul. This is my second year here and my pay has gone up by around £2,000 each year after my appraisal with the boss. She's on nearly £60,000, but she's responsible for the whole travel group and its 2,300 employees. That would frighten me at the moment, but that is what I aspire to .

Grading criteria

The table below shows what you need to do to gain a pass, merit or distinction in this part of the qualification. Make sure you refer back to it when you are completing work so you can judge whether you are meeting the criteria and what you need to do to fill in gaps in your knowledge or experience.

In this unit there are 3 evidence activities that give you an opportunity to demonstrate your achievement of the grading criteria:

page 154   **P1, P2, M1, D1**

page 166   **P3, P4, M2**

page 168   **P5, M3, D2**

To achieve a pass grade the evidence must show that the learner is able to...	To achieve a merit grade the evidence must show that, in addition to the pass criteria, the learner is able to...	To achieve a distinction grade the evidence must show that, in addition to the pass and merit criteria, the learner is able to...
P1 Use different contacts and resources to identify and describe two potential work experience placements in the travel and tourism industry, taking constraints into account	**M1** Explain how two potential work experience placements could provide opportunities to meet personal, career and curriculum objectives	**D1** Analyse the career progression potential of roles within the chosen work experience organisation and from that organisation into other areas of the travel and tourism industry
P2 Prepare for work experience by completing relevant documentation and setting objectives for the placement	**M2** Demonstrate effective skills, qualities and behaviour in a work placement, explaining how work undertaken has contributed to the key activities of the placement organisation	**D2** Evaluate own performance during work experience and produce an action plan with justified recommendations for future personal development
P3 Undertake work experience, monitoring progress of activities, including skills used and adherence to code of conduct	**M3** Explain the factors that contributed to the success of the work experience placement and provide supporting evidence to demonstrate personal effectiveness throughout the placement	
P4 Describe the nature of the work experience organisation, including own roles and responsibilities		
P5 Describe factors that contribute to an effective work experience placement, including supporting evidence used to track this		

21.1 **Know how to prepare for a work experience placement in the travel and tourism industry**

POTENTIAL WORK PLACEMENT ORGANISATIONS

You may already have strong preferences or interests in the type of work that you would like to do in the travel and tourism industry. However, while studying this course, your choices may be somewhat limited due to your location and the location of potential work placement organisations. Your school or college may already have existing relationships with travel and tourism organisations or you may know people who currently work in the industry.

The following table should be viewed as a starting point for you to be able to identify likely work placement organisations in your immediate area. It is important to remember that most organisations belong to larger groups or associations and these are excellent places to begin your search as they will provide you with comprehensive lists of members.

Table 21.1 Finding the right tye of work experience organisation

Type of work experience organisation	Associations or groups with comprehensive lists of members
Travel agent	The Association of British Travel Agents' website has a search function (www.abta.com). You can search by postcode, town or city or specialism.
Tourist Information Centres	A good place to begin to look for Tourist Information Centres is www.information-britain.co.uk/tic.cfm. Every English, Scottish and Welsh county or area has its own dedicated page with a comprehensive list of all TICs in that region, along with addresses and contact details.
Tour companies	Tour companies offer ready-made, usually specialist holidays, such as overland adventures. Useful places to begin your search are www.travel-quest.co.uk and www.thetravellerslounge.co.uk.
Tour operators	The Association of Independent Tour Operators (www.aito.co.uk) has 160 members. A full list of all members can be found at the bottom of the home page. Tour operators that run specifically British based services can be found at www.britainexpress.com. The Federation of Tour Operators tends to have members like the larger operators, such as British Airways and Cosmos (www.fto.co.uk). Selecting 'Resources' on the homepage and then selecting 'FTO members' from the drop-down menu finds their membership list.
Transport operators	A quick way of finding out the contact details for transport operators in your local area is to use your borough or county council website. This will have a full list, primarily of public transport or approved transport operators. The Guild of British Coach Operators has a full listing of members at www.coach-tours.co.uk. National Rail enquiries at www.nationalrail.com have a list of train operators, which can be accessed by selecting 'Train companies and maps' from the homepage toolbar and then selecting the 'Train operating company index'. Most airlines have their own websites and they also have potential opportunities at each of their transport hubs. For ferry operators, visit www.directferries.co.uk and select the 'Ferry operators' tab on the homepage.

CONTACTS

Contacts are any possible source of information or lead that could help you to find a work experience placement. You should leave no stone unturned in your search for a suitable placement and it is important to remember that there are several potential contacts who may have strong links with the travel and tourism industry. These people may be able to smooth your way into finding a suitable placement.

Your tutor will drive the work experience placement period or periods. They will be able to advise you with regard to the suitability of particular organisations and the likelihood of them taking students on for work experience. They will have had experience from previous years and possess a good idea of how the selection and application process works.

Be prepared to work as a member of a small group, pooling your resources, ideas and contacts. Travel and tourism organisations may be willing to take more than one placement.

Careers advisors are also very useful. While their primary role is to find full-time work, they will have established contacts in the travel and tourism industry and may personally know key managers or people working in the human resource departments of useful organisations.

Friends and family are also useful sources of information and contacts. They may know people who work for organisations in the travel and tourism industry. They could make enquiries on your behalf and find out who needs to be contacted in order to get a response from the business.

Direct contact with the human resource departments of travel and tourism businesses may also prove to be valuable. They may already have an ongoing policy with regard to work experience placements. They are probably in the strongest position to advise about the availability of placements and can liaise with particular departments or managers to gauge their reaction to your request.

Research tip

As a starting point, you might want to draw up a list of anyone you know who has even a remote connection with the travel and tourism industry.

Figure 21.1 Looking through books and magazines, searching on the internet and working with others are all good ways to find contacts

OTHER RESOURCES

It is highly unlikely that a travel and tourism organisation will actively advertise for work experience candidates. However, advertisements which are not just for current vacancies may provide you with useful leads. Advertisements for jobs imply that a business is expanding and that it may be in a position to offer a placement. Look through suitable newspapers that carry job advertisements or features related to the travel and tourism industry. There are also a number of trade magazines, which not only have job advertisements, but also information on trends and the type of work carried out by particular organisations.

Figure 21.2 The careers page on the Cosmos website is regularly updated

Research tip

A good place to look for potential magazines is www.mediauk.com/magazines. It also has a directory of all local, regional and national newspapers.

Example

The tour operator, Cosmos is an ideal example (www.cosmos.co.uk). By scrolling to the bottom of the homepage, there is a link to careers. It includes listings of the types of work available, current vacancies, useful links and contact details.

Your school or college may have a dedicated department that deals with work experience placements. They may have already set up an employer database, which includes all organisations that have previously taken or promised placements to students. It is important to remember that organisations do not want to be overwhelmed with enquiries about work placements and initial contact may be undertaken by your centre's own staff before the details are passed on to you.

You will already be aware of many of the websites related to the travel and tourism industry. It is valuable to look at the websites of particular organisations. Some have specific areas relating to working for the organisation. They may even have a page devoted to their policy on work experience.

The government run service, JobCentre Plus aims to assist people in finding full or part-time work and preparing them for work. They also have a website (www.jobcentreplus.gov.uk). This service has close and continued contact with most employers in a particular area. They may be able to give you valuable assistance in finding a suitable work placement and they may also be able to help you in finding seasonal or part-time work.

CONSTRAINTS

Many centres set aside a specific block of time for work experience. As far as this unit is concerned, you are expected to have at least 60 hours of work experience. The primary options are to do this in a block of two or three weeks, undertake the work at weekends or in the evenings or to arrange a placement during the holidays. For the last three options, you are more likely to be able to find part-time or seasonal paid work, which could be a distinct advantage.

As with any type of work, there are a number of constraints, which could mean that even the most attractive placement is not viable.

Location

The location of your work placement is very important. Ideally, it should be within easy travelling distance from your home or you should arrange to stay with friends or family in order to take advantage of the placement. There are some amazing work experience opportunities, but the very best ones expect you to pay for the privilege of working there.

Example

On the website www.gapyear.com, you could have two weeks work experience in China at the museum that houses the Terracotta Warriors for £1,295 plus flights and visas.

Transport access

Your centre might pay for any transport costs in getting to your work placement. However, you need to check to see whether it is feasible for you to get to the location at the required times. When considering transport methods, always bear in mind the risk of delays if you are using public transport. You should always investigate alternative routes in case there is a problem with your main mode of transport.

Travelling time

You do not wish to arrive at your work experience placement exhausted after a long or difficult journey. It is important to be sensible about travelling time and be realistic as to how long it will actually take, particularly considering that you may be travelling during the rush hour. It is a good idea to have a practice journey before you begin your placement, which will help to identify how long it will take and also to pick up on any potential travel problems.

> **Think** You may have an ideal placement in mind, but the location is difficult for you to get to. Are the disadvantages outweighed by the potential benefits of pursuing the placement as an option?

Hours of work

As a service-based industry, travel and tourism businesses often operate unsocial hours. You might not begin at 9am and finish promptly at 5pm. This is particularly true if you are opting for evening, weekend or holiday work. You are likely to be doing the hours that regular staff are unhappy or unable to do on a regular basis. **Shift work** may be a possibility.

Personal commitments

It is important to consider your personal commitments. There may be a range of these, including:

- work you may have to carry out for other units of this course

- existing part-time work

- family or carer commitments

- child care commitments

- other domestic commitments.

You need to take your personal commitments into account before accepting a work placement that may cause you any problems or concerns.

Key words

Shift work – working non-standard hours, such as beginning at 12 noon and finishing at 8pm

COMPLETE DOCUMENTATION

You will need to show evidence that you have completed any relevant documentation as an integral part of the assessment of this unit. It is highly unlikely that you will be able to secure a placement simply by making a telephone call or having an informal chat. With many students looking for placements, the most popular businesses have set procedures for dealing with applications and selecting the best potential candidates. This section looks at the different types of documentation that you may have to complete and retain copies of for your evidence.

Letter of enquiry

A letter of enquiry is a simple and straightforward letter, asking about the availability or possibility of a work placement. This can be fairly standardised, but should include the following information:

- your name and address

- the course you are studying

- your place of study

- your personal contact details and those of your tutor

- the ideal period for the placement

- a brief outline of the employer's role that has to be played in order for you to gather your evidence.

You may wish to use a **mail merge** in order to create several letters of enquiry, which you can send out at the same time. Make sure that you liaise with your tutor or your centre's work experience department to ensure that you are not sending a letter of enquiry to a business that other students have already approached. Make sure that you check the letter of enquiry thoroughly for spelling and grammar. It is also good practice to include a self-addressed envelope, so that the business can easily reply to your enquiry. Above all, make sure that you send enquiry letters several weeks before you intend to begin your work placement period.

Key words

Mail merge – creating a standard letter, with fields, allowing you to bring in names and addresses from either another document or a database

Letter of application

Some job advertisements ask the applicants for a letter of application along with a CV. Some businesses like letters of application to be handwritten. Letters of application should include the following:

- an opening paragraph that states where you saw the advertisement

- why the job appeals to you

- why you are applying for the job

- a summary of your main strengths, stressing your suitability for the job

- your enthusiasm for working in the travel and tourism industry

- when you are available for interview and when you could start the job.

The letter of application should be short, to the point and in a standard format for a business letter. The letter of application gives the candidate a chance to stress the key points in their CV or application form. It gives the business an opportunity to see a candidate's real writing skills and, in the case of handwritten work, a company may decide to analyse the handwriting.

CV

A curriculum vitae (CV) is a condensed life history. It contains various sections and should be short, but as complete as possible. The main information required of an applicant can be found in Unit 6, page 51.

It is important for CVs to be kept up-to-date. They may need to be adapted for different job applications. One of the major problems with CVs is that there is no commonly adopted format. They can appear in all kinds of designs and length and there is little agreement even as to the order of the sections or their headings.

It is therefore difficult to compare applicants' CVs as there might not be any common elements. CVs are nearly always typed or word-processed. This makes it difficult for the business to assess the communication skills of the applicant. Unless instructed otherwise by the advertising business, a CV should never be sent alone. It should always be accompanied by a letter of application.

Interview checklist

Interviews are an important form of face-to-face communication. It is reasonably likely that a job application will lead to an interview. Many interviews are quite formal and the candidate, or the interviewee, is interviewed by a panel of interviewers. The interview itself has two main purposes:

1) to give the organisation an opportunity to choose the right employee

2) to help the candidate decide whether or not the organisation is right for them.

The interview may be the only opportunity for representatives of the organisation to see a candidate before making a decision about who will be offered the job. They need to find out as much about the candidate as possible. The interview also gives the candidate the opportunity to find out about the organisation.

Less formal interviews also take place, sometimes on a one-to-one basis. The most important point is that all candidates are interviewed in the same way, regardless of what type of interview is used. Everybody should have an equal chance to prove that they would be ideal employees.

The assumption is that, no matter what type of interview is being carried out, the interviewees have all been checked to see that they at least meet the basic requirements for the job. It is possible that some of the interview panel members will have already looked at the applications and taken part in the **short-listing** process.

The interview is therefore designed to see whether a candidate that looks good on paper is actually good in real life. Candidates may have the skills, experience and qualifications, but they may not be the kind of person that would fit well in the business.

Key words

Short-listing – the process of selecting the best candidates who are then offered an interview

It is wise to find out as much as possible about the organisation prior to the interview, including:

- the nature of the organisation

- its products and services

- the markets in which the organisation is involved

- its typical customers

- its obvious competitors.

This information may be obtained from **company reports**, articles in the press, libraries or the organisation's website.

Key words

Company reports – the full title is Annual Reports and Accounts. These provide a summary of the activities and financial results for the shareholders of a company

Other pre-interview preparation could include:

- working out the most reliable and direct route to the organisation's offices and testing the route beforehand

- listening to the radio on the day of the interview to find out if there are any transport problems

- choosing suitable clothes to wear to the interview

- allowing enough travelling time to allow for any possible delays

- in the event of arriving early, not going into the building more than 10 to 15 minutes before the expected arrival time.

Any candidate that is preparing questions for an interview should take the following into account:

- ensure that the questions are clear and have been understood

- ensure that the questions are not repeating what has already been said

- do not ask questions that may be misunderstood as being sarcastic or cynical in tone

- try not to be funny

- ask the questions at the appropriate time

- never interrupt an interviewer, but wait for a natural pause or ask the questions when invited to do so.

The general rule is to make statements that are unambiguous and easy to understand. Regardless of the nature of the question, time should be taken to consider what is being said.

Remember that the interview time is restricted, so it is better to give clear and concise responses to questions asked by the interviewer and to ask any questions clearly, so as not to waste time.

Acceptance of offer

If you have attended an interview and are happy with the work placement offer, then you should verbally accept it at the time. Even if this is the case, you should follow up your verbal acceptance with a formal acceptance of the offer. This should simply restate what has been agreed and the fact that you will be attending at an agreed time on the agreed date.

You must make sure that you confirm your acceptance, no matter how the offer of the placement has been made. If you find yourself in the fortunate position of having more than one placement offer, immediately contact your tutor or centre, so that they can explore the possibility of passing the placement on to someone who has been less fortunate in their applications.

SET OBJECTIVES

An important part of this unit is to set a series of objectives for the placement. This effectively means setting out realistic skill or career development goals. On the other hand, it may simply be a question of collecting sufficient evidence for your assignment work.

The objectives must be realistic. If you manage to exceed the expectations of your objectives, it will be a considerable bonus and may give you the chance to take advantage of any opportunities that have arisen.

> *Think* Why is it important to be realistic about your objectives? How might high expectations lead to possible difficulties and frustration?

Personal

Any type of work experience gives you the opportunity to develop new skills. These may be dealing with customers for the first time, prioritising work, acting on instructions or following company procedures. You should identify a number of skills that you would like to develop and aim to have opportunities to do this throughout the placement.

Career

The work placement may be your first real experience of working in the travel and tourism industry. Use the opportunity to gain knowledge not just about the business you are working for, but the industry in general. You will encounter a number of people who can give you valuable advice about your future career. You will also meet people who may prove to be valuable contacts in the future after you have completed your studies and are looking for work.

Above all, the placement will give you an opportunity to gain experience. It will move you closer towards finishing your qualification and provide you with potential references when you apply for work. It is also important to remember that you should include the work placement on your CV and mention it in any future job applications.

Curriculum

The focus on this unit is on work experience. It includes the process of identifying and gaining a placement, showing a range of skills, qualities and behaviours, understanding as much as possible about the business and the industry and knowing how to make the best of the experience. At every opportunity, you should collect evidence by keeping your own records, obtaining feedback and encouraging your new work colleagues to provide you with witness statements.

EVIDENCE ACTIVITY

P1 – P2 – M1 – D1

You are expected to carry out at least 60 hours of work experience. This could either be in a block, at weekends, evenings or during holiday periods.

1. Identify two potential work placements. (P1)

2. Describe the type of organisation and potential roles you could fulfil. (P1)

3. Identify any constraints, in terms of issues such as location, access and travel time. (P1)

4. Provide evidence that you have obtained details for these potential placements from a variety of different sources. (P1)

5. Complete a letter of enquiry and application, as well as producing an up-to-date CV, interview checklist and letter of acceptance. (You will only need to do this for one work placement position.) (P2).

6. Ensure that your documents are suitable for sending out to a potential employer. (P2)

7. Set appropriate objectives for your placement. (You will need to identify key objectives for each of personal, career and curriculum.) (P2)

8. Choose two of your potential placements and explain how these would best provide you with the opportunity to meet the objectives that you have set out in task 7. (M1)

9. Analyse the potential progression routes and comment on how good the progression prospects are, both within the organisation and within the industry as a whole. (D1)

21.2 *Be able to demonstrate the skills, qualities and behaviours needed for effective performance in the workplace*

CODE OF CONDUCT

Codes of conduct are sets of expected skills, qualities and behaviours that you need to demonstrate during your work placement period. Many of them are standard qualities and behaviours that are expected of you in full-time work. As a student on work placement, you will be expected to follow the company's own code of conduct and to fall in line with expected behaviour.

Good timekeeping and attendance

It is an essential part of any placement to ensure that you arrive in good time, so that you are available during your agreed hours. If you have had the opportunity to test the transport and travel time to your placement, this should not present any great problems.

Your attendance also needs to be as full as possible for two main reasons:

1) Extended absence during your work placement does not give you the opportunity to fully experience all aspects of the placement and meet your set objectives. You will not have the chance to collect the evidence you need to cover the assessment of this unit.

2) Your employer may become frustrated with prolonged absence and may be less cooperative, both with you and with future students seeking placements with the organisation.

Demonstration of honesty and reliability

Regular timekeeping and attendance is a demonstration of reliability. This may be your first opportunity to acquire a meaningful reference and you need to ensure that you are both honest and reliable.

Honesty extends to accepting responsibility for mistakes and stating if you do not understand an instruction, rather than trying to muddle through and cause extra difficulties. You may have to handle money in certain circumstances and you will be accountable for it.

Reliability means ensuring that others are confident that a task will be completed to the necessary standards when they have given you a job to do. Reliability also refers to being in the right place at the right time and doing the work that has been assigned to you.

Accepting authority

Regardless of any permanent employee status at your work experience organisation, you should accept other people's seniority. They will have far more experience of doing the job and you may be able to learn a great deal from them, provided that you accept their authority. Obviously there are clearer lines of authority in an organisation, such as supervisors or managers. In all cases, you should accept their position and their right and responsibility to instruct you and discipline you when necessary.

Responding to instructions and accepting responsibility

These are two integral parts of being reliable and honest. If you are asked to carry out a particular task to a particular standard by a specified time, you should make sure that you achieve this. Make sure that you understand precisely what is being asked of you and set out to complete the task, following the instructions that have been given.

There may be cases when responsibility is delegated to you to carry out a task on someone else's behalf. This means you will be given the authority to complete the task and to make any necessary decisions. You should take these opportunities whenever they arise as they are valuable in gaining new skills, knowledge and experience.

Adhering to dress code

You may be issued with a uniform that you will have to wear during your placement. Uniforms are important because they form part of the company's image. It also makes it easier for customers to identify employees and seek help. It also means that everyone will arrive at work looking smart and well presented.

Men may have to wear shirts and ties, while it may be expected that females wear skirts. Sometimes there will be strict rules about hair, jewellery, nail varnish or the wearing of safety equipment. All of this will depend on the type of work and the specific dress codes of the company. You may have to wear a name tag or carry a pass with you for security reasons.

Please ensure that you are always smartly turned out for work and that your appearance meets with the requirements of the company by following the guidelines below:

- Please wear the company shirt provided (blazer optional)
- Ensure that it is not creased or dirty
- Male members of staff should wear smart black trousers
- Female members of staff should wear smart black trousers or black skirt (below the knee)
- Male member of staff should wear black shoes
- Female members of staff are expected to wear black shoes and are also permitted to wear conservative black heels, but no stilettos, etc
- No trainers
- Please refrain from wearing excessive jewellery
- Please wear your name tag at all times

Figure 21.3 Some placements may have a strict dress code

Although it may seem alien to you to dress as if you were attending a wedding or a funeral, adhering to the dress code makes you stand out less and helps you to fit into the working environment. It also proves to the employer and your new colleagues that you are taking the work experience seriously and that you value the opportunity they have given you.

Using appropriate language and being courteous

Although you will not be expected to know all of the jargon, key terms, shorthand or the names of all members of staff immediately, you should ensure that you try to use appropriate language at all times. This means avoiding the use of slang, swear words and **colloquialisms**. Using the appropriate language is important to help you fit into the situation, even if the working environment may seem unusual to you.

It is important to remember that the employer and your new work colleagues may be giving up their own time and putting off their own work in order to assist you. It is therefore important to be courteous and grateful for their assistance and to treat them in the same way as you would expect others to behave towards you.

This also extends to customers or visitors to the business. There may be recommendations as to how to address these individuals and you should make sure that you look at any company policies or procedures, if possible, and follow them at all times. It might be useful to look at Unit 4, Book 1 as a guide to dealing with customers in most situations.

Key words

Colloquialisms – words or phrases that you use when talking to your friends, but should not use in a business situation, such as 'know what I mean' or 'hang on'

Adhering to rules and procedures

There are various rules and procedures that you are expected to follow during your placement. Some are company specific, such as how to deal with customers, how to answer the telephone or the layout of a business letter. Others may relate to more potentially serious situations, such as health and safety, hygiene or security of information.

This does not necessarily mean that the working environment is a dangerous place. Rules and procedures are put in place in order to avoid accidents or misunderstandings between employees or between employees and customers. If you are ever unsure about the rules and procedures, you should ask your immediate supervisor or manager for assistance.

DEMONSTRATION OF SKILLS

During your placement you will have an opportunity to demonstrate a wide range of skills. It is vital that you note any of these as and when they arise. If possible, you should support your demonstration of the skills by either generating written evidence or asking for feedback or witness statements. Always make sure that you note down your use of skills in a diary or log book. These are valuable tools to support your evidence. The following table outlines the kinds of skills that you may need to demonstrate during your placement.

Table 21.2 The skills that you may need to demonstrate during your placement

Skill	Explanation
Social	The working environment is a social situation in which you are expected to interact with others. This gives you an opportunity to demonstrate your communication skills.
Technical	Many job roles in the industry require the use of standard computers with industry-specific software. Other companies may use particular equipment or machinery, which will give you an opportunity to broaden your technical skills.
Problem solving	You are often given tasks to complete that require a degree of problem solving in order to figure out how best to tackle the job. Problem solving is an important part of work and requires you to think through the possible options and select the most appropriate one for the situation.
Action planning	Preparing for a work placement is an example of action planning, but in the placement itself you will often have a number of tasks to complete at the same time and you will need to organise and prioritise, as well as plan your time. These are all important skills in action planning.
Self-motivation	You cannot expect to be supervised throughout the entire work placement period. There will therefore be times when you are left to carry out work alone. You should not take this opportunity to wander off, but stick to the tasks in hand and show that you are reliable and have the will and enthusiasm to complete work without supervision.
Customer care	Your placement may involve daily or occasional contact with customers. You should follow the company's procedures in dealing with customers and try to broaden your experience in handling a variety of different customer care situations.
Research	Not all tasks or duties can be easily completed without finding out more information. It is unlikely that you will be expected to complete a task without access to information, so you will need to know where the data can be found and how to use it. Research skills are very valuable and if carried out correctly can avoid mistakes being made in decision-making.
Presentation	Presentation can be understood in two different ways: your own personal presentation in terms of appropriate dress and behaviour or your ability to feedback information or report on a situation or give details of information you have researched.

Research tip

Look at Level 3 Key Skills, particularly for 'improving own learning and performance', as well as 'working with others'. These will give you some valuable leads as to the type of evidence you will be expected to generate.

MONITORING PROGRESS

There are three ways in which your progress will be monitored during your work placement. It is vital to ensure that you set aside time and effort to make sure this is carried out as it will provide you with invaluable evidence for this unit. It will also prove to be valuable to your work placement employer and your tutor in terms of judging you and assessing the value of the experience for everyone.

Keeping own records

The ideal ways in which to monitor your progress are to keep either a diary or a log book. You should try to set aside time every day in order to keep this up-to-date. Note down any time you have demonstrated particular skills or when you have had the opportunity to develop them or gained knowledge or experience.

The primary responsibility for monitoring progress lies with you and you will have the most complete record of your progress. You cannot expect either your placement employer or your tutor to keep these records for you. They may need to refer to your own records.

Employer feedback

Your teacher or tutor will give you a number of employer feedback forms. These will prompt the employer to answer specific questions about your demonstration of skills and your progress throughout the placement. Your supervisor, manager or placement work colleagues will be best placed to judge whether you have demonstrated particular skills and whether you have made any progression during the placement. These are valuable objective documents, which will provide useful supporting evidence in order for you to meet the grading criteria for this unit.

Tutor review

Your tutor will visit your work placement company periodically throughout your placement. They will have an opportunity to talk with you and to have discussions about your skills and progress with your supervisor, manager or colleagues. At that point, they will be in a position to feedback comments and suggestions in order to help you frame the rest of the placement period and fill in any skills gaps or improve your performance in a particular way.

At the end of the placement period, a longer and more formal review will take place. This seeks to identify your experiences of the placement and identify your strengths and weaknesses. These are derived from your own records, feedback from the employer and the previous tutor reviews.

Think In order to make the best use of the tutor review, what preparation will you need to have made? What documents and evidence will you need to assemble before each review?

21.3 Understand the nature of the chosen work experience organisation

ORGANISATION

It is difficult to predict the nature of the organisation in which you will be carrying out your work experience. You may already be aware, in the broadest sense, of the type of organisation and its main areas of activity. You need to be able to describe various features about your chosen work experience organisation. In this section, we look at how to collect that information and identify key characteristics.

Figure 21.4 Framlingham Castle

Type

Broadly speaking, the work placement organisation will be one of the following:

- a travel agent

- a Tourist Information Centre

- a tour company

- a tour operator

- a transport operator

- an attraction

- a historical site

- a museum

- an entertainment or exhibition venue

- an ancillary service provider.

It should be a relatively easy task for you to identify the type of organisation, but be aware that some organisations may be more than one of the above.

Example

The National Trust's Framlingham Castle in Suffolk is a tourist attraction and historical site. It is a museum, shop and restaurant, as well as containing other tourist facilities.

Ownership

You are probably aware that organisations fall into one of two categories. They are either privately owned, in which case the name will tend to end with the letters Ltd (private limited company), or publicly owned, in which case the name ends with Plc (public limited company). A Plc may belong to the government, a government agency, a charity or a local authority.

Example

In the seaside town of Great Yarmouth, the Pleasure Beach (www.pleasure-beach.co.uk) is a private limited company. The local authority owns the Marina Centre (www.marina-centre.com). The Time and Tide Museum is owned by Norfolk Museums (www.museums.norfolk.gov.uk), which is a charity.

Sector

As far as sectors of the economy are concerned, the vast majority of travel and tourism organisations are in the service or tertiary sector. It is important to remember that the primary sector includes businesses that extract products from the earth, such as mines, quarries and forestry. The secondary sector is largely manufacturing.

Figure 21.5 In certain areas of the world where tourism is developing, forestry often clears the way for hotel construction

Size and number of employees

The size of an organisation can be judged in many different ways. These could include:

- the sales revenue or **turnover**

- the number and size of branches, head offices or buildings

- the number of towns, cities, resorts or destinations in which they operate

- the number of employees.

It does not necessarily follow that organisations with a small number of employees are counted as being small. These employees may generate a great deal of income for the business. It also means that organisations with a large number of employees

and branches may not be considered to be very big as they may not generate a great deal of income.

Another key way of measuring the size of an organisation is its influence on the marketplace itself. This is usually measured in the **market share** that the business possesses. Each particular market, such as package holidays, generates a certain amount of income for all the businesses that are involved. Market share measures the percentage of that total, which is generated by one business. The higher the percentage, the greater the market share.

> **Key words**
> ------------------------------------
> **Turnover** – the amount of income generated by an organisation during a financial year
> **Market share** – the percentage of the total income from a particular market that is controlled by a single business

ORGANISATION CHART

An organisation chart is a pyramid shaped diagram that looks rather like the roots of a tree. It is usually narrow at the very top and gradually broadens like a pyramid as one goes lower down an organisation. There are relatively few key decision-makers at the top of the organisation, but there is an increasing number of managers and supervisors further down the organisation, ending with the bulk of the employees at the bottom of the structure.

Figure 21.6 A typical organisation chart

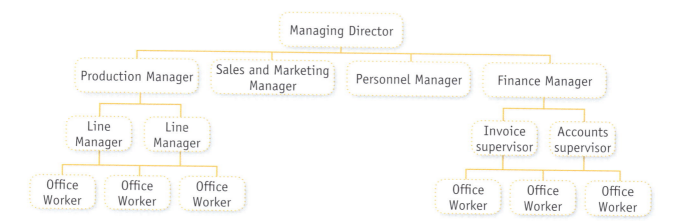

Type of structure

Not all organisations have multiple layers of management. Some can be described as being considerably flatter. The idea is for integrated work teams to be responsible for their own range of tasks and duties. A manager who directly reports to a more senior manager supervises them. Other organisations structure themselves into **functional** areas, supported by departments that work across the whole of the organisation.

Key words

Functional – part of the organisation responsible for a specific area of work provided by the business for its customers, for example, customer services

Example

A large tour operator may have a series of functional departments related to each of its brands. These departments concentrate on managing, promoting and selling products from the brand group. They are supported by an organisation-wide series of departments, including human resources, administration and accounts.

Line management and lines of communication

It should be possible to trace a line of authority and responsibility from your immediate supervisor or manager all the way up to the very top of the organisation. This line is a two-way communication and authority network.

The uppermost management in an organisation formulates broad instructions, policies and strategies. They pass these policies down the line through successive layers of management. These managers have to interpret the policies and strategies and turn them into workable instructions and solutions. As the instructions pass down the layers, they become more refined so that they eventually become very clear instructions to those who will carry out the policies on a day-by-day basis.

This is just one side of the lines of communication. Middle managers and senior managers would be unable to have a grasp of the day-to-day operations of the organisation without information being passed back up to them from the bottom of the organisation. It is the individuals who carry out day-to-day functions and have regular contact with customers that better appreciate the realities of the organisation's operations. By feeding back information through the successive layers of management, better decisions can be made and problems can be assessed and solved.

Think Your school or college will have clear line management and lines of communication. Try to identify this network and the successive layers of management and supervision.

KEY ACTIVITIES

It should be a relatively straightforward task to identify the key activities of your workplace organisation. However, it is important to emphasise that many organisations have several different key activities, which are integrated into overall packages provided to their customers.

Example

As part of the general easyJet brand, the key activity is selling airline seats for the various scheduled flights in easyJet's network. Other key activities provide additional products and services for customers to support and enhance the overall product offer. easyJet offers opportunities to purchase insurance, hire vehicles and book accommodation. It can also offer other ancillary services, such as parking and airport hotel accommodation and transfers.

The table on page 162 is by no means exhaustive, but it illustrates the typical key activities that may be present in your work experience organisation.

Table 21.3 Examples and descriptions of potential work experience organisations and their key activities

Key activity	Example and description
Tour operation	**Thomas Cook and Thomson** These companies provide whole integrated packages, as well as flight only and accommodation only options. They also offer a wide range of ancillary services, including currency exchange, car hire and insurance.
Sales	**Flightline and Freedom Direct** These are rather unfairly described as 'bucket shops'. They act as intermediaries between airlines and tour operators and customers. They can offer packages and flights, as well as accommodation from a huge variety of different suppliers. Their primary function is sales.
Providing accommodation	**Travelodge and Hilton Hotels** Not only do many of these accommodation providers offer short breaks for tourists, but they are also vital in the broader travel and tourism industry. They are often located at major transport hubs and provide packages, which include overnight accommodation and car parking. The range of accommodation is enormous, from room only through to all-inclusive and from the most basic accommodation to five-star luxury. They also offer a wide range of ancillary services, such as airport transfer and conference and meeting facilities
Marketing and promotion	**British Tourist Board and the English Tourist Board** These tend to be organisations that have a primary role in promoting and marketing all travel and tourism organisations and facilities in a given region or country. They are usually funded directly from central and local government. They also include Tourist Information Centres. All major travel and tourism organisations have marketing departments that are responsible for promoting products, services and brand names, both to customers and to the media.
Support services	**Post Office and Direct Line** These are just two examples of insurance support services. They provide ancillary products and services to support the travel and tourism industry. More generally, support services could include cleaning companies, catering suppliers, kennels and catteries and a host of other different indirectly related businesses.
Provision of information	**Tourist Information Centres and airline helpdesks** All organisations in the travel and tourism industry are providers of information. Customers need information in order to make a considered purchase. They may also need queries answered after the purchase has been made or during the use of the service that they have purchased. This is an integral part of an overall customer care package, which is of vital importance to all businesses in the industry.
Entertainment	**Theme parks, theatres and art galleries** Although we associate theme parks with being a major part of the travel and tourism industry, we often forget that tourists visit locations in order to attend the theatre, an art gallery or the cinema. They are all, broadly speaking, tourist attractions. They provide entertainment services and often offer a range of additional services, including food and drink, guides, printed brochures and ticketing.

PRODUCTS AND SERVICES

The key activities of your work experience organisation might be varied and encompass more than one major function. The key activity clearly determines the types of products or services offered by the organisation.

- Package holidays – offered by travel agents, tour companies, tour operators, airlines and 'bucket shops'.

- Insurance – either offered directly by the holiday provider or airline (usually in association with a named insurance company) or directly through a specialist insurance company.

- Conference services – this is an important area of the travel and tourism industry and revolves around major event venues all over the UK, including the NEC in Birmingham (www.necgroup.co.uk) or the Excel Centre in London (www.excel-london.co.uk) Conference services are also provided by most of the accommodation providers, including the Premier Travel Inn (www.premiertravelinn.com) and the Hilton Hotel International Group (www.hilton.co.uk).

- Accommodation – this is not solely provided by major hotel or motel chains. There are literally thousands of smaller bed and breakfast accommodation or guesthouses in the UK (www.bedandbreakfasts.co.uk).

- Support for businesses – many of the small to medium-sized travel and tourism organisations rely on a range of other businesses to ensure that they can continue to run their operations smoothly and efficiently. This includes computer support, cleaning, security, banking, building maintenance and insurance, as well as health and safety and transport.

- Transportation – there is a wide variety of established transportation networks, both in the UK and into and out of the country. Transportation includes air flights, coaches, ferries, rail (both overland and underground), buses, car hire and other specialist transportation, including canal boat and waterways boat hire (www.hoseasons.co.uk).

Figure 21.6 The Excel Cetnre in London hosts conferences and major events all year round

HEALTH AND SAFETY ISSUES

There are specific sections on health and safety as far as legislation is concerned, which are covered in other units. They will address the majority of situations in which you may find yourself during your work placement. It is important to remember that all businesses with employees and especially those whose premises are accessible to visitors or customers have to adhere to very strict government legislation.

Legislative and regulatory requirements

As a general rule, the most important health and safety legislation is the Health and Safety at Work Act (1974). The Health and Safety Executive are in charge of managing it (www.hse.gov.uk).

The Health and Safety at Work Act has been considerably refined over the years. It has also been the subject of additional regulations, as laid down by a number of different European Directives. All employers have a responsibility to provide their employees with a safe and healthy place in which to work. They must also ensure that there are secure working systems, so that employees can do their jobs safely.

Even as a student on work placement, you too will have responsibilities under the act:

- you must take reasonable care to preserve the health and safety of yourself and others who could be affected by your actions

- you must cooperate with your employer when operating any safety equipment or systems

- if you come across a hazardous situation, you must report it immediately to a responsible person

- you must never remove or interfere with any safety equipment or devices that have been put in place by the employer in order to comply with the legislation.

> **Think** In addition to health and safety, a work placement organisation has to have liability insurance. Why might the terms of this insurance make it difficult for them to offer a placement?

163

Policies and procedures in the workplace

All organisations have a series of policies and procedures in place, which detail recommended and safe ways of carrying out work. Organisations routinely carry out risk assessments that look at the workplace and the activities that take place there in order to identify hazards and risks. It is important to make the distinction between a hazard and a risk:

- a hazard is anything that has the potential to do harm to an individual

- each hazard is looked at in order to establish the likelihood of harm taking place. This harm is known as the risk.

It is usual for organisations to have policies and procedures in place that go beyond the basic legislative or regulatory requirements related to health and safety. You should familiarise yourself with these policies and procedures at the earliest opportunity as they may be considerably different from those at your school or college or at any other place where you have worked or studied.

Emergency procedures

Emergency procedures come into place when there is a major problem in the workplace, such as a fire. If a fire is discovered, you should operate the nearest alarm call point. Do not attack the fire unless you are absolutely confident that you can deal with it using appliances that are available.

You should leave the area immediately if you hear an alarm, making sure that any fire doors are closed. The building will have arrows that show you the nearest escape exit. Never use lifts or go back to collect your personal belongings. You should make sure that you know where your designated assembly point is located outside the building. Never re-enter the building without being given explicit instructions or permission to do so by your supervisor. If you have difficulties in using stairways, find out where the nearest **place of safety** is located. You should make sure that you read all of the fire notices in the building, which summarise the key fire or emergency procedures.

Key words

Place of safety – designed to act as a refuge point where there is a call point, so that you can contact someone who will assist you in evacuating the building

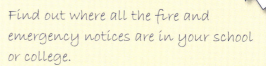

Research tip

Find out where all the fire and emergency notices are in your school or college.

Think Do you know where all the assembly points are in the different areas of your school or college?

Security in the workplace

Security falls into four major categories:

- Losses to the company – these include thefts, suspicious activities, property accidents and other crimes. You should usually report any of these directly to your supervisor, who will contact a designated individual responsible for liaising with the local police.

- Personal losses – these are crimes, suspicious activities or property accidents that personally affect your own belongings. You should follow the same procedure as losses to the company.

- Property security – larger organisations have their own security, which extends to building access, fire codes, traffic regulations and the grounds surrounding the buildings and parking areas.

- Building access control – many businesses now use key codes or swipe cards in order to restrict access to particular buildings or rooms in buildings. As a temporary member of staff, you will only be given the codes needed to allow you to access buildings or rooms where you are based. You must keep these codes or cards in a safe place and act responsibly.

Security also includes access to company information. Businesses that hold information about customers are required to keep it secure under the terms of the Data Protection Act. This means that customer information will have limited access by the use of passwords and codes.

OWN ROLE

In order for your tutor or teacher (and later on the Edexcel representative who looks at your portfolio) to understand your role during the placement, it is important to give as much detail as possible about your duties, responsibilities and reporting structure. It is a major part of the basic grading criteria for you to describe your own roles and responsibilities, as well as describing the nature of the work placement and your experiences.

Duties and responsibilities

In full-time work, you will have a job title and **job description**. These documents give precise details about your role in the organisation and what is expected of you in terms of duties and tasks. You will not have this luxury, especially if you are doing your work placement in a block. You may have access to a job title and job description if you are using part-time, weekend or holiday work as the basis for your evidence on work experience for this unit.

If you have a job title and a job description, they should provide sufficient evidence. If you do not have either of these, you should outline all of the main duties that you have performed throughout the placement and outline any responsibilities that have been passed to you by others. It may be possible for you to compare your role with that of a permanent member of staff and ask them for a copy of their job description to provide you with a basic list of duties and responsibilities.

Reporting structure

This simply means the individual or individuals to whom you are directly responsible. It could be a **mentor**, someone you are **shadowing**, a supervisor or a manager.

You should extend your description of the reporting structure beyond your immediate supervisor or manager. If you have already obtained a copy of the organisation chart, it will give you a clearer indication of the organisation's whole reporting structure.

> **Key words**
>
> **Job description** – a document that outlines the tasks, duties and responsibilities of a post and its holder
> **Mentor** – an individual assigned to you to act as a guide and assistant throughout your work placement
> **Shadowing** – accompanying a permanent member of staff and assisting them in their work, seeing the range of duties and responsibilities that they perform

» Job description

A tourism officer develops and promotes tourism in order to attract visitors and produce significant economic benefits for a particular region or site. Tourism officers often work for local authorities, but may also work within private companies or other public sector agencies.
The tourism industry covers a broad scope and so the role is varied and may include many different types of work. Key areas include marketing and the development of services and facilities.
Tourism is increasingly focused on economic development or urban and rural regeneration, particularly in local authorities. Tourism officers therefore usually work closely with the residents and businesses in a local community.

» Typical work activities

As well as maintaining visitor services and attractions, tourism officers are usually involved with strategic planning and development. Their work involves liaising with the public and with local and public agencies, and also a great deal of behind-the-scenes preparation and planning.

General aspects of the job include:

- responding to enquiries from members of the public;
- undertaking factual desk and market research with members of the public and visitors to particular attractions;
- providing a range of information on local resources and facilities;
- providing funding advice and sending email newsletters to local businesses;
- running training courses to encourage networking and economic growth in the tourism industry;
- giving talks to local parties, community groups, and schools, as requested.

Figure 21.8 A job description for a tourism officer

OTHER STAFF ROLES

In order to get a fuller picture of the overall structure and organisation of your work placement, it is important for you to note the nature of other staff roles. You are not necessarily expected to detail every staff role within the organisation. It is easier and more reasonable for you to focus on individuals with whom you have daily contact and those who carry out similar work to your own duties and responsibilities.

Duties and responsibilities

You would naturally expect individuals in more senior positions to have a wider range of duties and responsibilities. The ideal situation is to ask them either for a brief description of how they see their duties and responsibilities or to ask them whether they would be willing to give you a copy of their job description. By comparing a number of these, you will be able to assess the range of different duties and responsibilities. It will also help you when you look at progression opportunities.

Reporting structure

Looking at the organisation chart will give you an idea of the organisational and reporting structure of the organisation. Even the managing director of a company reports to others, such as the **shareholders**. Within the rest of the organisation, all staff, including supervisors, managers and **board members**, have someone that they must report to and receive instructions from.

> ### Key words
> **Shareholders** – individuals or other companies that own a part of a private or public limited company because they have bought shares
> **Board members** – senior managers appointed by the shareholders as key decision-makers in the business

Progression opportunities

The actual progression opportunities for employees can be very different to those on an organisation chart. Progression relies on a number of different factors including the abilities, skills and experience of an individual; the existence of a vacant, more senior job role and continued expansion by the company, requiring more senior posts to be filled.

EVIDENCE ACTIVITY

P3 – P4 – M2

These are activities that relate to your actual placement. They are designed so that you produce sufficient evidence of your successful placement.

1 Undertake your work placement and monitor the activities throughout. (P3)

2. Describe your activities and make sure that you mention the skills and behaviours that you have demonstrated. (Ideally recorded in a logbook.) (P3)

3. Provide sufficient records to facilitate feedback from your employer and tutor. (P3)

4. Describe the activities of the organisation, its products and services and any health and safety issues you may have come across. (P4)

5. Obtain or create an organisation chart. (If your work placement is in a large organisation then provide a chart simply of the department in which you worked.) (P4)

6. Describe your own role and responsibilities. Relate this to other employee roles and how they interlink, along with progression opportunities. (P4)

7. Produce a written report or give an oral presentation, supported by visual aids and witness statements. (P4)

8. Provide supporting evidence to confirm that you have been successful in completing your work placement. (M2)

9. Incorporate employer feedback and tutor review. (Your tutor will complete observation sheets and the employer witness statements.) (M2)

21.4 Understand the factors contributing to an effective work experience placement

FACTORS

The main consideration in this final part of the unit is for you to identify any factors that have contributed to an effective work experience placement and for you to generate or produce supporting evidence to back up your claims. Many of the potential factors affecting your placement have already been covered and others may have become apparent to you during the work placement. Broadly speaking, the factors that contribute to an effective placement will relate to skills and career development, as well as gaining new contacts for future employment.

Research tip

It is a good idea to prepare yourself for this evidence gathering exercise before you begin your placement. Put together a folder with plastic pockets and plenty of blank witness statements, observation records and employer feedback records. Prepare a blank attendance record and make sure you keep your diary and log book up-to-date. Set aside time each day to ensure this is completed.

Skills development

You may have had the opportunity to experience industry standard technical equipment, including hardware and software for the very first time during the placement. This represents a significant skills development. If you have completed work experience in a travel agency, you will have encountered the company's search and booking systems. Technical skills revolve around the use of machinery, software and other equipment.

Interpersonal skills may also have been developed during the placement. You will probably have been in situations where you have had to respond to questions, follow instructions, take part in discussions and deal with customers on a face-to-face basis. Where you have had the chance to use your communication skills, including non-verbal communication, your writing skills and developed your ability to work as a member of a team, you will also have developed valuable interpersonal skills.

Attendance and punctuality

Adhering to requested working hours and modes of attendance are important achievements and necessary requirements for future full-time work in the travel and tourism industry. You will be relied upon to attend your agreed work sessions at the appropriate time. This includes returning back to work from tea or lunch breaks. It may also involve having to work after hours if requested.

Behaviour in the workplace

Certain companies may have specific requirements with regard to dress code, honesty, reliability, the acceptance of authority and responding to instructions. In all dealings with work colleagues and especially with customers, you will have been expected to use appropriate language and to be courteous at all times. You will also have been expected to follow any specific rules, regulations, policies or procedures, as outlined by your supervisor or in the staff handbook.

Career aspirations and employment opportunity enhancement

If you were able to make a wise choice in your work experience placement, this could provide you with a vital springboard in terms of your career. At the very least, it may have identified an area of the travel and tourism industry in which you now do not wish to work. This is an equally valid view to take as the actual practice of doing a particular job may not always necessarily match the description or your perceptions of that type of work.

The placement should put you in a position where you can begin to make firm plans for future employment. You will have identified your key strengths and weaknesses and should now be in a position to make best use of your strengths and address your weaknesses before you complete the course.

In terms of employment opportunity enhancement, there is a strong possibility that you could acquire part-time or seasonal work with the organisation if you have made a sufficiently good impression during your placement. The company may even offer to keep you in mind when you successfully complete your course and offer you either a position or at least an interview.

Having displayed your existing range of skills and had the opportunity to receive feedback from your employer during the placement, you will have a clear idea as to how they view your present range of skills, attitudes and behaviours. This puts you in a stronger position to fit more easily into the organisation if a suitable vacancy arises.

Networking

For many students, work experience provides the first real taste of the working environment. It also provides an ideal opportunity to meet and interact with individuals working in the industry. All employees have a range of contacts and they could provide valuable connections with potential employers.

Any new contact should be welcomed and it may be an ideal opportunity for you to continue your contact with them, especially to remind them that you are actively seeking work at the end of the course.

Your work placement supervisor or manager will also be able to provide you with a suitable industry-related reference. This is invaluable for students who have not had any real work experience through part-time work as it provides a real life rather than academic reference.

EVIDENCE ACTIVITY

P5 – M3 – D2

You are required to make a presentation, identifying the key factors that contribute to an effective work experience placement.

1. Describe the factors that contribute to an effective placement. (Ideally this should be carried out prior to the placement and you should make direct references to your own objectives during the placement.) (P5)

2. Explain the aspects of the placement that were the most successful from your own point of view. (M3)

3. Mention any areas where your skills have been developed or any contacts that you have made that may be significant in the future. (M3)

4. State clearly how the factors have contributed to the success of the placement. (Bear in mind that you will need to link these to the objectives that you have already set.) (M3)

5. Identify your own strengths and weaknesses. (You should analyse whether you met your original objectives during the work placement.) (D2)

6. Identify what went well and what did not go so smoothly. (D2)

7. Produce a personal action plan in order for you to identify and develop your skill base and knowledge for your future career. (D2)

SUPPORTING EVIDENCE

In order to back up any claims you may make with regard to positive factors that have contributed to an effective placement, you will need to provide documented evidence. Table 21.4 briefly outlines the source and value of various types of supporting evidence.

Table 21.4 Types of supporting evidence

Type of supporting evidence	Source and description
Diary	Self-generated. This needs to detail the type of work that you have done on a particular day and may need to be cross-referenced to feedback records and witness statements.
Log book	Self-generated. Similar to the diary, but it could be specifically designed to list specific skills, codes of conduct and duties and tasks that have been carried out. This should be cross-referenced to feedback records and witness statements.
Employer feedback record	School or college-generated pro-forma document, completed by employer. This will detail how you have performed in your demonstration of particular skills from the employer's perspective and can also be invaluable in monitoring your progress, as well as outlining any of your duties and responsibilities during the placement.
Attendance record	Employer-generated (although this may be on a pro-forma document provided by your centre). This will be completed either weekly or at the end of the placement. You may have to enter the details yourself and then have them verified by your immediate supervisor or manager. This confirms your hours of work, punctuality and attendance.
Skills audit	Either centre or self-generated. This should be a comprehensive list of skills that are outlined in the specification for this unit. You should note down as many potential skills as possible and then detail any occasions where you have had the opportunity to demonstrate them. This can be used as a means of comparing your skill range before the placement and afterwards.
Witness statement	Centre-designed pro-forma document. It will be your responsibility to ask or prompt your work placement colleagues to complete witness statements, confirming that they have seen you demonstrate specific skills, carry out particular duties or taken on identified responsibilities. These will form a major part of your evidence, which you should cross-reference to your diary or log book and use as the basis for creating your post placement skills audit.

Current issues in travel and tourism

unit 26

Unit 26 is essentially a research and report project. The unit is designed to help you prepare for necessary research that you may have to do in higher education. The unit focuses on current issues, which are defined as those that have occurred during the past five years.

You will have encountered many different issues in the travel and tourism industry throughout the other units. This unit now gives you the opportunity to look at one of those issues in depth. You will need to develop your skills to carry out effective research. You also need to use current, accurate and relevant data and liaise with the industry to collect information.

You will be required to analyse the data and to present your findings in a clear and logical manner.

By the end of this unit, you will:

26.1 Understand methods that can be used to research a current issue affecting the travel and tourism industry   page 173

26.2 Be able to conduct research into a current issue affecting the travel and tourism industry, using appropriate resources   page 178

26.3 Be able to communicate findings on a travel and tourism issue using appropriate media and conventions   page 188

26.4 Understand the impacts of a current issue on the travel and tourism industry   page 194

So you want to be a...

Market Research Manager

My name Ivana Berkoff
Age 25
Income £23,000

Are you a person with a good head for numbers, who would feel confident both accumulating data and presenting it? Then take a look...

What do you do?

I collect and analyse market research information to help my company make informed decisions in the holiday package tour market.

What responsibilities do you have?

To design surveys and questionnaires, write and plan project proposals and conduct qualitative and quantitative surveys. I have also had to learn to use statistical software, so that I can look for patterns and solutions. I also create reports and often have to present these to key managers and board members.

How did you get the job?

I gained my BTEC National Diploma in Travel and Tourism and then I went on to university to study tourism and statistics. One of the main things is to be very numerate, pay attention to detail and have a creative streak when carrying out research.

How did you find your current job?

I actually saw the same job being advertised in a national newspaper and on the website www.totaljobs.com. That's just one of dozens of websites advertising jobs, but be careful because a lot of them only lead you to agencies rather than the business taking on the researcher.

> **"I gained my BTEC National Diploma in Travel and Tourism"**

What training did you get?

I was lucky enough to convince my company to let me do the British Market Research Bureau's Diploma in Research. I have also been on some professional training courses with the British Market Research Association and the Royal Statistical Society.

What are the hours like?

In theory, it's a standard 37-hour week. I'm not usually expected to work any weekends, but if there's a rush job on or people are late getting the research data to me, I tend to take it home and work on it, or I come into the office for an hour or two on Saturday mornings.

What skills do you need?

Interpersonal skills are important, as are communication skills. You also need to have commercial awareness, be good at analysing and an additional language can be useful, particularly if you are researching overseas resorts.

How good is the pay?

They started me on £18,000 straight out of university. I am hoping that once I've been here for five years, my salary will have increased to around £30,000. More experienced researchers can earn up to £45,000 a year, which would mean moving to London or the southeast of England – something I will consider in the future.

Grading criteria

The table below shows what you need to do to gain a pass, merit or distinction in this part of the qualification. Make sure you refer back to it when you are completing work so you can judge whether you are meeting the criteria and what you need to do to fill in gaps in your knowledge or experience.

In this unit there are 5 evidence activities that give you an opportunity to demonstrate your achievement of the grading criteria:

page 177   P1

page 183   P2, M1

page 188   P3, M2, D1

page 193   P4, M3

page 195   P5, M4, D2

To achieve a pass grade the evidence must show that the learner is able to...	To achieve a merit grade the evidence must show that, in addition to the pass criteria, the learner is able to...	To achieve a distinction grade the evidence must show that, in addition to the pass and merit criteria, the learner is able to...
P1 Explain different methods that can be used to research a current issue affecting travel and tourism	**M1** Explain how the proposed research plan enables exploration of the current issue	**D1** Evaluate the research undertaken and recommend improvements to your own research skills in the future
P2 Propose a research plan to investigate a current issue that is affecting the travel and tourism industry	**M2** Conduct independent research into a current issue, using at least four different types of sources of information, showing awareness of limitations of sources	**D2** Use findings from research into the current issue to recommend actions for the travel and tourism industry
P3 Use appropriate sources of information to research a current issue, using a standard referencing system	**M3** Communicate information about a current issue clearly, concisely and coherently, using specialist vocabulary and making connections and synthesising arguments	
P4 Communicate a current issue that is affecting the travel and tourism industry, using appropriate conventions to convey findings	**M4** Provide a comprehensive analysis of the current issue researched, combining and recognising different points of view	
P5 Explain how a current issue impacts the travel and tourism industry		

26.1 *Understand methods that can be used to research current issues affecting the travel and tourism industry*

RESEARCH METHODS

Before even the sources, type of data or the issue are considered, it is important to note that there are various different types of research methods. The way in which the research is carried out will determine precisely how you will go about collecting and dealing with any information over the course of the research project.

Intervention research can be seen in two ways. It can be viewed as the researcher establishing their impression of a current issue and then deciding to research it. Sometimes this makes it difficult to separate the researcher's own views from the evidence as it often drives the way in which the researcher carries out their task. At times, this can mean that the researcher is actually looking for evidence to support their views.

In any case, intervention research focuses on the introduction of a change to a current situation and then studies the consequences. For example, there may be a change in the law that alters procedures at an airport or the way in which airline tickets are booked. The other way of viewing intervention research is that as someone is researching a situation, they are intervening, as something different from the normal status is taking place.

Non-intervention research tends to look at well-established procedures and situations. No particular changes have occurred, but the purpose of the research is to monitor the situation and analyse it. The major difference between intervention and non-intervention research is that the former looks at something new, while non-intervention research tends to look at the existing situation.

Action research is another way of dealing with research methods. It usually involves the researcher working with members of an organisation in order to arrive at a workable solution to a problem. The major advantage with action research is that the researcher can deal with a real life organisation and problem or issue. The organisation can obtain a completely objective outside view of the situation and a solution to the problem that they could not have seen themselves.

The action research model is actually very useful in terms of the demands of this unit. It will help to frame a workable research plan and identify where you may need to adapt your research at various stages.

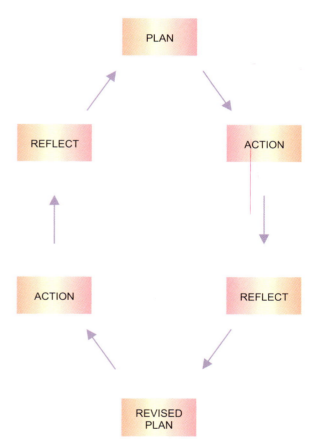

Figure 26.1 Action Research Model flow diagram

As seen in figure 26.1, an initial research plan can be created. As it is put into action, there is an opportunity to judge its effectiveness and arrive at a revised plan, which generates sufficient information in a more effective manner.

RESEARCH SOURCES

Research sources and their availability are clearly key aspects of your investigation into a current issue. To some extent, your chosen research topic will be highly dependent on the availability of data, but this begins when you access the research sources.

There is a great deal of written material on the travel and tourism industry. There is also a considerable amount of information on the Internet. Some travel and tourism organisations may be willing to share information. Representatives from travel and tourism businesses may be happy to be interviewed.

All of these are potential sources of information, but it is important to remember that without adequate sources, any research topic, no matter how interesting or important, may prove to be impossible to carry out.

Primary

Primary sources actually enable the researcher to get as close to real data and information as possible. Primary data is usually defined as something that has never been collected before. It is in its original format and it has probably never been analysed or considered thoroughly in the past.

For most research projects, this would involve actually collecting the data for the first time. This could be in the form of results from a questionnaire or information that you have collected by observing a situation or talking to someone during an interview.

Primary research sources should tell you what people are thinking and planning. It should reveal their goals, beliefs, strategies or assumptions. As we will see, most primary research is opinions or expert views, which is known as qualitative data.

Secondary

It would be foolish to dismiss secondary sources of information just because the data already exists. It may have even been analysed, reported on and quoted in various books, journals and newspapers and on websites. This does not mean that secondary research sources are worthless. In fact, most researchers will begin by looking at what is readily available about their research topic. This involves examining existing secondary research sources. It gives the researcher a far better view of the situation and helps them to identify what additional primary sources they may need to use to obtain the full picture of the current issue they are researching.

Secondary data sources will generally mean looking at statistics, research papers and printed material. It is important to remember that unless the source is 'raw', (in other words, the information is presented as it was found and not commented upon), it will have the opinions and the analysis of the original researchers. This can make some researchers reluctant to consider secondary research sources as they may feel that the information is not pure enough to act as a basis for any kind of comment.

Research tip

There are many secondary sources of information relating to the travel and tourism industry. Secondary data sources available on the Internet include:

www.tourismtrade.org.uk – the corporate pages of VisitBritain, the national tourism agency for the UK. Click 'Market Intelligence and Research' from the menu on the homepage to access data and statistics.

www.staruk.org.uk – the official website of the UK Research Liason Group, made up of representatives from the UK national tourist boards.

www.world-tourism.org – the official website of the World Tourism Organisation, a specialised agency of The United Nations. Click 'market' in the Programmes menu on the homepage for global research data and statistics.

RESEARCH DATA

In theory, all research data has a value, provided that it has been collected in a reasonable and objective way. It can provide you with an insight that you may not be able to achieve by researching it yourself. Research data carried out by large organisations, such as the Office of National Statistics, may contain data on hundreds of thousands of people. This is beyond the scope of even many of the largest businesses in the travel and tourism industry.

> **Research tip**
>
> Look at www.statistics.gov.uk to find out more about the Office of National Statistics.

Businesses in the industry routinely collect data. For example, an airline may collect data on the payment methods or gender of their passengers, a travel operator may have a popularity league of resorts and a rail network may keep a log detailing the number of trains that have run to schedule. The problem with much of this information is that it is commercially sensitive. This means that the business is unwilling to share their data with anyone outside the organisation. They may be obliged to provide certain information to regulatory bodies. If they are a public limited company, they are obliged to reveal certain aspects of their operations to their shareholders. For the most part, however, information that has been collected from within an organisation will remain there.

> **Think** Why do you think that most organisations are reluctant to share their data?

Qualitative data

Qualitative data can be extremely varied in its nature. The only common aspect of qualitative data is that it is not numerical. Usually qualitative data is collected through interviews or by observation. It tends to capture actions, views or attitudes at a particular time.

Qualitative data can give great depth of information about a situation. It is harder to analyse because it is sometimes difficult to make a judgement about the importance of what has been said or seen. Qualitative data is considered to be very valid, but it must be approached with a degree of caution as you are obtaining an opinion during an interview and your presence may affect what is happening.

> **Think** Why might your presence in an interview situation affect the opinions given by the interviewee?

Quantitative data

Many people view quantitative data as simply being statistics. It is usually numerical data that can be transformed into tables, graphs and charts. A researcher normally asks the same questions to a number of people and then adds the scores or responses together for each question in order to create a graph or table to show the spread of responses.

If the right kinds of questions are being asked and the researcher is careful about how the responses are recorded, this can be a simple way of collecting a large amount of information and then transforming it into an easily understandable format. The only problem that arises is that quantitative data collection tends to lack depth. It is fine for 'yes' and 'no' questions and it is also perfect if you offer a series of multiple choice questions. Once you begin to ask deeper questions, the process then moves closer towards qualitative data, which is harder to process.

TYPES OF CURRENT ISSUE

Choosing a suitable current issue may be of secondary importance as your ability to research it will be determined by the availability of sources and data. There are various ways of approaching this:

- How old is the current issue or how long has it been an issue? This will determine how much has been written about the issue and whether any research has already been done on the situation. It may also determine the availability of the data. If the issue has been ongoing for some time, then there may already be a wealth of qualitative and quantitative data available.

- If it is a current issue that has only come to prominence in the last few days or weeks, there is likely to be a great deal of opinion about it, but very little in the way of hard facts. This type of situation would be ideal for qualitative research, but you may not be able to rely on collecting any quantitative data.

- Although interesting and rewarding, obscure or odd current issues that only affect a tiny part of the travel and tourism industry may prove to be almost impossible to research. If you have access to individuals who are affected by a particular current issue, then this may be a possibility. Current issues that only affect an overseas country with which you may have difficulty in terms of language or culture should also be avoided as research will become problematic. There will also be very little quantitative data and the opportunities for collecting qualitative data will be limited.

Broadly speaking, there are four key types of current issue that you may consider for your research topic:

1) A current issue that has caused a change in demand for products or services in the travel and tourism industry – this could be a trend or fashion or a change that has been brought about by an economic factor.

2) A current issue that relates to current affairs – this would include political, economic, social or cultural situations or legal changes. A prime example is the introduction of the Green Tax on airline tickets, which was introduced in early 2007.

3) Environmental issues – the current dominant issue is the carbon footprints of travellers. This could be examined from the point of view of holiday-makers, transport providers and green pressure groups. Environmental issues generally concern the impact of travel and tourism on particular areas and how this has affected the environment.

4) Health issues – health scares, such as the SARS virus and bird flu, have had marked effects on the travel and tourism industry at various times. Health scares and problems have a drastic impact on the demand for products and services related to particular destinations.

Figure 26.2 There have been several protests against the planned expansion of Stansted Airport

Example

In 2010, South Africa will host the Football World Cup. Considerable investments are being made in infrastructure and yet there are serious concerns about the country's crime rate. There are also problems with HIV and AIDS as one in seven South Africans has the disease. There are many sources and considerable research data available on the probable impacts on the country and its ability to attract tourists up to and including the World Cup in 2010. Much of the data will be secondary, although there is a mixture of quantitative and qualitative data.

Research tip

Useful websites to begin research are:
www.worldcup2010southafrica.com
www.fifa.com
www.southafrica2010.org.

TRAVEL AND TOURISM INDUSTRY

Your research into a current issue affecting the travel and tourism industry may actually affect the whole industry in general. An example of this could be increased disposable income from potential customers.

Think Can you think of other examples of current issues that are affecting the whole travel and tourism industry?

It is more likely, however, that your research will involve one or more specific sectors of the travel and tourism industry:

- Accommodation providers – either those in a local or regional area, national or international chains, or trends in the way in which accommodation is offered (such as the increased numbers of all-inclusive hotels in certain resorts).

- Transport providers – either a specific transport provider or a particular type of transportation, such as air, sea, rail or road. The impact or issue could affect a single area, country or world travel.

- Attractions – options may include theme parks, museums, historical sites or zoos. The current issue could relate to accessibility, pricing or visitor figures.

- Tour operators – trends in the types of products and services sold, recent takeovers and mergers, the activities of tour operators in particular resorts or how some of them have contributed to the development of particular destinations.

- Travel agents – how the balance of bookings by customers is gradually shifting away from the high street in favour of the Internet and telephone bookings, or activities and initiatives undertaken by travel agents to attract customers back to the high street, so that they can receive face-to-face customer service.

- Trade associations and regulatory bodies – the activities of these organisations and how they control or bring members into line, as well as providing a framework for good practice and working within the law.

- Ancillary service providers – activities and trends either in integration between tour operators and other providers or the activities of independent ancillary service providers and their links with other parts of the industry.

EVIDENCE ACTIVITY

P1

As a consultant to the travel and tourism industry you have been asked to carry out a research project on current issues in travel and tourism. You are to focus on issues that have arisen in the last five years.

1. Explain the different methods that can be used to research a current issue. (P1)

2. Present the advantages and disadvantages of at least two potential sources of information. (P1)

26.2 Be able to conduct research into a current issue affecting the travel and tourism industry, using appropriate resources

RESEARCH PLAN

As we have seen, any research plan will depend on the information you need and the resources available. Bear in mind that you will be carrying out research with fairly limited resources, so it is important not to be overly optimistic about what you will be able to achieve.

A research plan aims to set out precisely what you will be researching, how this will be achieved, where you will find sources and resources and how you will manage the whole process. Work carried out at this stage can be extremely valuable as it will highlight areas that will present difficulties. It may even mean scrapping the original research idea or perhaps focusing on a smaller aspect of a current issue. The broader the topic, the more information is potentially available. This means that you will have far more information than you probably need and it will be much more difficult to decide which sources are useful and what data is relevant.

By following the stages in creating a research plan, you can prove, to yourself, but also to others that your research idea is feasible and achievable.

Example

Hilary decides that she wants to look at the growth of Norwich Airport. Five years ago, very few international flights left the airport each week. Now over two dozen leave every day during the peak season. At this point, her research plan is not very focused. She needs to identify precisely what to look at so she decides to research the impact that the growth of the regional airport has had on the local area. This outline is still quite broad and her research will depend on what kind of sources and resources she is able to find.

Setting of hypothesis

A hypothesis is a statement, suggestion or assumption that the research is intended to either prove or disprove.

The idea is that the research plan will test the hypothesis. The hypothesis is effectively the objective of the research. A hypothesis should be testable. An example of a poor hypothesis that cannot be supported by evidence is 'people visit the Himalayas because the Yeti lives there'.

An example of a hypothesis that serves no useful purpose is 'more people travel to Spain than Greece because it takes 20 minutes less time to get there'. Even if this were found to be true, it would not serve any useful purpose to know this information.

A good example of a hypothesis is 'more people travel to Spain because the infrastructure is better suited to British tourists than the Greek infrastructure'. Although this hypothesis is quite a broad one, there are useful and measurable criteria. Reasons for visiting both destinations can be investigated (qualitative data) and statistics can be examined, looking at visitor figures to support the qualitative information.

Research tip

If wanting to conduct research into a major UK airport then a good place to start is the BAA website at www.baa.com. The company is responsible for the day to day running of some of the worlds most well known airports and from here you can navigate to the home pages of airports throughout the UK, as well as others in Europe and around the world, including: Heathrow at www.heathrowairport.com, Southampton at www.southamptonairport.com and Glasgow at www.glasgowairport.com. Each of these sites includes information on all aspects of airport life, from community matters to the choice of restaurants in terminal buildings, and is a useful resource for contact information.

Example

Hilary decides to focus her research plan and set out her hypothesis. She decides to state 'the growth of Norwich Airport will encourage more business travel and stimulate growth in Norfolk'. This gives her some clear terms of reference, aims and objectives and helps her focus on possible sources of information.

Think Can you think of any other good hypotheses that Hilary could have chosen instead?

Terms of reference

Terms of reference describe the structure and the purpose of the research. It is important to create detailed terms of reference as they basically define what will be done. It usually includes:

- what has to be achieved

- how it will be achieved

- when it will be achieved

- for whom it will be achieved.

In other words, the terms of reference look at the scope and extent of the proposed piece of research.

Example

Hilary decides that her terms of reference will be:

- to examine the growth of Norwich Airport over the past five years

- to identify business travellers' use of the airport

- to investigate the advantages of the airport's location and connections

- to estimate the long-term impact of the growth of the airport on Norfolk.

Aims and objectives

The aims of the research plan should include terms such as 'identify', 'describe', 'produce' or 'analyse'. The research aims to look at a current issue and then, taking the hypothesis into account, state precisely what the researcher hopes to achieve.

With regard to the earlier example of South Africa's 2010 World Cup, the aim might be 'to identify, describe and produce an analysis of the impact of the 2010 World Cup on South Africa's tourism'.

This clearly sets out the aim of the research, but the objectives also need to be stated in order to be clear about precisely what will be included in the research plan. Again, using the same example, the objectives could be that the researcher wants to find out:

- how the marketing of South Africa has changed since winning a World Cup bid

- what steps South Africa has taken to prepare for the large expected influx of tourists in the lead up to the World Cup

- what South Africa is saying and doing about fears of crime and other problems in the country that could jeopardise its success

- how the travel and tourism industry views the prospects for sales related to the World Cup in 2010.

There is a great deal of research to be carried out here in order to achieve these objectives. Some of the data will be available on official websites, showing the progress being made in improving the infrastructure. Contacting chosen members of the travel and tourism industry who deal with tours to South Africa can also help in collecting qualitative data.

Planned outcomes

Planned outcomes seek to set out precisely what will be achieved by using research sources and data to find out information related to the terms of reference, as well as the aims and objectives. Planned outcomes could include:

- a solution to a problem

- a suggestion as to how things might change in the near future

- the likelihood of something happening

- whether the current issue is a short-term fashion or trend

- whether there are major reasons to be concerned

- whether the issue will add additional costs to either the industry or customers

- whether the issue means that new products and services have to be developed.

Example

Hilary has worked out that her planned outcomes will be:

• whether the continued growth of the airport will have a positive or negative effect on the city of Norwich

• whether the airport's connections will attract further investments from abroad in the long term, creating more jobs in travel and tourism.

> **Think** Can you think of any other planned outcomes for Hilary's research plan?

Possible sources and resources

You have probably come across a particular issue that has interested you during the course of your studies in travel and tourism. This part of the research plan is the beginning of your search for possible sources and resources that will help in fulfilling your research.

> **Think** Which current issues have interested you? Why?

It is important to remember that without sufficient sources and resources, there is little hope that you will be able to complete your work. As we will see, there are several potential sources of information, but there may be more or less information available, depending on the actual issue. Remember that the issue has to be sufficiently important or significant for others to have written about it. If the issue is too obscure, few people may have noticed it. This means that while your research will be original, you may encounter more problems collecting information than if you had chosen something more mainstream.

You should not view possible sources and resources as simply a list of books, journals or websites that you have not actually looked at. Simply typing a term, phrase or destination into a search engine and jotting down the first handful of websites will reveal nothing of any value to you. You will need a range of sources and resources that is as diverse as possible. You will have the time to create questionnaires and collect your own primary research material. However, you need to know who will complete the questionnaires and how you will collect the survey data from them.

Example

Hilary does not live very far from Norwich Airport, but this is not necessarily useful. The first thing she does is to visit Norwich Airport's website, only to discover that she needs to be a journalist in order to use their media centre. She searches the website and finds very little information that is of any use. The next logical thing to do is to look at the regional newspapers. Luckily, they are online and she can begin to find comments about the growth of the airport and what it might mean for the area. She also finds two other organisations, Invest in Norfolk and Shaping the Future. Both of these are concerned with encouraging people to bring their businesses to the area. She now needs to begin to see if there is any data that breaks down the types of travellers using the airport.

Figure 26.3 Logo of Shaping Norfolk's Future

Research tip

For more information on Norfolk's Shaping the Future visit:
www.shapingnorfolksfuture.org.uk

Task dates and review dates

Although you may have a considerable amount of time to carry out your research, you may be surprised about just how long it might take for industry professionals to get back to you with useful information. You may also find it difficult to access information immediately that you thought would be readily available.

> **Think** What strategies could you use to minimise any risks to your project plan of people not responding to your enquiries?

Looking at your hypothesis, terms of reference, aims and objectives and planned outcomes, you can begin to break down precisely what you need to do by particular dates in order to produce your research on time.

Try to break down each task into as many different components as possible. Set realistic dates for their completion, taking into account that you will have to rely on others at some point to provide you with information.

You should also set review dates on a weekly or monthly basis. This will give you an opportunity, hopefully with your teacher or tutor, to look at your current progress, check to see whether you have met your task dates and to then review and amend the dates, if necessary.

Monitoring progress

Although you need to carry out much of the research independently if you hope to gain a merit or distinction, your teacher or tutor will be at hand to assist you in monitoring your progress.

At the outset, you may have decided to carry out the research in a particular way. At first, you may have sent out a number of letters requesting information. This is a reasonable approach and if it is done early enough, then information should start coming back in a timely manner. However, when you are monitoring your processes in collecting information, you may discover that very few have actually replied and need to be prompted. Time needs to be set aside to send a second letter or to make a telephone call to remind them.

The monitoring process gives you the opportunity to make amendments in the way in which you are collecting data and helps you with your priorities. It can also alert you to the possibility that a serious problem is about to happen, which could throw your whole research plan into chaos.

Example

Hilary has been waiting for a Norwich City councillor to write and let her know when he could be interviewed about the impact of Norwich Airport on the city. He is a well-known local expert on transport matters and he even owns two or three local tourist attractions. Hilary is relying on his expert information and feels that she can obtain valuable insights from him. The day before the interview, she receives a telephone call from the councillor's assistant. He has been called away on urgent business and will not be available for another three weeks.

> **Think** How would a monitoring process help Hilary to deal with this set-back?

Contingencies

In the worked example on the previous page, Hilary needs to rethink. This is what contingency planning is all about. What will you do if certain circumstances occur that mean that you cannot complete a task or obtain information that you had banked on?

Contingency plans mean having a second plan of action, something that you can do instead or another way in which you can obtain the same information. It is not always possible to come up with a viable contingency plan, but there is usually almost always another way of getting the information you need. Think carefully about the organisations or individuals you could approach if your first choice of source lets you down or doesn't deliver on time. Bear in mind this will involve building in extra time for gathering information.

Always try and build in enough time for you to use your contingency plan. There is no point in discovering that the information you had hoped would arrive the following day will not be ready for another fortnight. There may simply not be sufficient time to find the information elsewhere. It would have been better to set the task date for the receipt of that information a week before you needed it.

Example

Hilary did have a contingency plan. She had already asked the councillor's business partner whether he would mind being interviewed if the councillor was not available. The business partner pencilled her in for the same day and only asked that she call the day before to confirm whether or not he was required. Hilary can now make that call and tell him that she will meet him as planned.

Ethical issues

If you are using primary qualitative data from interviews or comments that you have collected from participants during your research, it is advisable to obtain permission from them to use it. The following sample form suggests how this permission might be gained.

I voluntarily agree to participate in the research carried out by

-------------------------------. I understand that this is designed to

form the basis of a research project for a BTEC National in Travel and

Tourism. I understand this may involve:

- Recorded observations
- My completion of a questionnaire
- My participation in a 30-minute interview

I grant my permission for this interview to be recorded and used for

the research project.

RESEARCH PARTICIPANT SIGNATURE:

_____

DATE: --

Figure 26.4 Example of a permission form to be filled out by a participant

Think Why do you think some people wish to remain anonymous?

It is important to make sure that individuals you are interviewing or questioning from the travel and tourism industry are aware of the purpose of your research. They may wish to remain anonymous and you must not note their names in your final report.

These ethical issues are important as you will encounter the issue of the use of personal information in the workplace.

Evaluation

Having created your research plan, it is now important to step back from it and try to review it objectively. You must ask yourself a number of questions:

- is my research too broad and does it need to be more focused?

- have I been clear about my hypothesis, terms of reference, aims and objectives?

- do these match my planned outcomes and are my planned outcomes achievable?

- have I checked my possible sources and resources thoroughly? Are they reliable and accessible?

- have I built in enough time to carry out each task?

- how often will I carry out a review of my research progress and what will be my actions if I find that dates have been missed?

- what monitoring processes are in place? How often will I need to see my teacher/tutor?

- do I have a contingency plan? What fallback sources and methods can I use if a major part of the research proves to be useless?

- have I obtained permission or can I obtain permission from any participants and have I taken ethical issues into account?

This final evaluation period should alert you to any remaining problems with your research plan. Your research plan will have changed gradually as you have created your hypothesis and then transformed it into achievable, timed tasks, using accessible data or contacts.

EVIDENCE ACTIVITY

P2 – M1

Having outlined potential research methods and sources, you now must turn your attention to the research itself.

1. Propose a research plan to investigate your chosen current issue that affects the travel and tourism industry. (P2)

2. Explain how your proposed research plan will enable you to explore the current issue. (M1)

SOURCES OF INFORMATION

Without knowing precisely what the current issue is that you will be researching, it is difficult to give any definitive advice about sources of information. You will have to use as broad a range as possible. Some of these will already be published and some will be relatively easy to access and find, while others may require a considerable amount of thought or your own work to collect the data.

There are some comments that can be made about particular sources of information, which could prove valuable as you begin to collate a comprehensive list of information sources that you will use.

Books

The first two things to look for in a book are the date when it was published and why it was written. The date will reveal to you whether the information contained in the book is current or whether it is referring to a period some time in the past. As you are expected to be looking at a current issue, this means that the book must not be more than around five years old. It is important to bear in mind, however, that the book may have been written up to several years before the publication date, so check the period that it covers. The second aspect to look at is why the book was written. Is it a simple description of something that has happened or is it the opinion of the author on a particular issue?

If it is the latter, then they will have done their own analysis and be offering their own interpretation. You may need to look for another book that puts forward a contrary view.

Research tip

Look at www.amazon.co.uk. By typing in key words, you can find out whether books have been written on particular subjects.

Journals

Journals are usually be published by professional organisations that are related to the travel and tourism industry. They tend to be very academic. The authors will have spent a great deal of time researching a particular issue and may have written the information in a format that is not always user-friendly. The date of the article and the reason why the article was written are also important indicators of how useful a particular article might be.

Research tip

Go to www.sprig.org.uk. This is an organisation that promotes information sources in leisure, tourism and sport. By clicking on their guides, you will find another page where you can select tourism, which provides you with a list of all UK and worldwide journals.

Think How would you go about finding relevent journals or articles?

Magazines and newspapers

Magazines related to the travel and tourism industry can also be valuable sources of information. They tend to highlight a particularly newsworthy issue, but the magazine may lack the space to go into the issue in any great detail. It is important to check any sources of information that the writer or writers have used. You may be aware of information that they could not have had access to at the time. Look at when the article was written as the situation may have changed. The same can be said for newspapers. Most newspapers, particularly at the weekends, have extensive travel sections. Sometimes they have lengthy articles that deal with a particular travel and tourism issue or destination. However, what has been written may only have applied at the time and the situation may have changed considerably since then.

Research tip

There are a number of newspapers that have searchable databases if you use key words. These include www.ft.com, www.guardian.co.uk, www.independent.co.uk, www.telegraph.co.uk, www.observer.co.uk and www.timesonline.co.uk.

Websites

These should always be approached with caution. There are no controls over who can put up a website with information on it and there will not necessarily be any guarantees that the information is correct. It is better to rely on industry recognised websites, but this does not mean that you should trust travel and tourism providers' websites completely as they will tend to be upbeat and positive and not highlight any particular problems. It is best to check any facts and figures with other sources before quoting them.

Figure 26.6 *The UNWTO website is a good resource for global tourism issues and statistics*

Published research papers

You will normally need access to an academic website to be able to read published research papers. These are usually extended pieces of research that have been carried out by people studying for higher-level degrees. They may be highly focused on a small, yet significant issue. They have a fixed format with many cross-references and some of them are difficult to understand. They have been written to match specific criteria, but the research will have been fairly rigorous. The research papers will set out to prove or disprove a particular hypothesis, just as your research should do.

Research tip

A good place to start is www.theses. com, but it requires a subscription. Your school or college may have a licence. At the time of writing, there were nearly 500,000 research papers on this website and there is a search option.

Research tip

www.world-tourism.org is a good place to start if your current topic has a world dimension. You can select 'Regions' to find specific information. There are also links to a number of World Tourism Organisation publications.

Official statistics

The first place to begin when looking for official statistics is government websites, as well as trade associations and regulatory bodies. Tourist boards are also quite a useful source for facts and figures. It is important to make sure that you find the latest statistics, but this is not always possible as there is usually a delay of a year or more in producing complete sets of statistics. For example, in 2008, you will be fortunate to find completed statistics covering a period any later than 2006.

Television

There are very few travel and tourism-focused television programmes. Travel and tourism tends to be featured only when there is a major issue or problem. This means that hoping there will be television coverage on your chosen current issue could be fruitless. You can always check with websites, such as www.bbc.co.uk, to see if there are any upcoming programmes that will feature your issue or a particular destination.

Research tip

www.euromonitor.com can provide general market research information. Other sources include www.mintel.co.uk and www.europa.eu.int where you should choose the 'Eurostat' option. Most countries will have their own tourism statistics on their main tourist information websites.

Questionnaire results

You will have used questionnaires as part of your collection of research material. These will provide you with a range of qualitative and quantitative information. If you have organised your questionnaire efficiently, this should be a relatively simple task. However, you must make sure that your questionnaires have been distributed to a reasonable number of people. Basing your findings on six completed questionnaires does not provide you with any valid results. You must decide how many questionnaires you can handle within the time period you have been allotted to complete your research.

Portals

Although, strictly speaking, these are websites, portals are also very valuable. One of the most useful is www.waksberg.com/research. It contains links to government sources of information, journals, news, organisations, ongoing research, travel and tourism related resources on sustainability and transportation. At the very least, portal sites such as this and www.intute.ac.uk provide you with quick access to useful websites that you may have otherwise overlooked. On the Intute website, select 'Social Sciences' and click on 'Travel and Tourism' under the 'Browse by heading' option. This reveals another set of sub-listings, from adventure tourism through to wildlife and nature tourism. Each page has dozens of useful links that are regularly checked to ensure they are still working.

REFERENCING

It is an expected practice for you to credit the source of your information. This serves a dual purpose:

- it acknowledges the fact that you have carried out research and recognised the value of someone else's work in your own research

- it also authenticates facts and figures that you may have collected from a variety of sources. It proves to the reader that your information is valid, current and accurate.

You may use **superscript** to number any quotations, facts or figures that you have taken from another source. This will allow you to state the source in the **footnotes** or the bibliography at the end of your research paper.

Example

"Brochures use codes to identify different accommodation offered and these need to be cross-referenced with a particular month or departure date[1]."

1 – Foundation Leisure and Tourism, Jon Sutherland and Diane Canwell, Hodder and Stoughton, 1996, p131.

Standard system

An equally easy way in which to acknowledge your source of information is to name the author and the date when it was written. You can then put the full details of the book, journal or article into the bibliography at the end of your report.

Key words

Superscript – an option in Word that produces a small, elevated number or letter. Highlight the number or letter and select 'Format', then 'Font' and the 'Superscript' option
Footnotes – text or references that are located at the bottom of a page or document

Bibliography

A bibliography is an alphabetical listing of the sources that you have used during your research. It has three major purposes:

- it acknowledges the sources that have been used

- it gives any reader the opportunity to identify and look at the sources used

- it also allows readers to check whether the information in the research is accurate.

The way in which the bibliographical entries are written depends on the type of source. The following order is adopted for books:

- the names of the author or authors, with their surname before their forenames

- the title of the book (italicised)

- the publisher of the book

- the year of publication.

Example

Kerr, A., Lindsay, V., Sutherland, J and Sutherland, D., *BTEC National Travel and Tourism Book 1*, Edexcel, 2007.

If you are using a magazine or newspaper article, the following order is used:

- the name of the author or authors

- the title of the article

- the magazine or newspaper name

- day, month or issue number

- the year of publication

- page numbers.

If you are quoting from the Internet, the following order is used:

- the name of the author or authors (this may be an organisation)

- the year of publication

- the title of the web page

- the date accessed

- URL or web address.

Example

Canton, Naomi. How the Jobs Market is Shaping Up for 2007. Viewed 28/03/07. http://www.eveningnews24.co.uk.

Key words

URL – Uniform Resource Locator or website address

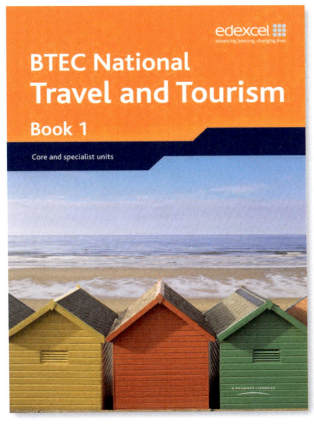

Figure 26.6 *Any book you take an extract from must be referenced in your bibliography*

EVIDENCE ACTIVITY

P3 – M2 – D1

Having had your research proposal approved, you must now undertake your actual research.

1. In your findings show that you have used at least three different sources of information. (P3)

2. Use accepted conventions for referencing sources, such as a bibliography, in your report. (P3)

3. Show that you have obtained your information independently. (M2)

4. Show that you have used at least four different types of sources of information. (M2)

5. Highlight the limitations of any sources that you have used. (M2)

6. Identify and evaluate the key areas of strengths and weaknesses in your own research. (D1)

7. Make recommendations as to how you could improve your research techniques in the future. (D1)

26.3 *Be able to communicate findings on a travel and tourism issue, using appropriate media and conventions*

COMMUNICATE FINDINGS

You may be required to either present your findings in the form of a written report or as an oral presentation, supported by a summary of your findings. In either case, you must remember to make sure that you have provided sufficient evidence, you have followed your research plan and you have used the widest possible range of sources of information and referenced them, where appropriate.

Communication skills are vital in any job role in the travel and tourism industry. It is a people-based business. Interactions take place between colleagues and customers and these take the form of either written or oral communication.

However, in this particular instance, the communications that you will be using are somewhat formal. A report has a specific format and needs to follow particular conventions. An oral presentation must be clear and in a logical sequence and supported by illustrations and documentation, where necessary. In both cases, you will need to engage the reader or the audience and to focus on communicating your findings on a travel and tourism issue.

Presenting your own argument and those of others

There is rarely one view that is commonly held by all commentators about a particular travel and tourism issue. Commentators will have their own opinions and their own motives for putting forward particular arguments. Some will view particular aspects, facts and figures in a completely different way, placing a greater or lesser emphasis on them. It is important to incorporate and give equal weight to differing points of view in any investigation into an issue.

You will be required to present your own views, but these should not dominate or be considered more important than other individual's arguments. It is always wise to try to balance advantages and disadvantages, for and against.

During your investigation, you will have discovered that what may be considered to be positive for one group of individuals is eyed with suspicion or negativity by another.

Example

Hilary has discovered that the owners of Norwich Airport are very upbeat and positive about the airport's continued expansion. It has the support of many business leaders in the area. There are plans to extend the airport and to increase the number of flights into and out of the city. Hilary thinks that the progress is a positive thing for the city and for the area and that it will stimulate tourism. However, she must not conduct her investigations on this purely pro-airport stance. There are local residents who are upset with the number of flights coming into and out of the airport; their lives are being disrupted by the aircraft noise. Local residents are also concerned with the amount of traffic in the area and feel that the road network is not adequate. There are also environmental pressure groups that are fundamentally opposed to airport expansion. They point out the pollution and the creation of greenhouse gases that the airport generates and want the airport's owners and business leaders to reconsider any future expansion. Hilary would be advised to present both sides of the argument in order to give a balanced view.

Drawing conclusions

Conclusions are essentially the high points or the most important features of all of the findings of a particular research project. In the travel and tourism industry, like many other sectors of business, long and carefully written reports are rarely read from cover to cover. Instead the audiences, for which the reports were intended, move directly from the terms of reference to the conclusions of the report.

They can look back into the findings if they want clarification about a particular conclusion. The conclusions should, therefore, summarise the main points of information that have been gathered during the research.

In an oral presentation, in particular, you may not have the opportunity to present in any length or detail all of your findings. You must therefore make the judgement as to which parts of your findings are important. You can then draw conclusions and present these instead.

Summarising data

Just as there may be no time to present all of your findings, you should also not expect your audience to allow you to read out every element of the data that you have discovered. It needs to be summarised and the main data points highlighted. This means that data that does not necessarily add anything to your argument should be dealt with quickl, leaving more time to focus on more important information.

By all means, you should present tables, charts and graphs of your data, but these will be summaries, so that they can easily be understood and appreciated as you refer to them.

Engaging the audience

No matter how interested or focused the audience for your presentation may be, a person's concentration span is only very limited. The following points are important to remember when making an oral presentation:

- have a clear introduction

- do not put all the details of your findings into your talk

- do not count on the audience remembering anything in detail, so avoid referring back to something you may have said earlier

- try to build your talk into a coherent story, cutting out as much unnecessary information as possible

- try to help the audience understand where you are heading

- it is sometimes a good idea to give an overview first, then add detail toyour overview

- use illustrations, if necessary. Depending on the technology available, you may be able to use a PowerPoint presentation on a laptop computer, projected onto a large screen. If you are using PowerPoint, do not try to cram too much information onto each slide

- alternatively, if you have access to an overhead projector, then you can create transparencies. These can either be hand-drawn or they can be printed out using a computer if your centre has the technology to do so.

> **Think** Can you think of any other appropriate ways of engaging the audience's attention during your presentation?

APPROPRIATE MEDIA TO COMMUNICATE FINDINGS

Broadly speaking, your communication options fall into one of two categories, although you could use a combination of the two.

- A written report, containing your terms of reference, findings, conclusions and recommendations, supported by appendices with additional information.

- An oral presentation, either as an individual or as a member of a group, supported by illustrations, graphs, tables, charts and handouts.

- A shortened report and an oral presentation.

- A full report and a question and answer session to confirm your process, understanding, conclusions and recommendations.

Report writing

An extended formal report is not an opportunity to write everything you know about the travel and tourism industry and thinly disguise it as research into a current issue. A good report has the following features:

- it is about a single clearly defined issue

- it is up-to-date and accurate

- it includes everything that the reader needs to know

- irrelevant information is not included

- the reader can understand it and does not find it a strain to read

- it is clearly and neatly presented

- it follows the correct format (see below)

- it is concise and simple

- it is well organised and structured

- it does not contain unexplained jargon or technical terms.

Ideally, a report should have the following structure:

- 1.0 Terms of reference – the reason for the report and what it hopes to achieve

- 2.0 Procedures – how the information contained in the report was found

- 3.0 Findings – what information was actually discovered

- 4.0 Conclusions – the edited highlights of the findings

- 5.0 Recommendations – what should be done or what might happen in your opinion, having researched the issue

- Appendices – this is where all charts, tables, graphs and other information that does not fit comfortably into the first five sections are placed.

You will have noticed that each of the sections is numbered. Each different point you are making will effectively become a separate numbered point.

Example

Looking back at Hilary's original terms of reference, she formats this part of the report in the following way:

1.0 Terms of reference

In order to research the impact of Norwich Airport fully, the following terms of reference were agreed:

1.1 To examine the growth of Norwich Airport over the past five years

1.2 To identify business travellers' use of the airport

1.3 To investigate the advantages of the airport's location and connections

1.4 To estimate the long-term impact of the growth of the airport on Norfolk

Presentation skills

Although we will look at some of the conventions in communications in the next section, it is important to establish whether you will be required to produce written or oral communications in the presentation of your research findings. Presentations can be no less demanding than completing a fully referenced report. Getting presentations right can mean the difference between proving that you have carried out an effective research project and are able to convey the key results, or that you have made a serious mistake somewhere along the line and you are simply unprepared to make the presentation.

Although the following checklist is by no means exhaustive, it will begin to give you an indication as to the kind of issues that you need to consider in the lead up to making your presentation. You should not be referring to this checklist in the last few days before your presentation. The checklist needs to have been considered from the moment you were told that an oral presentation was necessary as the major conclusion for this unit.

Table 26.1 Presentation Checklist

Presentation	Checklist
Identify aims of the presentation	
Identify audience characteristics and needs	
Identify time allowance for the presentation	
Check out the room for seating and lighting etc (and use of power)	
Double check materials needed for the day	
Decide on a format and structure	
For group presentations, divide up roles and tasks for preparation and on the day	
Make speaker's notes	
Prepare visual aids	
Prepare the delivery: the beginning, the middle and the end	
Prepare for the question session	
Be calm; better to be prepared and early than nervous and in a rush	
Be organised on the day	

APPROPRIATE CONVENTIONS TO COMMUNICATE FINDINGS

Certain conventions, or expected ways of doing things, are essential to communicating your findings in the most appropriate manner. Many of the comments in this section are equally as valid for written reports or oral presentations. The expectation at this level is for you to be able to use your communication skills so that they can enhance the way in which you present your work.

Use of vocabulary

You will have noticed as you progressed through the National Curriculum in the run up to your GCSEs that there were certain expectations of you in terms of your spoken communication. The same levels of development are required at this level. These would include:

- using a more formal vocabulary and tone of voice when required

- varying the use of your vocabulary and the level of detail

- having an appreciation of what standard English means and when it is used

- being able to use standard English in formal situations and being fluent, particularly in oral presentations

- showing a confident use of English, both in written and in verbal communication.

In terms of actual written work, you have clearly passed the point where it is acceptable to produce handwritten material. Virtually everything that you need to present as evidence for this course will have to be word processed. Although word processing software can help to a large degree in sorting out spelling mistakes and grammatical errors, there is still an art in the construction of sentences and arguments.

- Ideas should be developed in a sequence of sentences.

- You should be able to extend ideas in a logical manner.

- You should widen your vocabulary and use technical or industry-specific words, where appropriate.

- It is perfectly acceptable to use grammatically complex sentences with extended meaning.

- You will be expected to organise your work into complex paragraphs, using a range of punctuation. If you are writing a report, the numbered sections will help you to achieve this.

- Your writing should be impersonal and you should not normally refer to yourself when describing processes or research undertaken.

Grammatical expression

The English language has many peculiarities. It can be easy to fail to convey exactly what you mean, even though you may have all of the information to hand. Grammatical expression is best described as the ability to explain complex ideas, issues and situations in a clear and understandable manner.

In terms of written communications, this might mean:

- the use of appropriate headings

- organising your work into a logical sequence

- cross-referencing information may need additional explanation.

It can also mean using the right kinds of words and phrases at the appropriate time. For verbal communication, it tends to be about sentence structure. It is also to do with the ability to deliver a presentation that is logical, which uses the appropriate level of language and is clear to the audience.

Grammatical expression also means using the correct tense.

- Past – what has happened or the ways in which things were done, e.g. the industry enjoyed growing sales in the 1990s.

- Present – what is currently happening, e.g. the industry is enjoying a growth in sales.

- Future – what might happen, e.g. the industry expects a growth in sales.

It is important to remember that grammatical expression is an integral part of Key Skills at Level 4. This unit is a Level 4 qualification that was originally designed for the BTEC Higher.

Emphasis, structure and logical sequence

We have looked at many of these aspects already. Emphasis refers to your ability to identify and highlight the key aspects of your findings. In terms of a written report, your emphasised aspects will be included in the conclusions and recommendations. They are the highlights or main points of your entire research project.

It may be more difficult to emphasise key findings in an oral presentation. The structure of a presentation will always begin with a simple introduction. You then move towards more detailed findings. As a conclusion or highlight of the presentation itself, you construct an ending that initially summarises the key aspects of your findings and then proceeds to make recommendations as a result of them. It is good practice to create a handout, which can be given to the audience and outlines the main points that you are making in your conclusions and recommendations. This should give them sufficient emphasis.

In terms of structure, if you are producing a written report, the format already dictates how it should appear. It is important to remember not to incorporate any raw data or information into the report itself. If you feel that this information is of value and can add to the strength of your report, then it should be placed in an appendix at the back of the report. If you wish to refer briefly to it in your findings, then you should indicate in which appendix the material could be found. It is

important to stick to the accepted report format and to make use of sub-headings to give structure to your report.

We have already seen that an oral presentation needs a beginning, middle and an end. The introduction is important as it frames everything else within the presentation. Your findings should be the main part of the presentation, but you should leave sufficient time in order to present your conclusions and recommendations. It may also be necessary to set aside time for questions and answers from the audience.

Figure 26.7 Presentations must be clear and concise

EVIDENCE ACTIVITY

P4 – M3

You must now present your findings as a consultant.

1. Present the findings of your research, either in the form of a written report or a verbal presentation. (P4)

2. Use appropriate conventions to convey your findings. (P4)

3. Clearly, concisely and coherently communicate your research findings. (M3)

4. Make use of specialist vocabulary. (M3)

5. Make connecting and contrasting arguments. (M3)

26.4 Understand the impacts of a current issue on the travel and tourism industry

IMPACTS

It is difficult to predict the kinds of impacts that you will discover during your research into a current issue. However, in order to be a significant current issue, one of a number of outcomes or impacts may have been registered in the travel and tourism industry. They will generally include the following, but bear in mind that there may have been more than one impact.

Loss of customers

This would refer to a serious situation where either the reputation of a business, region or destination has caused a drop in the number of bookings or a spate of cancellations. A prime example would be the impact on the Maldives in 2004 when a tsunami wiped out many of the islands' key resorts. There was complete chaos in the area and significant loss of life. The continued effect of the tsunami meant that the Maldives took a considerable amount of time to recover. This affected not only the Maldives and its people, but also airlines and tour operators that included the area as a destination.

Figure 26.8 The 2004 tsunami in the Maldives had a disasterous effect on visitor numbers

> **Think** Can you think of some other examples of natural or man-made disasters that have resulted in a loss of customers in the travel and tourism industry?

Developments of new markets

New destinations are identified each year as being the next best or unexploited region to visit. The current trend in 2007 is for areas along the Adriatic, which were formerly parts of Yugoslavia. Countries such as Croatia are becoming key travel destinations as it was very difficult to holiday in these areas for many years. Other key markets that the travel and tourism industry are developing are Green Tourism and what is referred as the Pink Pound, which is better known as Gay Tourism. (The American market is said to be worth over $54 billion a year.)

Loss of revenue

Unexpected expenses or significant drops in the number of customers can cause businesses in the travel and tourism industry to make far less money than they had predicted. There has been a gradual decline in certain types of tourism, such as the package holiday to Spain. Businesses that had traditionally relied on this type of tourism as their main source of revenue have seen their incomes drop. This is a long-term trend and can also be described as a changing demand. However, immediate loss of revenue can occur when there is a major problem for an airline.

Example

In August 2006, there was a terrorist alert and the airline easyJet had to cancel 469 flights. There was an immediate loss of income of £4 million. In the aftermath, they also had to fund tougher security measures, which led to delays and extra costs for the airline.

Changing demands

The most significant and long-lasting change in demand in tourism is customers' requirements for higher quality service and generally higher standards. The travel and tourism industry sees the way in which they handle quality issues as a key way to deal with competitors. This change in demand is definitely customer driven, but it is being used by many travel and tourism businesses to gain a competitive edge.

Additional costs

As we have seen with loss of revenue, emergency situations can cause an immediate drop in revenue and a sudden increase in costs.

- -

Example

Budget airlines easyJet and Ryanair have introduced charges and restrictions on items of checked-in luggage. easyJet impose the charges on any second item of luggage, whilst Ryanair charges per item. Both airlines offer a discount for customers paying for their luggage in advance or online and a standard charge for those checking in on the day.

Both companies also place additional charges on any passenger checking in luggage that exceeds a set weight restriction.

These measures have been seen as a way for the airlines to offset the costs of tightened security at airports since the terrorism attacks of September 11th 2001.

Research tip

For the most up-to-date information on easyJet and Ryanair baggage definitions, restrictions and charges visit the websites http://www.ryanair.com/site/EN/conditions.php?pos=MYFLIGHT and http://www.easyjet.com/EN/Planning/baggage.html

Changes to products and services

Passing on additional costs to customers can be seen as changes in products and services. It has certainly not been the case that people could carry anything onto an airline within limits. The trend now appears to be to reduce the amount people place as baggage into airline holds. There have also been considerable changes in other products and services in the travel and tourism industry. There are an increased number of flights from regional airports and there is also a trend towards all-inclusive holidays. Equally, there have been new products and services developed to cater for the older traveller. Tour operators such as Saga have spearheaded many of these initiatives.

EVIDENCE ACTIVITY

P5 – M4 – D2

You have now been asked to explain the probable effects of the current issue on the travel and tourism industry to an assembled representative group of travel and tourism organisation members.

1. Explain how the current issue affects the travel and tourism industry. (P5)

2. Provide a comprehensive analysis of the issue. (M4)

3. Highlight different viewpoints on how the current issue will affect the industry. (M4)

4. Make clear, detailed, appropriate and realistic recommendations of action for the travel and tourism industry arising out of your findings. (D2)

INDEX

Edexcel
190 High Holborn
London WC1V 7BH

ISBN: 978-1-40586-808-2

Printed in Great Britain by Scotprint
Illustration by Oxford Designers & Illustrators Ltd
Indexed by John Holmes

Acknowledgments
The Publisher is grateful to the following for their permission to reproduce copyright material:

Co-op Travel; Greek Sun Holidays; Mark Warner; Ski Lebanon, for more information visit www.skilebanon.co.uk; Travel Trade Gazette

Crown copyright material is reproduced with the permission of the Controller of HMSO.

Picture Credits
The publisher would like to thank the following for their kind permission to reproduce their photographs:

(Key: b-bottom; c-centre; l-left; r-right; t-top)

ABTA: 70, 126t; AITO (www.aito.co.uk): 123t; Alamy Images: AA World Travel Library 132; Biphoto 100; Danita Delimont 101; Mark Dyball 38r; Andrew Holt 19l; Peter Horree 160; Jon Arnold Images 134; Justin Kase 121; Barry Mason 139t; National Trust Photolibrary 38l; Photofusion Picture Library 47; Robert Harding Picture Library Ltd 99; Jack Sullivan 135; Best Western International: 61; ; Comos Holidays (www.cosmos.co.uk): 149; Thomas Cook: 19c, 69; Club 18-30 19r, 130; Corbis: Randy Faris 94-95, 96, Brian A. Vikander 112; Mark Karrass 15b; Sergio Pitamitz 118-119, 120; Somos Images 64-65, 66; Henrik Trygg 24; Empics: Associated Press 111t, 115, 176; Excel Centre, London : 163; Federation of Tour Operators (www.fto.co.uk): 123bl; Flickr: David Barrington 39; Gideon Ben-Ami (www.letthemtalk.com) 108; Christopher Hylarides 17; Ross Mackenzie 159; David Quick 111b; Getty Images: AFP 126b; Angelo Cavalli 10-11, 12; Jon Feingersh 193; IHG (InterContinental Hotels Group): 87; Investors in People: 60; iStockphoto: David Cannings-Bushell 75; Jeff Moore (jeff@jmal.co.uk): 15t, 67; Nick Kiehl Photography: 98, 102, 170-171, 172; Kosmar Villa Holidays PLC (www.kosmar.co.uk): 125; lastminute.com: 77; PunchStock: Corbis 34-35, 36, 144-145, 145; Digital Vision 187; Pixtal 105; Radisson Edwardian Hotels: 76; Reuters: Anuruddha Lokuhapuarachchi 194; Saga Holidays Limited: 127; Shaping Norfolk's Future (www.shapingnorfolksfuture.org.uk): 181; STILL Pictures The Whole Earth Photo Library: Jeff Greenberg 21; Tourism Concern (www.tourismconcern.org.uk): 110; Travel Trade Gazette, published in 9 June 2006 issue page 8 of: 44; UKinbound: 123br; Mark Warner Ltd (www.markwarner.co.uk): 33, 131; World Tourism Organization (www.unwto.org): 185; World Travel Market (www.wtmlondon.com): 106

Cover images: Front: PunchStock: Digital Vision

All other images © Pearson Education

Picture Research by: Liz Moore

Every effort has been made to trace the copyright holders and we apologise in advance for any unintentional omissions. We would be pleased to insert the appropriate acknowledgement in any subsequent edition of this publication.